THE FUTURE IS FEMINIST

THE FUTURE IS FEMINIST

WOMEN AND SOCIAL CHANGE IN INTERWAR ALGERIA

SARA RAHNAMA

CORNELL UNIVERSITY PRESS
Ithaca and London

Copyright © 2023 by Cornell University

All rights reserved. Except for brief quotations in a review, this book, or parts thereof, must not be reproduced in any form without permission in writing from the publisher. For information, address Cornell University Press, Sage House, 512 East State Street, Ithaca, New York 14850. Visit our website at cornellpress.cornell.edu.

First published 2023 by Cornell University Press

Library of Congress Cataloging-in-Publication Data

Names: Rahnama, Sara, 1988- author.
Title: The future is feminist : women and social change in interwar Algeria / Sara Rahnama.
Description: Ithaca : Cornell University Press, 2023. | Includes bibliographical references and index.
Identifiers: LCCN 2023024084 (print) | LCCN 2023024085 (ebook) | ISBN 9781501772993 (hardcover) | ISBN 9781501773006 (epub) | ISBN 9781501773013 (pdf)
Subjects: LCSH: Feminism—Algeria—History—20th century. | Muslim women—Algeria—Social conditions—20th century. | Women's rights—Algeria—History—20th century. | Social change—Algeria—History—20th century. | Feminism—Religious aspects—Islam.
Classification: LCC HQ1791.5 .R456 2023 (print) | LCC HQ1791.5 (ebook) | DDC 305.420965—dc23/eng/20230608
LC record available at https://lccn.loc.gov/2023024084
LC ebook record available at https://lccn.loc.gov/2023024085

ISBN 978-1-5017-8134-6 (pbk)

For Parichehr and Hadi

Contents

Acknowledgments ix
List of Abbreviations xiii
Note on Translation and Transliteration xv

Introduction	1
1. The Rise of the Woman Question in Interwar Algeria	18
2. Domestic Workers in a Changing City	47
3. The Educated Muslim Woman and Algeria's Path to Progress	75
4. The Haik, the Hat, and the Gendered Politics of the New Public	103
5. French Feminists and the New Imperial Feminism	130
6. Muslim Women Address the Nation	154
Conclusion	180

Notes 187
Bibliography 215
Index 227

Acknowledgments

My first debt of gratitude is to my parents, Parichehr and Hadi, who have lovingly supported me at every stage of this process. They encouraged a commitment to discipline and rigorousness that has fueled this project. My brother Mehdi has been a constant, steady stream of love and support that I am so grateful to always be able to lean on. My sister Mona has been right next to me cheering me on through all of the toughest moments of my life, including finishing this book and childbirth. Her sisterhood was the first I ever knew, and it sparked something so deep in me that I continue to seek it out and study it. I have been blessed with not one supportive family but two. I am grateful to Ilhan Cagri, Younos Mokhtarzada, and the Mokhtarzada family for their patience, understanding, and encouragement throughout this process.

I have been fortunate to have many excellent history teachers. At Richard Montgomery High School, I learned from Robert Thomas and Robert Hines, whose engaging pedagogy pulled me into a love of history as a teenager. At the University of Maryland, this excitement for history was nurtured in the classrooms of Madeline Zilfi, Julie Taddeo, Arthur Eckstein, David Sartorius, and Peter Wien. My friendships with many of them, as well as with David Libber, have made this project so much richer. This project was also born out of the intellectual community at Johns Hopkins, and the epicenter of that community for me is Todd Shepard. He has nurtured and encouraged my vision for this project for a decade now. For all those times he pushed me to write better, clearer, and stronger and refused to accept what I produced as good enough, I am (now) immensely grateful. I am grateful for the opportunity to learn from Nathan Connolly and Judy Walkowitz. I miss Pier Larson, who provided so much thorough, invaluable feedback on this project. Nathan Marvin and Amira Rose Davis continue to inspire me and have become family.

ACKNOWLEDGMENTS

I am indebted to the many archivists who made this project possible and treated me with patience and kindness as I tested the limits of the rules for researchers. I owe gratitude in particular to the archivists at the National Archives in Algiers as well as the Wilaya Archives in Algiers, Oran, and Constantine, many of whom helped me navigate their holdings with a special warmth. I thank Mohamed Benani of Beit Benani in Tunis for his kindness to both me and my husband. Many thanks to the John Kluge Center at the Library of Congress for the grant that allowed me to complete this book. This project would not have been possible without my Arabic teachers and tutors, and especially May Rostam. Thank you to Siham Eldadah for the excellent discussions and Arabic help in the final days of finishing this book. No words are sufficient to express my gratitude to Fatma Zohra Benaik and Dahbia Lounas, who agreed to talk with me about their lives and whose oral interviews add texture to this book, and I thank Sarah Djebli and Sumi Dabaoui for making those connections possible.

I owe a debt of gratitude to several intellectual communities. Morgan State University has offered me a supportive scholarly home base, and I am particularly indebted to Brett Berliner for his ongoing support. The Women Historians of the Middle East have offered sisterhood and mentorship. This book was made much better by the thorough feedback offered by James McDougall, Marylin Booth, Beth Baron, and Judith Tucker. I am also very grateful to my family of fellow scholars of Algeria. I am grateful to be in community with fellow scholars of Algeria and friends, Sam Anderson, Muriam Haleh Davis, Sarah Ghabrial, Liz Perego, Terry Peterson, and Chris Silver. From the early days of this project, Arthur Asseraf has helped me develop my ideas in critical ways, whether during lunches shared at the Bibliothèque nationale de France, on long walks in Paris, or on patient international phone calls while my kids play loudly in the background. When I've lost faith, he has reminded me of the urgency of this work. Every chapter of this book has benefited from his advice.

Many incredible women have supported me on this journey. My friendship with Lindsey Stephenson has been a welcome reminder of the fullness of life beyond this book and academia. Beeta Baghoolizadeh, my rock jan, has been a steady support in my corner helping me navigate the decisions of not only this book but also my career. Sadiqeh Agah, Anais Eslami, Behnaz Haddadi, Yasmina Khan, and Nayereh Paterrov have continually offered encouragement, love, and sisterhood throughout this project and beyond. Amira Rose Davis's friendship has nourished me as both a scholar and a mother. Marcia Chatelain, Sara Saljoughi, and Neda Maghbouleh have offered thoughtful advice and support at critical moments. I thank Maryam Asgari for her constant love, support, and encouragement.

Writing, revising, and finishing this book while on a four-four teaching load with two small children would not have been possible without Idris. I thank him for believing in my vision for not just this project but my career and the world I want to live in. May the future be feminist for Yara, Raha, and all of us.

Abbreviations

AAA	Archive of the Archdiocese of Algiers
AEMAN	Association des étudiants musulmans d'Afrique du Nord
AFMA	Association des femmes musulmanes algériennes
AIOIA	Association des Instituteurs d'origine Indigène d'Algérie
AN	Archives nationales d'Algérie
AOMA	Association des oulémas musulmans algériens
ANOM	Archives nationales d'outre-mer (Aix-en-Provence)
BNF	Bibliothèque nationale de France
FLN	Front de libération nationale
MTLD	Mouvement pour le triomphe des libertes democratiques
PCA	Parti communiste algérien
PPA	Parti du peuple algerien
SFIO	Section Française de l'Internationale Ouvrière
UFSF	Union française pour le suffrage des femmes
UDMA	Union démocratique du manifeste algérien
UPA	Union populaire algérienne

Note on Translation and Transliteration

All translations are mine unless otherwise noted. I have followed the conventions of Cornell University Press, including not italicizing Arabic words that appear in the *Merriam-Webster Collegiate Dictionary*, eleventh edition, and adopting the spelling that appears in the dictionary. For Arabic, I have adopted a simplified version of the *International Journal of Middle East Studies* transcription style, omitting diacritical marks to ease reading. For city names I have used the French colonial city name (which was most often used in my sources) with the Arabic city name in parentheses. Names of organizations and political parties appear in the original language in their first usage with a translation and abbreviation in parentheses, and with the abbreviation only in subsequent usages.

Introduction

On Saturday, July 7, 1934, Muslim elites gathered in Constantine to celebrate the marriage of two of their own, Miss Bensaci and Mr. Salah Bey. The couple were both from families involved in the colonial legal system. Salah Bey was a lawyer from the nearby town of Khenchela, and his father was a qadi, a judge who presided over a Muslim court, in the town of El Khroub. Miss Bensaci's father was a distinguished magistrate in Constantine. During the wedding celebrations, a guest named Abou-Ezzohra made an impassioned speech to the influential families in attendance in which he proclaimed that "the feminist movement gaining terrain every day" in the Middle East was a "completely Islamic movement."[1] He argued that Muslim women in Algeria needed better access to education so that they could "certainly and tangibly contribute to the to the rebuilding of the Muslim world," alongside their accomplished Middle Eastern sisters.

Abou-Ezzohra's speech was so powerful and compelling that it was published less than a week later by *La Voix Indigène*, the anticlerical newspaper run by schoolteacher Rabah Zenati. Throughout the interwar years, press coverage of women's and girls' issues flooded the Muslim press in Algeria.[2] These debates bubbled up in all the spaces where an urban Muslim public gathered in the interwar years: cafés, mosques, theaters, cinemas, community halls, political rallies, association meetings, and schools. Within the pages of the French- and Arabic-language press, thinkers debated a range of questions, including the utility of women's education, the appropriateness of women's work, the necessity of the hijab, and whether Muslim society or the French colonial state was responsible for limiting women's possibilities. While most of these commentators were men, several Muslim women also joined the discussions.

For Abou-Ezzohra and other commentators, this story of Middle Eastern upheaval and advancement was inextricably linked to women's possibilities. In their formulation, the equation was simple. Women's education had led to women's advancement, which in turn uplifted entire societies. While Algerian women remained uneducated, Turkish, Egyptian, Syrian, and Iraqi women were "the foundation of the renaissance" taking place across the region, which had "woken up after a long slumber." In contrast to many of the interwar calls for women's rights globally, which focused on women's capacity as mothers, he lobbied for more than strengthening their ability to raise children. Abou-Ezzohra admired how these Middle Eastern women were not only "doctors, teachers, artists, employees in public administrations" but also leaders within "literary, scientific, athletic, [and] even political movements." In Algeria too, Abou-Ezzohra called for women to be treated as "equal without any restriction." While Abou-Ezzohra's vision of women's advancement was particularly egalitarian, he was part of a broad segment of interwar Algerian society calling for women's advancement.

Algeria and the New Muslim Middle East

Abou-Ezzohra never mentioned France or even Europe in his speech, even though some of these Middle Eastern regimes and women's rights movements he admired looked to Europe as a model. Instead, he articulated the progress of Middle Eastern nations in terms of Islam, not the region or the specific countries in question. The education and leadership of "our Muslim sisters," he reflected, was "the foundation" of the "renaissance of Islam." Abou-Ezzohra referred to the Algerian woman sometimes as simply "the Muslim woman" and elsewhere as "the Algerian woman." Women of the Middle East were specified by their country of origin—"the Egyptian, Syrian, Iraqi woman." This fluidity of language, between "Muslim" and "Algerian," was common in interwar Algeria. Muslims themselves most often referred to themselves as Muslims, but occasionally as Algerians.

Scholars of Algeria are thus forced to negotiate these terms and ambiguities. I refer to the Muslim population of colonial Algeria as "Muslims" because this is often how they called themselves. The term "Muslims" over "Algerians" refuses the assumption of the inevitability of a future, independent Algeria, which more accurately corresponds to the ambiguity of the national question in the interwar years. I use the geographic language of the Middle East in spite of its Eurocentric origins because it most accurately describes what commentors often meant when they spoke of "Muslims" in the region.[3]

The status of women in the Middle East was changing rapidly. By the end of World War I, the Ottoman Empire had been steadily losing territory for almost a century, a process that began with the French occupation of Algeria in 1830. Much of the territory once under Ottoman rule was now under European control either as colonies or as "mandates," unofficial colonies. By 1919 Algeria, Tunisia, Morocco, Syria, and Lebanon were under French control, while Egypt, Palestine, Transjordan, and Iraq were under British control, Libya was under Italian control, and northern Morocco under Spanish control. Much of the world around interwar Algerians was under European control.

By 1923, after the four-year-long War of Independence, Mustafa Kemal Atatürk (in power 1923–1938) and the Turkish National Movement had successfully wrestled control of Turkey away from not only what was left of the Ottoman Empire but also the French, British, and Italian forces who had occupied Istanbul since the end of World War I. In the following decades, the newly independent Turkish Republic underwent a broad range of reforms designed to strip Turkey of its former perch as the center of the Muslim world and elevate it to a modern nation-state. This process compelled a range of women's rights reforms, including the abolition of polygamy, equal rights to divorce for men and women, and most revolutionary of all, universal suffrage.

Mustafa Kemal Atatürk was not the only new leader in the region to prioritize women's rights as an avenue toward modernization. In 1919, after the third Anglo-Afghan War, Afghanistan won back the right to control its foreign policy from Britain. The new Afghan monarch, King Amanullah Khan (r. 1919–1929), also pursued a project of modernization that included women's rights. He campaigned against polygamy and the veil, and he encouraged women's education in both urban and rural areas. In 1921 Reza Pahlavi led a largely bloodless coup in which he took control of Iran as prime minister. By 1925 he was named Reza Shah (r. 1925–1941), thereby marking the end of the

Qajar dynasty and the beginning of the Pahlavi dynasty. Like Mustafa Kemal Atatürk, Reza Shah sought to marginalize the clergy's influence as part of his project of modernization. He enacted a series of reforms, such as granting women entry into colleges of law and medicine, a measure that facilitated Iranian women taking on a more public presence. Atatürk, Reza Shah, and Amanullah Khan all enacted state feminism, defined by Marya Hannun as "the state's implementation, co-option, and instrumentalization of women's rights and ostensibly 'feminist' reforms often with the explicit purpose of establishing its modernist credentials and breaking with an older regime."[4]

Yet women's advancement was not only a top-down project of statecraft. It was equally a key issue for social and political movements across the region. Egyptian women were particularly well organized. Women marched in the streets alongside men as part of the 1919 Egyptian Revolution against British occupation. In 1923 Huda Sharawi formed the Egyptian Feminist Union (EFU). In 1925 the EFU created their own journal, *L'Égyptienne* (published in French and eventually in 1937 in Arabic), which they used to publicize their positions on social and economic questions. In 1925 the EFU succeeded when their demands for compulsory primary education for both boys and girls were finally met. In Palestine, Muslim and Christian women organized together, led protests against the British Mandate, and demanded a broad platform of women's rights. In Syria and Lebanon, the Women's Union formed in 1924 and called for greater access to education and voting rights for women. In 1926 four thousand women marched in Damascus to demand an end to the French bombing of Syria.

For Muslims in Algeria, news of these developments in the Middle East provoked both excitement and despair. On one hand, they were inspired by the positive correlation they saw between women's advancement, modernization, and broader societal uplift. On the other, they compared this regional transformation to how they remained constrained by settler colonialism. The de facto segregation of colonial life forced most Muslims to live with limited access to schooling or employment and dilapidated, overcrowded housing. The colonial economy offered Muslims few opportunities for stable work. The status of women in Algeria, they argued, reflected the impoverished material conditions of everyday life.

Politically as well, settler colonialism continued to stifle opportunities for Muslim advancement and equality under the law. Already a century into France's colonial occupation of Algeria, Muslims there had long been forced to endure a subordinate status with respect to the European settler population. This status was codified by the *Code de l'indigénat* (Native code, hereafter *Indigénat*), a series of laws that arbitrarily restricted freedoms for Muslims and cemented their secondary status.[5] Citizenship rights too remained extremely limited. Muslims could apply for French citizenship only if they were willing to renounce their Muslim personal status—a move most Muslims interpreted as apostasy. Even for those willing to do so, applications were frequently denied for arbitrary reasons. The Blum-Violette Proposal of 1936 aimed to extend citizenship rights to between twenty and twenty-five thousand Muslim elites without requiring them to renounce their Muslim personal status but was never even voted on because of the outrage it sparked from European settlers in Algeria. By the interwar years, most Muslims had lost hope that reform was possible within the French colonial system. Anti-colonial nationalism, while initially marginal in the interwar years, became an increasingly compelling and attractive political ideology.

Algeria was also inextricably changed by World War I. During and immediately after the war, economic prospects were so dismal that many men migrated to metropolitan France in search of opportunity.[6] In 1914 thirty thousand Muslim men from Algeria were working in France.[7] By April 1917, almost 3 percent of the total Algerian Muslim population was in France as soldiers (173,000) or as factory workers (120,000).[8] By 1924 another 120,000 Muslim workers had arrived in France. By the interwar years, then, Algeria had experienced a mass exodus of its Muslim male labor. For those who remained, there was little reliable work. While some veterans who returned to Algeria were initially optimistic their service might grant them additional rights, the French colonial regime repeatedly failed to deliver on their promises.[9] The Jonnart Law of 1919, for example, gave 421,000 Muslim veterans the right to vote for Muslim members of municipal councils, but many felt it did not go far enough.

In the realm of rights for Muslim women too, Muslim voices were stifled. Judith Surkis has demonstrated that European fantasies about Muslim sexuality, including women's strict sequestration and subjugation by their husbands, were not just Orientalist fantasies that appeared in European art.[10] They also shaped Algerian legal and political realities. French administrators returned to such fantasies to legitimize the confiscation of land and denial of political rights to Muslims. Despite the considerable public support for increased education for girls, the French colonial regime was slow to open schools. Administrators claimed that the domination of Muslim women by Muslim men was such a salient feature of Muslim life that to offer women an education risked provoking anger. Such claims absolved the state of any responsibility to work toward improving Muslim women's possibilities.

It was these conditions established by settler colonialism that rendered interwar Algeria so different from other Middle Eastern spaces, even as there were sometimes parallels in its debates about women. It lacked the state feminism of Turkey, Iran, or Afghanistan. It also lacked the organized women's movements established by the elite women of Egypt, Palestine, Syria, and Lebanon. The colonial economy and the French colonial regime's continued dismantlement of Muslim institutions in Algeria left only a very small (albeit growing) middle class.

As a country positioned geographically between Europe, Africa, and the Middle East, Algeria's discourses around women were equally a product of its status within the Mediterranean, as an extension of the French metropole, as a predominantly Muslim former Ottoman territory, and as a culturally Arab and Amazigh (popularly known as "Berber") space within North Africa. Understanding their multidirectional gaze requires a multidirectional analysis that is attentive to the north-south, east-west, and south-south orientations of their references. This analysis pushes beyond the scholarly obsession with political and legal dynamics between France and Algeria in isolation and instead explores how social questions about women equally animated public life in the interwar years and connected Algeria to the Middle East. While scholars have increasingly been thinking about North Africa's relationship to other Mediterranean spaces since Mary Lewis's *Divided Rule*, they are only beginning to map its connections to the Middle East.[11]

Still, there were transformations underway in Algeria that created dynamics similar to those taking place in the Middle East. Urbanization provoked profound transition and crisis in Algeria. Long-standing distinctions that had structured Algerian public life became blurred. Rural people became city dwellers as hundreds of thousands of migrants from rural Algeria now crowded into the Muslim neighborhoods of cities. Association meetings, theaters, cinemas, and markets were all sites of increased heterosocial proximity. Women who recently migrated to cities dramatically joined the labor force and traversed the boundaries of their streets, neighborhoods, and markets en route to work. Sartorial norms began to shift as some members of the growing Muslim middle class began adopting European-style dress. The Muslim reform movement that emerged out of Egypt at the turn of the twentieth century rapidly grew in popularity across Algeria.

The language of "progress" and "modernity" permeated Muslim discourse in Algeria. Samira Haj has recently, in conversation with other scholars like Talal Asad, modeled how scholars can use the category of tradition to refer "not simply to the past or its repetition but rather to the pursuit of an ongoing coherence by making reference to a set of texts, procedures, arguments, and practices."[12] This understanding of tradition enables scholars to situate Muslim intellectual production within a longer Islamic discursive tradition in order to better analyze how Muslims played with and redefined the categories of modern or traditional. *The Future Is Feminist* brings a gender analysis of a settler-colonial context into these ongoing scholarly discussions.

Despite a century of settler claims that Algerian culture and Islam were backward, Muslims in Algeria took recent Middle Eastern political and social shifts as evidence of Islam's capacity to be modern and to facilitate progress. Similarly, invocations of Islam were not stagnant references that simply celebrated a past golden age. Instead, commentators ordered and reordered the corpus of Islamic knowledge to reframe Islam as emancipatory, flexible, and modern. I use "Islamic knowledge" as an umbrella category to hold together references to the Qur'an, hadith literature, and Islamic history. Together, these references to Islamic knowledge and to news from the Middle East enabled Muslims in Algeria to organize the world on their own terms. Their praise for the modernization of the Middle East decentered Europe and enabled them to articulate new aspirations for the future. These discourses offered them a path forward amid growing frustration and resignation about what the French colonial project could offer Muslims.

Algeria's Future Is Feminist

As Abou-Ezzohra lamented the contrast between the stifled Muslim women of Algeria and their more emancipated Middle Eastern counterparts in his wedding speech, he also looked to Algeria's future. He wrote that there was still "hope for a better future" in Algeria. The number of Muslim girls attending school was slowly increasing. Nearly twenty Muslim women had even become schoolteachers. These developments suggested that there was a path forward for Algeria, toward a more feminist and prosperous future. He was clear about who was responsible for ushering in change: "The male elite has a role to play."

The Future Is Feminist argues that discussions of the woman question in interwar Algeria opened up new horizons of feminist possibility, and understanding these discussions requires attention not only to the colonial divide but also to the multiple social divides—between rural and urban, poor and elite, Sufi and reformist—that were also being negotiated as Algerian Muslims imagined their future. This analysis, which keeps both feminists and their detractors in view, works not to squeeze Algerian discourse into our understanding of feminism, but rather to expand the frame of feminism itself. Judith Butler has summoned scholars to "emancipate [feminism] from the maternal or racialist ontologies to which it has been restricted."[13] If we adopt Margot Badran's definition of feminism as "the awareness of constraints placed upon women because of their gender and attempts to remove these constraints and to evolve a more equitable gender system involving new roles for women and new relations between men and women," many of the commentators analyzed within the pages of this book qualified.[14] They envisioned themselves as beginning the discussions that would lead to such a removal of the impediments that constrained women, including, for example, their limited access to employment or education. Most of them also envisioned a more equitable society. Many still envisioned women's social role to be confined to the family, but even they imagined a woman's potential future as a more empowered, educated household manager. Others were open to women taking on a greater variety of public roles, including within traditionally masculine professions. Muslims in Algeria referenced models of feminist advancement from the Middle East and, through these references, theorized their own versions of a hybrid feminist project adaptable to Algerian realities. Yet they have largely been left out of the growing body of scholarship on Middle Eastern and African feminisms. To insist that Algerian feminism be legible in today's terms functions much like interwar calls for Muslim women to be liberated according to French models.

The frame of feminist possibility also illuminates how interwar developments created openings of which women took advantage to work toward feminist outcomes. Zuhur Wunisi, for example, grew up during the intense debate in the interwar years about what the end goal of girls' education should be. She and other girls educated in Muslim reformist schools capitalized on interwar feminist possibility to expand what was possible for Muslim women. They were educated, became teachers and authors, some unveiled, and Wunisi herself would later become one of Algeria's first women politicians and government ministers. The book's final chapter also turns to the postwar period to demonstrate how these interwar discussions paved the way for later conversations in which women used nationalist discourse to critique both French colonial society and Muslim men.

Attention to how Islam informed these commentator's arguments is critical to any serious analysis of these questions about interwar Algerian feminism. Margot Badran has recently analyzed what she differentiates as Muslim secular feminism on one hand, and Islamic feminism on the other.[15] Secular feminism, she writes, emerged in Muslim societies in the late nineteenth and early twentieth centuries. Responding to the Islamic modernist teachings of Muhammad Abduh, this feminism called for gender equality in the public sphere and was often tied to nationalist movements. Islamic feminism, on the other hand, developed in the late twentieth and early twenty-first centuries and emphasized "the Qur'anic principles of human equality and gender justice" to preach gender equality in society as well as within the family.[16] Interwar Algerian discussions borrow from both of Badran's types of feminism. They appeared in the context of emergent Algerian nationalism and yet cited forms of Muslim regional belonging that transcended Algeria's borders. While the interwar discussions were largely concerned with public life, including women's labor and education, the postwar discussions also analyzed here were more concerned with familial dynamics. Notably, Islamic knowledge for them was not about mastery of a static set of historical texts but rather something malleable to be worked into a vision for a modern and sometimes feminist future Algeria. The goal here is not to valorize Algerian commentators as undiscovered feminist heroes but rather to explore how feminist imperatives can be simultaneously encouraged and constrained, sometimes by the same voices. This analysis thus works to "release the term [feminism] into a future of multiple significations . . . and to give it play as a site where unanticipated meanings might come to bear," as Butler has called for. Through its analysis of these tensions, *The Future Is Feminist* also offers a fresh perspective on the intersections of Islam and feminism—an urgent undertaking given the enduring depictions of Muslim women as oppressed that persist in both popular culture and academic circles.[17]

While critically important, the growing body of scholarship on feminism in the Middle East has focused largely on either women-led movements for women's rights or state feminist projects, which were more developed elsewhere in the Middle East in the interwar years and well underway by the later twentieth century.[18] Attention to a space peripheral to the Middle East, Algeria, offers a model of how to consider feminist possibilities and horizons where there was not yet any such women-led movement for women's rights. *The Future Is Feminist* explores which feminist possibilities could exist under settler colonialism and how they became central to both working through the social divisions of the present and the imaginings of possible Algerian futures.

While the commentators who raised questions about women in the Muslim press were largely male, this book is not another story of women's "silences" and "absences." This study—unlike those on the women's rights projects that swept the Middle East in the interwar years—begins with working-class women. In Algeria women's changing status was not measurable through new access to consumption patterns, education, or activism—the key markers of "new women" and "modern girls" elsewhere. Instead, it looked like women struggling to support their families through continued poverty, with the occasional splurge on nonessential groceries, like black market coffee. Still, women becoming primary earners within their households had a profound impact on power relations within the home. Outside of the home, these women also left their mark on the explosion of interwar public life. Women who worked by day as domestic workers also performed on stages in some of the country's largest theatrical avenues. They campaigned for causes in the streets and marched among crowds in protests. They frequented cinemas and theaters. Their presence was felt within association meetings or political rallies by offering *youyous* (*zagharid*) of approval.[19] The details of their lives and questions about these details animated debate across all the institutions of the emergent Muslim public: the press, association life, schools, urban space, and the theater. This book explores how women, both working-class and elite, and concerned men identified, pushed back against, and worked within the constraints placed on them both by the French colonial state and by Muslim society. A *mujahida*, or female fighter, in the Algerian War, Louisette Ighilahriz described her mother, who would have been of the interwar generation, as "illiterate but hyperpoliticized."[20] The interwar discourses on women, then, while perhaps not conventionally feminist, contained feminist possibilities, which made possible the activism and militarism of the next generation.

In its attention to the future's feminist possibilities, this analysis contributes to the growing body of scholarship on the future as a category of historical analysis, which has ranged from the heavily theoretical to the everyday evocations of the future. My analysis is particularly informed by other scholars who have examined the political uses of the future as a language to work through anxieties about the present and shape particular versions of the past. In *Future Tense* Roxanne Panchasi has written about how the future became a powerful "way of framing potential changes to French society and ways of life (already underway in some cases) as out of step with the nation's history and cultural traditions" in interwar France.[21] More recently, in *Familiar Futures* Sara Pursley has offered a layered and multifaceted analysis of the different ways concepts of the future were mobilized and familiarized during the Iraqi revolutionary era.[22] She analyzed, for example, the narratives produced by Iraqi schools and military not for their nationalist content but for how they sought to produce bodies that were oriented toward a particular future.

In the interwar Algerian discussions about Muslim women, too, the future became a container for ideas about how women's advancement could create a social uplift, which in the interwar years was often located in an ambiguous future. By the postwar years, as nationalism became a more dominant (albeit still disputed) ideology, commentators more consistently referred to a nationalist, anti-colonial future. Yet part of what this book seeks to map is how in the interwar years multiple futures were still possible. Commentators' calls for the urgent need for change in the present in order to achieve later prosperity constituted visions of the future, even if they were unspecific about when that future would take place and what it might look like.

The Future Is Feminist engages theoretically with the frame of colonial internationalism and its "future-oriented politics" proposed by Manu Goswami. Goswami argued that attention to internationalist politics of colonial subjects can illuminate "an open-ended constellation of contending political futures" that has been otherwise eclipsed by the scholarship's enduring focus on nationalism. In colonial internationalism, she argued, the present was envisioned as "a transformative juncture," which could lead to "a potential transition to a new egalitarian world order." She focused on the work of the sociologist Benoy Kumar Sarkar, whose internationalism involved "three interlocking strands: an emphasis on the historical category of the possible, a dual rejection of imperialism and cultural nationalism, and an insistence that equality was the central problematic of political and epistemological struggles alike."[23] The "new egalitarian world order" proposed by Sarkar and his contemporaries was envisioned as an equality that would push back against the assumptions of Orientalism and reflect itself "in the discussions of learned societies, in school rooms, theatres, moving picture shows, daily journals, and monthly reviews."[24]

The Algerian case illustrates how some of these uniquely interwar imperatives were also at work in discussions about women and the future. Muslim commentators also believed the contrast between how Algeria was stifled under settler colonialism while there was advancement and modernization across the Middle East made the present a moment of both crisis and possibility. They too imagined what more egalitarian futures could be possible in ways that were often ambiguous about nationalism. In fact, the precise parameters of this future better Algeria were often unspecified. The Algerian case illustrates how a wide set of references—including to Islamic knowledge and regional developments—could be marshaled to diagnose the problems of the present and to argue for a more egalitarian future—both in terms of men and women, but also between colonizer and colonized. For almost all commentators, women's advancement was envisioned as the pivotal key that could propel Algeria forward in the new international world order.

Within the scholarship on Algeria, the teleology of the Algerian War of Independence remains so powerful that it has dictated which societal actors merit historical attention. Decades of recent scholarship has focused on political questions, including the tensions that resulted in the ultimate success of anti-colonial nationalism. Even histories of the interwar period have demonstrated how the anti-colonial nationalism of the 1950s would not have been possible without intellectual and communal developments of the interwar years—including the rise of the reformist movement and its histories of precolonial Algeria and the rise of communal culture through associations and cafés.[25] James McDougall has argued that Algeria was so remade by colonialism that even intra-Muslim discussions were shaped by the French because of their reliance on French categories, including "the Muslim world." I argue instead that such claims flatten the way interwar commentators stretched such categories to contain multiple meanings. As they debated developments in Algeria with references to the Middle East, for example, they played with notions of belonging in ways that rendered the concepts of Islam, nation, or the Muslim world unstable.

My analysis takes seriously how colonialism shaped Muslims' lived realities and worldviews while simultaneously remaining attentive to the ways Muslims drew connections to the Middle East that transcended colonial boundaries and sometimes remained ambivalent toward anti-colonial nationalism. This book charts a different type of revolt: one that focused on the status of women rather than the political project of nationalism. In its attentiveness to feminist possibility, my analysis is in dialogue with what Manijeh Moradian has called "a methodology of possibility." She writes, "A methodology of possibility takes the collective feeling of hope or possibility itself—however fleeting or naïve—as a legitimate object of study, as a way of rethinking the legacy of anti-imperialist revolutions."[26] In the Algerian case, attention to feminist possibility, over feminism as a cohesive movement or feminists as intentional actors, reveals a whole world of transnational feminist imagining and aspiration. These previously underexamined articulations of feminist possibility were radical in the ways they wrote back against French colonial claims about Muslim misogyny—the very ideological underpinnings of French empire in Algeria.

The enduringly powerful teleology of the Algerian War has also implicitly suggested that women's ability to actively shape Algerian society began with their participation in the Algerian War. The narrative posits that women's emancipation was uniquely possible alongside national liberation. Until now, the longer history of women's eventual involvement in the Algerian War remains untold, although some have described the interwar years as a turning point. In 1955, for example, the French historian Roger LeTourneau wrote, "In the last twenty years or so the emancipation of Muslim women [in North Africa has] begun."[27] The search for women's presence in interwar public life requires a look beyond the most obvious markers of what advancement looked like. Indeed, if we rely on figures and state archives alone, change appears miniscule. Despite all the interwar agitation for more schools for girls, the number of schools open to Muslim girls remained small. In terms of literacy, for example, in 1954 on the brink of the Algerian War, women's literacy was only at 4.5 percent.[28] For men, the literacy rate was 13 percent. Yet literacy rates do not reflect the dynamic processes by which Muslims encountered news, information, and commentaries. While walking down the street, men and women alike would hear young boys selling newspapers shouting recent headlines. Men who congregated in cafés would listen as someone read aloud (and even translated) from a newspaper or journal. The women who worked as domestic workers in European homes would listen to the radio left on while they worked. Women would gather and discuss community developments and news on rooftops or in associations. Press archives illuminate how women occupied a central role, symbolically and physically, in interwar Algerian intellectual and social life. While many women's lives remained constrained, their life circumstances and possibilities became the object of heated debate.

This book treats women's participation in the Algerian War of Independence not as an inevitability but rather as one possibility among many. Nationalism is of course part of this story. It explains why it was so important for Muslim reformists, for example, to have their own ideal for Muslim women who contributed to a distinct Muslim Algerian identity. Yet even within discourses we may firmly label as nationalist, authors played with other forms of belonging, including to a Muslim *umma*, to solidarity among women globally, and to other modernizing nations. Decentering nationalism allows us to take seriously the wide range of voices who were unconvinced or ambivalent that an independent future Algeria was the most ideal future for Muslim women and Algeria broadly, and who would otherwise be written off as assimilationist, insufficiently subversive, or marginal. In terms of the question of women's rights too, my analysis holds in equal view those who advocated women's equality with men, those who were more skeptical, and those who suggested that any education at all for women could emasculate men and upend Muslim society.

There has been so much focus on eventual anti-colonial revolt as a pathway to liberation, but what other forms of liberation were available to Algerians? What forms of liberation could be imagined while everyday circumstances remained constrained both materially and politically? For many, the status of women was key. *The Future Is Feminist* offers a window into a society working through their anxieties about the future through a multidirectional and multivocal inquiry into the status of women.

Methodological Considerations for Algeria's Multivocal Muslim Press

The French- and Arabic-language Muslim press makes up the key source base of this work, as it illuminates the social concern about women only peripherally present in state archives in France and Algeria. This project has been driven by an imperative that histories of Algeria (especially social histories) require Arabic-language sources and sources beyond colonial archives. Scholarly conclusions about Algeria have been predetermined by their overuse of French-language sources and heavy reliance on French colonial state archives alone. As Augustin Jomier has written in his important article on interwar Mzabi women's agency, while women were virtually "invisible" in the French language sources, Arabic-language sources help reveal a whole world of women's power and agency that complicates scholarly assumptions.[29] My attempt to offer a social history of gender in interwar Algeria contributes to the growing body of new social histories of Algeria, including by Arthur Asseraf on the media, as well as by Charlotte Courreye and Augustin Jomier on Muslim reformists.[30]

My use of Arabic-language sources and paying attention to the work "Islam" does within discourses about women does more than expand our sources; it also radically transforms our view of this historical moment. Whereas many intellectual histories narrowly focus on a few key thinkers or a single community, my analysis of multiple overlapping Algerian communities in tandem through both French and Arabic sources maps the complexities of the debates about women. My commitment to multivocality allows for an analysis of how discourses from a broad range of commentators intersected, overlapped, and clashed as they posited their versions of feminist possibilities in the present and the future. This attention to multivocality examines a broad range of voice without privileging either secular or religious voices, or assuming there was a neat divide between the two. Khaled El-Rouayheb has critiqued the enduring focus of intellectual histories of the Middle East on "European 'modernity' and its challenges while breezily ignoring the continuing tradition of *madrasah* scholarship in the modern period."[31] Community members, religious leaders, and imams of both traditional Sufi and reformist traditions published regularly in dozens of publications. Also, religious authorities were not the only figures to marshal Islamic knowledge. Rather, the corpus of Islamic knowledge provided a language for commentators to use to justify their arguments about women. Even Muslims who may not have adhered to Islamic practices in their private lives cited the Qur'an and hadith in their appeals to the broader public. While this analysis is attentive to evocations of Islam and the work those evocations performed for commentators, it is also attentive to other social divides, which illustrate that Islam alone cannot explain Muslim behavior and society, as was theorized by colonial-era ethnographers and administrators and persists today among some contemporary thinkers.

More traditional archival sources play a role as well. French colonial surveillance reports, correspondence, and memos illustrate the multiple meanings assigned to debates in the press about Algerian women. French colonial surveillance reports, for example, interpreted Muslim efforts to reform women's status as a marker of the success of the French civilizing mission, even though some discussions were quite critical of the colonial regime. Master's theses completed at Algerian universities reveal how Muslim women's labor and Muslim family life in Algiers transformed between the 1920s and the 1950s. Minutes from local government meetings illustrate how representatives made use of press analyses to level legislative or legal arguments about women.

The book begins with a chapter that builds the world of interwar intellectual life in terms of its communities, publications, and spaces. Chapter 1 offers an overview of how after World War I, the number of Muslim presses in Algeria grew exponentially, sparking new levels of public engagement with news from the region and lively debates about social changes both abroad and at home. Chapter 2 then moves straight into an exploration of migrant domestic workers who changed the optics of Algerian cities as they traversed the boundaries of Muslim and settler neighborhoods every morning en route to work. Chapter 2's analysis is both attentive to the spatial, in its look at how domestic workers moved through the city, and the intellectual, in its analysis of how within the press these women became markers of colonialism's social and economic upheaval and provoked masculine anxieties about growing female power. Chapters 3 and 4 go deeper into the realm of intellectual discourse around women, focusing on education and dress. Chapter 3 examines how diverse Muslim commentators agreed that women's education was the first step in women's larger empowerment and social progress. As they advocated for women's education, they looked east to other countries in the region and inward to Islam's own history of feminist reform to challenge French colonial ideology about Muslim misogyny and offer a vision of Algerian Muslim belonging to the modern world. The debates about both women's hijab and men's headwear mapped out in chapter 4 illustrate that it remained contentious what precisely such a Muslim modernity would look like in Algeria. The final two chapters move to two different but interconnected contexts. Chapter 5 examines how these ongoing debates in Muslim society were so fluid that they also intersected with French feminist discussions. French feminists too were preoccupied with Muslim women's education and advancement, but most often so they could advance their own case for suffrage. The book's final chapter moves to the postwar context, as an extended conclusion of the book's themes. It illustrates how in the postwar period, nationalism offered Muslim women a language that would counter the interwar discourses of which they were the subject. They used nationalist language to challenge not only colonialism but also Muslim men and the limits they imposed on women's labor, education, and dress. Together these chapters explore how Muslim commentators envisioned feminist futures as a path forward out of the problems of the Algerian present.

CHAPTER 1

The Rise of the Woman Question in Interwar Algeria

In November 1934 the editorial staff of the Muslim reformist newspaper *La Défense* published an open call to their readers.[1] Two decades earlier, Abdelhamid Ben Badis had ushered the Muslim reform movement into Algeria after studying at Zeitouna University in Tunis. By the 1930s the movement was growing in popularity across Algeria. *La Défense* was the movement's publication aimed at a younger generation. Its editor, Lamine Lamoudi, was a student of Ben Badis and a socialist. The editorial staff of *La Défense* wrote that they wanted to delve deeper into the woman question, a subject "that preoccupies our intellectuals in all the Muslim countries." What should be done about women's limited possibilities? Should women be educated? Should women work? They welcomed all "young Muslims who have an idea to put forth or an opinion to express on this important subject" to write into the newspaper and have their thoughts published. The newspaper offered a brief explanation of their own position. They wrote that they were committed to Muslim women's education and cited the hadith of the Prophet Muhammad that "education is an obligation for every Muslim man and woman." They argued that this education should be designed by Muslims themselves with the greatest respect for Muslim customs and traditions, a jab at French colonial schools for girls. To initiate the discussion, they reprinted an article from a

Moroccan newspaper, *La Presse Marocaine*, about the urgent need to educate Muslim women.

That year, 1934, was *La Défense*'s first year in print, and throughout the year it had continually printed articles about Muslim women. The paper reprinted an article from the schoolteacher publication *La Voix des Humbles* about how Iraqi women were enjoying a revolution in their rights and status, and then in a later issue they published a letter they had received from a Muslim woman in Algeria who responded to the article and questioned why so little was being done for Muslim women in Algeria. In November they turned to their audience, open to hearing their perspectives on the subject. Other publications also facilitated debate about Muslim women. From January until April 1937, for example, another reformist paper, *al-Bassair*, published a multipart debate on whether Muslim women's veils needed to cover their faces.[2] The debate became so heated that commentators made personal attacks on one another, and the publication then printed commentaries that sought to mediate the divergent perspectives. Debates about women swept the Muslim press across intellectual communities in the interwar years. As the number of Muslim presses in Algeria grew from a handful to dozens after World War I, their proliferating debates about social changes both abroad and at home constituted a key site in which Algerian Muslims, colonial authorities, and French feminists advanced different, often conflicting, visions for Algeria's future and women's role in creating it.

Interwar Algeria in Flux

The interwar years were a time of enormous social transformation for Algerian society because of a variety of factors, including Algerian men's participation in World War I, their labor migration to France, urbanization, and more Muslims having access to positions within the French colonial bureaucracy. Social classes among Muslims were in flux. Allison Drew has offered a helpful description of the social classes. At the top, she writes, were the *vieux turbans* (old turbans), the Muslim landed elite who were socially and religiously conservative, often with ties to particular Sufi saints.[3] In the interwar years this group's power started to decline, unless they reinvented themselves through new access points to power, including employment in the French colonial bureaucracy or courts.[4] There was also a newer "economic elite composed of factory owners, managers, high-level civil servants and professionals." These were the most assimilated to European culture; they spoke French, may have even lived in or near European neighborhoods, and were "generally conservative or moderate in their politics." Next was a growing middle class of "small and middle businessmen, civil servants, professionals, technicians, white collar workers and certain skilled workers." Finally, below them was the large Muslim working class, who in rural areas often performed agricultural labor and in cities often took on irregular work, as day laborers or dockworkers, for example.[5]

In spite of these divisions, however, the interwar years were characterized by a fluidity in which intellectuals straddled multiple communities. These new social, political, and religious formations reflected a society in flux as the divisions between European settlers and colonial subjects became increasingly murky socially, even as they remained relatively rigid legally. McDougall has described the fluidity and interconnectedness of the interwar social climate: "Among intellectuals and professionals, journalists, schoolteachers and social reformers, in schools and at university; in cafés, political parties and freemasons' lodges; in rural medical clinics, markets and post offices; and at particular, brief moments, especially in the enthusiastic mobilisations around the Popular Front in 1936, Algerians of all confessions and languages, citizens and non-citizens, met, disputed and agreed, worked together and across the divisions of colonial society."[6] In this single sentence, McDougall identifies some of the major actors and settings of the interwar social worlds. Most key, however, is McDougall's description of how these various individuals and communities "met, disputed and agreed, [and] worked together." This gets at not only the collaboration between communities but the extent to which there were overlaps and intersections across the different communities as they convened in various spaces.

Many of these zones of cross-class contact and connection were male-dominated. Yet women of various classes also gathered in some spaces of urban public life, including in schools, theaters, cinemas, Popular Front demonstrations, mosques, and cemeteries. Women also participated in urban culture in varying ways depending on their class. In terms of shopping, for example, working-class women's buying power was limited by their meager wages. Any extra money would go toward something small like cigarettes or black market coffee.[7] Upper-class urban women, on the other hand, many of whom would have been part of families of landed elite or civil servants, were "eager to purchase new things, whether they come from Europe or from the East," according to French functionary Marguerite Bel.[8] This class of women were also the consumers of luxury items for household use, including textiles produced with linen or silk.[9] Dahbia Lounas, a woman born in 1933 from the rural town of Mirabeau (today Draâ Ben Khedda) near Tizi Ouzou, saw the city as "beyond our means and our culture."[10] She described urban spaces like cafés, theaters, and cinemas as spaces that in her childhood she envisioned were solely "for the French." Despite how urbanization continued in the decades after the interwar years, the public life it created did not affect all Algerians the same way.

Living quarters too reflected varied lived realities. In Algiers, while all classes of Muslims intermixed in the casbah, the conditions under which they lived varied. The Ottoman-era buildings of the casbah tended to be two or three stories high, with three or four rooms per floor, and a courtyard in the middle. The vast majority of casbah dwellings were overcrowded, with extended families sharing a home and many people sleeping in a single room. By the end of the interwar years, more families were moving into the bidonvilles (shantytowns) on the outskirts of town. The first bidonville appeared outside Algiers between 1926 and 1930, and their numbers continued to swell from thirteen in 1938, sixteen in 1942, fifty-eight by 1947, and 164 by 1954.[11] These cramped living conditions were one urban reality that reflected how the colonial divide between settlers and Muslims remained stark. Scholars have studied many aspects of Algeria's settler colonialism including, among others, its architecture, its urbanism, its bifurcated legal system, and its violence.[12] A closer look at the Muslim press and its discussion of women illustrates how Muslims diagnosed the problems of the Algerian present and proposed paths toward better futures in ways that were both shaped by the settler-colonial context and pushed beyond it to look toward the Middle East.

The Growth of Muslim Presses and Publics

There was an explosion of the Muslim press in the interwar period, facilitated by new printing technologies that made printing a newspaper less expensive. Consequently, the number of Muslim newspapers exploded from a handful to dozens, and there were more spaces for Muslim communities and editors to broadcast their points of view. In the interwar period the European settler press in Algeria had consolidated into several newspapers that reprinted international wire news and featured less editorial analysis.[13] In contrast, the Muslim press in Algeria, which emerged strongly in the 1920s and 1930s, frequently granted Muslim editors significantly more power to control editorial content. Since Muslims also read European newspapers for news, Muslim publications often printed commentaries on the news, as well as on social and political questions.

Many editors in the Muslim press adopted several strategies to make the pages of their publications a space for community exchange, rather than a consistent expression of a single viewpoint. Content was generated not only by editors but also by community members. Readers were regularly invited to contribute, and editors regularly published their letters. Some of these letters were from remote, rural areas, which reflected the press's broad reach beyond Algeria's urban centers. Contributors frequently commented on recently published editorials in other publications. Editors published opinions with which they themselves disagreed. Publications solicited readers to write on particular questions and often hosted debates that were published across multiple issues between contributors with opposing perspectives.

In his thorough study of Algerian media, Arthur Asseraf has recently complicated Benedict Anderson's famous thesis that the press brings people together ideologically. The interwar Algerian press certainly helped create community, as Anderson describes presses broadly doing. Yet Asseraf has shown how in Algeria the press also further fractured an already divided settler-colonial society. I argue that discussions about women illustrate both the contours of these fractures and surprising convergences among various political, religious, and social groups. Scholars of the Algerian press have often divided the Muslim press into distinct ideological groups, such as the French-language assimilationist press or the proto-nationalist Muslim reformist press, but such neat categorizations risk oversimplifying the nuanced positions contained within each publication.[14]

Some publications of course had clear ties to particular political or religious projects, such as the official and unofficial organs of the Muslim reformist movement, *al-Shihab* (The Meteor), *al-Bassair* (The Insight), and *La Défense*, or those affiliated with the community of schoolteachers, like *La Voix des Humbles* (The Voice of the Poor) and *La Voix Indigène* (The Indigenous Voice). These two communities, Muslim reformists and schoolteachers, constitute two of the most important communities who reappear throughout this book, and yet they were hardly neatly defined, contained communities. Other publications were less transparent in their allegiances. While French colonial officials described it as favorable to the French cause, the largest Muslim publication, the Arabic-language *al-Najah* (Success), published editorials that straddled a range of religious and political opinions. Even schoolteacher publications, which could be easily written off as assimilationist, raised important critiques of French colonial policies and practices. One of the central contentions of this book is that interwar intellectual life was messy, and the elite Muslims who participated in it often maintained multiple religious, cultural, and political allegiances.

Anderson draws a neat line between the emergence of the press and eventual national unity. Stephanie Newell has argued that historians too frequently turn to nationalism to explain press activity and shows instead that both editors and readers were motivated by a wide range of political, social, and cultural allegiances.[15] Discussions about women show how the press was also a place for multiple imaginings, some of them ambivalent about nationalism. The history of debates about women is also a history of how a new communal intellectual life developed within interwar Algeria, even as most Muslims struggled to eke out a living. The press is not simply a source base that offers access to these debates. It is also an integral character within the story of how women's status became such a contentious and important issue within interwar Algeria.

Competing Visions at the Newsstand

The Muslim press in the interwar years was a mouthpiece to a wide range of political, religious, and social communities who used their publications to both preach to their existing following and court new followers. This vibrant communal intellectual exchange planted the seeds that grew into the activism (anti-colonial as well as feminist) of later generations. A closer look at some of the key publications offers an important context to their role within the world of the press. Debates about women help illustrate how these communities were interconnected in a larger network of interwar Muslim public life.

La Voix des Humbles (1922–47) was the official organ of l'Association des instituteurs d'origine indigène d'Algérie (the Association of Schoolteachers of Indigenous Origin, AIOIA). Many of the schoolteachers did not come from elite families, but their education in French colonial *écoles normales d'instituteurs* in Bouzareah, Oran, and Constantine enabled them to teach in French colonial schools. Over its long lifespan, the review featured the voices of 367 contributors, ninety-six of whom were former students of the école normale and graduated before

1912. Despite their middle-class status, these schoolteachers and the other contributors claimed to speak on behalf of the impoverished Muslim masses ("les humbles"). The editors wrote they wanted *La Voix des Humbles*, which was published in French, to speak to the state and European settlers as well as Muslim readers. Every cover page of *La Voix des Humbles* included the journal's subtitle, "For the evolution of the indigenous by French culture." This subtitle reflected their role as primary schoolteachers who were trained to facilitate the transmission of French culture.[16] Farther down the cover page featured an illustration of a man in an *'amama* (turban) building a building, brick by brick, with the caption: "Let's build a new society." These two slogans together illustrate how the schoolteachers envisioned themselves as vanguards encouraging a new hybrid society in which Muslims would assimilate to French culture and in turn enjoy more rights and a more prosperous society. Interestingly, the man remains dressed in the *'amama*, perhaps suggesting they envisioned the older elite of the *vieux turbans* were the ones to build a new society, or maybe the turban reflected a respect for Islamic culture.

La Voix des Humbles was not a newspaper but a significantly longer review, with the average issue about thirty-five pages. It frequently published longer pieces, including the minutes from association meetings or political assemblies, as well as serialized fiction pieces. The publication also acted as a mouthpiece for their community of middle-class Muslims, often congratulating recently married couples or posting about the death of a community member. One of the most central groups of actors in the discussions about women were the French-educated Muslim schoolteachers who were part of a small but growing Muslim middle class. Some of the details that appear in the historical record about their editors and milieu illustrate how this community was set apart from the vast majority of Muslim society in a number of ways yet was also connected to other communities. Fanny Colonna has described the schoolteachers as part of "a few thousand members of a 'cultivated elite,' the start of a true national elite and a well-formed middle class, fairly militant, with a progressive bilingual press representing several tendencies; open to the rest of the world, but careful not to risk an open break with the metropolis (mainland France) and the colonial authority."[17]

Some of those who were able to become schoolteachers enjoyed some social mobility. *La Voix des Humbles* cofounder Saïd Faci, for example, was born into a family of poor rural peasants and only began his schooling at age fifteen.[18] The editors and contributors to *La Voix des Humbles* were also exceptional because they were among the 2.1 percent of Muslim men literate in French.[19] Although they published in French, they also envisioned themselves as educators of the broader Muslim community. They wrote about Islam's feminist possibilities in order to educate the broader public that women's education was not a foreign imposition but an essential part of the Islamic tradition.

The papers' founders maintained multiple connections to other publications, political parties, and associations. Faci, Rabah Zenati, and Mohand Lechani, three of the four *La Voix des Humbles* cofounders, all published their own books, including novels, alongside their articles.[20] From 1945 to 1946 Lechani was elected *conseiller général*, or departmental administrator, of the Kabyle town Fort National (Larbaâ Nath Irathen). He was against nationalism until he reluctantly signed the "Motion of 61" in 1955 and allied with the Front de libération nationale (National Liberation Front, FLN). Faci, Zenati, Lechani, and the fourth *La Voix des Humbles* cofounder, Larbi Tahrat, were also all members of the Socialist Party, the Section française de l'Internationale ouvrière (French Section of the Workers' International, SFIO).[21] Even these political choices to some extent reflect the exceptional middle-class status of the cofounders, as the SFIO attracted predominantly middle-class Muslim members, unlike the Parti communiste algérien (Algerian Communist Party, PCA), which drew in more working-class Muslims.[22] They formed connections, through both the party and the École Normale de Bouzareah, to other interwar notables, including the lawyer of nationalist leader Messali Hadj Ahmed Boumendjel and the militant socialist from Oran, Joseph Begarra.[23] The party was equally a platform within which European women in Oran took up the "colonial maternalist" cause of Muslim women's advancement.[24] Many schoolteachers were active members of a range of associations, including the Association of Indigenous Intellectuals, the Association of the League of French Citizens of Muslim Origin, and the Committee for the Defense of Indigenous Liberties.[25]

Not all the contributors to *La Voix des Humbles* and *La Voix Indigène* were themselves schoolteachers. Some contributors also had roles within the French colonial bureaucracy.[26] Brothers and judiciary interpreters Ali, Amar, and Ahmed Hacène published in *La Voix des Humbles* and *La Voix Indigène*. *La Voix des Humbles* was also the first Muslim publication in Algeria to have regular female contributors, who were photographed and featured on the cover of the March/April 1932 issue (figure 1.1). The clothing donned by *La Voix des Humbles*' female contributors suggests they were middle- or upper-class and fluent in European sartorial norms.

Many nationalist and Muslim reformist commentators critiqued the schoolteachers' claim to speak on behalf of the impoverished Muslim masses ("les humbles") and questioned whether naturalized French citizens like cofounders Faci and Zenati and contributor Abderrahim

Figure 1.1. Muslim women on the cover of *La Voix des Humbles*, March/April 1932.
Source: BNF

Bendiab were connected enough to Muslim society. Nationalist leader Ferhat Abbas and *La Défense* editor Lamine Lamoudi, for example, critiqued Zenati and *La Voix Indigène* for their support for assimilation.[27] Zenati and Faci both became naturalized French citizens in 1903 and 1906, respectively. Very few Muslims held French citizenship, in part because applying for it meant renouncing one's Muslim personal legal status—a gesture many interpreted as a betrayal to Islam—and in part because of the exclusionary practices of French colonial administrators, who frequently denied applicants for arbitrary reasons.[28] The numbers of Muslims naturalized were generally very low with respect to the total population. Between 1905 and 1914, for example, on average forty-three Muslims were naturalized each year.[29]

The question of naturalization was thorny. Throughout the colonial project in Algeria, colonial theorists debated the best approach for the French colonial state to take with its Muslim colonial subjects.[30] Put briefly, "assimilation" in its political sense was the nineteenth-century idea that Muslims could become modern subjects and gain more rights if they could be imbued, through education and other measures, with the universally good values that the French cherished, like civilization.[31] Yet by the turn of the twentieth century, many had become disillusioned with this political project and argued instead for "association," which suggested Europeans and their colonial subjects should evolve independently according to their own cultural norms and constraints. The term "assimilation" can thus refer to either this political project or cultural assimilation, in which Muslims adopted European styles of dress or believed in the transformative impact of a French education.

In 1865 a *sénatus-consulte*, or French law, defined the parameters of personal status and naturalization. It was introduced to the Senate with the claim that it helped undertake the "patient and consistent work of assimilation, of progressive initiation into the benefits of civilization."[32] Yet the law separated French and Muslim subjects, arguing that Muslim norms, customs, and religion rendered them ineligible for French citizenship, so they should thus be governed by Muslim law, while French subjects would be citizens governed by French law. Claims about Muslim sexuality, polygamy, and family customs were central to how lawmakers justified this exclusion of Muslim subjects from French citizenship.[33] In terms of both colonial law and ideology, it cemented difference. As McDougall has written, the 1865 law "combined the preserving principles of 'association' with the universalist aspiration of 'assimilation' in a powerfully reassuring idea of colonization as progress, while in fact it made 'progress,' towards the resolution of the colonial situation in the ultimate emancipation it affected to imagine, impossible."[34]

In the first decades of the twentieth century, some Muslim intellectuals, including *La Voix des Humbles* cofounders Faci and Zenati, abandoned their Muslim personal status to become naturalized French citizens—a move most Muslims interpreted as apostasy.[35] Yet in the aftermath of World War I, as anti-colonial sentiment began to percolate globally, even assimilated intellectuals were treated with suspicion by the French colonial regime.[36] *La Voix des Humbles* also was subject to censorship and surveillance like other Muslim newspapers, especially for their occasional criticism of the French colonial regime.

The schoolteachers occupied a complicated position with respect to the colonial regime. They were educated in Algeria's three écoles normales (Bouzareah outside Algiers, Oran, and Constantine), which certified instructors to teach in French colonial primary schools.[37] These schools trained schoolteachers in their most primary task, deemed more important than any particular curriculum: the transmission of French culture.[38] French colonial administrators even sought to export the successful practices of the école normale of Bouzareah to other colonies. The governor-general of French West Africa (AOF) praised the school for how it did not "strain the religious and social convictions of its audience" but also managed to transmit "the prestige of France and French ideas."[39] They were trained alongside settler colleagues in the écoles normales in how to effectively transmit French culture to their students. As Jonathan Gosnell has described it, Muslim schoolteachers were "anointed as substitute fathers by the French colonial administration."[40]

Yet as Muslims they were still subject to the arbitrary whims of the *Indigénat*, a set of laws that cemented Muslims' secondary status and made them subject to arbitrary punishments. While French administrators praised them for their loyalty to the French cause,[41] the schoolteachers themselves described how, like other Muslims, they continued to be subject to the *Indigénat*, state surveillance, and "arabophobia."[42] As David Prochaska has written, in a settler-colonial society "the maximum points of friction occur . . . [between] those at the top of indigenous society and at the bottom of settler society."[43] Therefore schoolteachers, as part of Algeria's growing middle class, likely encountered particular forms of prejudice from settler society. Their publications, like other

Muslim periodicals, were subject to censorship. In 1923 Faci was forced to cede direction of *La Voix des Humbles* to Zenati in order to maintain amicable relations with the French colonial regime after they had censured one of his articles in which he blamed the state's negligence for the outbreak of tuberculosis. By 1927 Faci had moved to Toulouse, although he continued to publish in Algeria.

While many of the schoolteachers advocated assimilation and disavowed nationalism in later years, the community of schoolteachers as a whole should not be hastily written off as agents of empire. Later generations, including Fadéla Mesli, a nationalist fighter in the Algerian War of Independence, described how some schoolteachers took advantage of their position and the space of the classroom to teach potentially subversive material that would inspire pride in students' Muslim identity. Of her grandfathers, Mesli wrote:

> My grandfathers—maternal and paternal—were part of the first intake of teacher training students. France tried to draw from well-known middle-class families, whose children were talented, to get them to go to the Ecole Normale d'Instituteurs d'Alger. The objective was to train them in French language and culture so that after they could instrumentalize them to win over the rest of the population. [My grandfathers] did not fall into the trap and they kind of rebelled, they did the opposite of what they were meant to do. They taught their Muslim pupils the true values of our country, our culture and our identity.[44]

This suggests that some schoolteachers made use of their liminal position between the French colonial state and Muslims to teach beyond the curriculum.

Another newly formed community with its own publication was the Fédération des élus indigènes algériens (Federation of Indigenous Elected Officials), founded in 1927.[45] The Fédération des élus eventually had over a thousand members, all of whom held roles within the French colonial administration. Several of their first members were former members of the Young Algerians, a diverse French-educated group united by their calls to end the *Indigénat* and for equal taxation of settlers and Muslims, and sartorially by their mixing of European-style clothes with the tarbush, or fez. The group had two organs: *L'Entente Franco-Musulmane* and *L'Echo Indigène*. Their most outspoken leader was Dr. Mohammed Salah Bendjelloul, who directed *L'Entente Franco-Musulmane*, first published in 1935.

Some members of these communities would later start other publications. *La Voix des Humbles* cofounder and schoolteacher Zenati also edited his own newspaper, *La Voix Indigène* (1929–46), later renamed *La Voix Libre* (1947–52), until his death in 1952. As a member of the Fédération des élus, Ferhat Abbas critiqued the inequalities perpetuated by the French colonial regime but called for assimilation. By the late 1930s, however, he became increasingly disillusioned with the idea of reforming the existing colonial system and more committed to nationalist politics. He founded his own nationalist political parties, first the Union populaire algérienne (UPA) and later the Union démocratique du manifeste algérien (UDMA).

There were also publications affiliated with religious communities. The Muslim reform movement was ushered into Algeria by Ben Badis and organized through the Association des oulémas musulmans algériens (AOMA). The movement's mouthpieces in print were three major publications: *al-Bassair* (1935–39, 1947–56), *al-Shihab* (1925–39), and *La Défense* (1934–39). Of their Arabic-language publications, *al-Bassair* was the more traditional newspaper, often eight pages in length. Their other Arabic-language publication, *al-Shihab*, published longer essays on social, political, and religious questions alongside Ben Badis's Qur'anic commentary (*tafsir*). *La Défense* was their French-language newspaper run by a younger generation of reformist students.

The reformist movement established itself in opposition to the popular Sufism practiced in Algeria. While popular Sufi practice included pilgrimages to local shrines and allegiance to local Sufi saints and their families, reformists insisted intercession through shrines and saints was entirely unnecessary and Muslims could simply read the Qur'an for themselves. Sufi clergy members also collected payment from the French colonial state, a practice that reformists disavowed. Instead of a fundamental religious or doctrinal incompatibility, however, the tension between Sufis and reformists reflected a struggle over leadership.[46] The first generation of the AOMA was largely composed of scholars trained in Sufi *zawiya* (institutions), an illustration of how the communities were initially more connected than diametrically opposed. Still, they differed in their priorities. For the oulémas, it was incredibly important that Muslims in Algeria have their own distinct identity influenced by the Middle East as Arabic speakers, as Muslims, and as Algerians. The AOMA enjoyed wide support, and donors (many of them merchants) helped fund their publications and schools.[47]

Politically, reformists were connected to multiple communities. Ben Badis supported his cousin, Dr. Bendjelloul, and reformists supported Abbas's UDMA. Lamine Lamoudi, who was the secretary-general of the AOMA from 1931 to 1935 and the editor of *La Défense*, maintained ties to communist groups in Algeria. In the interwar period the reformists' vision of a distinct Arabic-language, Muslim, Algerian identity lent itself to a nationalist vision of a future Algerian nation, independent from French colonialism, but the group was largely focused on schooling and its publications. The AOMA became decidedly more political under the leadership of its second president, Sheikh Bashir al-Ibrahimi, when they became more involved with Ferhat Abbas's nationalist party, the UDMA.[48] As they became more vocally committed to anti-colonial nationalist politics, their tension with French colonial authorities increased, culminating in the creation of an AOMA office in Cairo in 1949 to operate with less scrutiny.

There were many Sufi orders (*tariqa*) in Algeria, but the most important were the Rahmaniyya, Qadiriyya, Tijaniyya, and Derqawa orders.[49] Although Sufi Islam was widely practiced across Algeria, Sufi communities did not have the same widespread, enduring presence in the press as the reformists.[50] In general, Sufi publications, like the majority of Muslim publications, were small and short-lived because of financial insecurity.[51]

In the 1920s a new order emerged in Mostaganem, the Alawiyya, under the leadership of the Sheikh Ahmad Ben Aliwa.[52] The Alawiyya order's mouthpiece, *al-Balagh al-Jazairi* (1926–47, The Algerian Messenger), voiced virulent opposition to the assimilationist tendencies of the schoolteachers, and it critiqued reformists as well. While other publications called for women's education, *al-Balagh al-Jazairi* questioned whether Muslim girls' virtue would be tainted by education or even by regular movement outside the home. They argued that essentialist patriarchy, or men's natural, innate dominance, was the foundation of Muslim society in Algeria, and any change to it would weaken their society as a whole. While the Mostaganem order lost influence in the 1940s, it still produced a handful of other short-lived publications after the end of *al-Balagh al-Jazairi*.

While there were many overlaps and connections between these various communities, there were other strict dividing lines. For example, while reformist and Alawiyya communities were staunchly against naturalization, several schoolteachers and contributors to their publications (*La Voix des Humbles* and *La Voix Indigène*) were naturalized French citizens.⁵³ Another obvious division was the choice to publish in French or in Arabic.

Some publications defied such neat categorizations entirely. The newspaper *al-Najah*, which was in print from 1920 to 1956 and was the largest Muslim paper in terms of printed copies, was less ideological than many of its interwar counterparts and would become the largest Muslim publication. Its cofounder and owner, Abdelhafidh ben El-Hachemi, was from an elite family in Biskra connected to the Sidi Ali ben Amar Sufi order.⁵⁴ He was educated at Zeitouna University in Tunis and then moved to Constantine in 1918, where he maintained multiple connections to both Sufi and reformist communities. Like Sheikh Abu Ya'la al-Zawawi, the imam of the Sidi Ramadan mosque in Algiers who published regularly on women in *al-Najah*, El-Hachemi maintained ties to both traditional Sufi communities and the emergent Muslim reform movement.

Despite these connections, he never became a nationalist. While *La Voix des Humbles* and the reformist publications were produced by a team, *al-Najah*'s editorials were mostly written by either El-Hachemi or the paper's editor, Smaïl Mami ben Allaoua. Unlike El-Hachemi, Mami was born into an impoverished family in Constantine, but they had similar connections to other important families, like the Ben Badis and Benlabed families. Like El-Hachemi, he too studied at Zeitouna, and despite his humble origins, he was well connected to multiple Muslim milieus across North Africa. Although colonial censors described *al-Najah* as "favorable to the French cause," Mami's regular travel was monitored closely and documented in French colonial surveillance reports.⁵⁵ Even in Tunisia, colonial agents tracked and reported on his connections to Tunisian activists.⁵⁶

Al-Najah capitalized on new wire technology to publish the latest news from the Middle East. In the second half of the 1920s, *al-Najah* offered a steady stream of coverage of Mustafa Kemal Atatürk's rise to power in Turkey and the reforms he undertook in the new Turkish Republic, including new rights for Turkish women. News from Tunisia, Egypt, Syria, Iraq, Iran, and Afghanistan equally illustrated for readers in Algeria that women's advancement was an integral part of modernization and uplift. As *al-Najah* reported this news, commentators in a wide range of publications began framing women's education in Algeria as an opportunity to participate in the broader renaissance underway in the "the Muslim world."

This overview is most concerned with the publications that discussed Muslim women, so there are many other Muslim publications, like the nationalist publication *Étoile Nord-Africaine*, for example, unanalyzed here.[57] Settler papers were rarely engaged in discussions about Muslim women's status, except for the occasional publishing of ethnographic accounts of Muslim women. The major exception here were papers by French feminists. The settler feminist paper *Femmes de Demain*, for example, offered continuous coverage about the status of Muslim women. Some contributors to *Femmes de Demain* highlighted the contributions of settler women who maintained ties to the Muslim community as educators, nurses, journalists, and amateur ethnographers. The paper claimed that as settler women, their shared bond of femininity made them better able to reach Muslim women than the French colonial regime. Their ability to successfully maintain their intermediary status between the state and Muslim women proved, they argued, that they deserved the right to vote in France. Such claims reappeared in the metropolitan feminist newspaper *La Française*.

Another settler paper analyzed within this book is *Oran républicain*, a communist newspaper launched in February 1937, with the agenda of "republicanism and opposition to anti-Semitism and Muslim oppression." As Allison Drew has mapped, the Parti communiste algérien (PCA) was directed by the Communist International (Comintern) to ally themselves with Muslim anti-colonialism.[58] As such, one of *Oran républicain*'s goals was to foster understanding between Europeans and Muslims, including through their weekly "Muslim Page," which appeared on Fridays, with articles written by socialist Mohamed el Aziz Kessous. Their "Women's Page," which appeared on Saturdays, sometimes featured articles about Muslim women's impoverished lived realities and limited possibilities, written by its editor, Yvonne Mussot.

In both the Muslim press and the French feminist press, articles frequently went unsigned. While reformist papers were developed by a large team, other newspapers had a smaller staff. Unattributed articles in *La Voix Indigène* were likely written by its prolific editor, Rabah Zenati, while unattributed articles in *al-Najah* were likely written by either its editor, Smaïl Mami, or its owner, Abdelhafidh ben El-Hachemi. In both the Muslim and French feminist presses, authors also frequently used pseudonyms or initials. Colonial subjects adopted pseudonyms for a wide range of reasons, including to play with notions of authority or to evade colonial censorship or social backlash.[59] As Stephanie Newell has illustrated, though, the anonymity of sources does not diminish their usefulness in historical analysis.

Readership

The press both reflected and produced community. Publications rendered local events accessible to readers across Algeria. Quotidian events otherwise difficult for historians of colonial subjects in Algeria to access—weddings, association meetings, speeches, conferences, public protests—left their traces within the pages of these publications. They reprinted and commented on speeches, association meetings, and events. Algerian readership practices also produced community around the press. Unlike the European press, subscriptions were infrequent for Muslim newspapers. News was also consumed communally in Algeria, which allowed it to expand its reach beyond the small literate population.[60] Young men on street corners called out and sang the news to passersby. Both in order to save costs and because of the high rates of illiteracy, a single newspaper was frequently purchased, read aloud, and sometimes translated in its entirety in a café, and then passed along to others. For Muslims, then, to quote Arthur Asseraf, the newspaper was "usually seen or heard rather than read."[61] This practice was common across the Middle East and made news accessible to the illiterate.[62] In Algeria, it made news particularly accessible because material in French could also be translated, thus further expanding its reach. Thus the interwar Muslim press was diffused across multiple sites of exchanges in which larger communities could participate in the debates about women, whose status was inextricably linked to Muslim society writ large.

Cafés themselves constituted entire social and intellectual worlds, which were inextricably tied to the social world of the press as well. Not only were newspapers regularly read aloud, but prominent figures associated with different newspapers gathered in particular cafés. In his memoir, the reformist writer Malek Bennabi devotes considerable attention to the café Ben Yamina in Constantine. It was located on rue des Rabins Ech-Charif, down the street from Ben Badis's office and the reformist printing press that published *al-Shihab*.[63] He labeled this street as the "intellectual artery" of Constantine. Bennabi describes all the characters one would encounter at the café Ben Yamina, including Smaïl Mami, the editor-in-chief of *al-Najah*, among other notable intellectual figures, like Younès Bahri.

Some Muslim women also read newspapers. Elite families had subscriptions to newspapers. Several of the women who wrote in to Muslim newspapers in the interwar years described being compelled to contribute to ongoing discussions after having read specific articles. There were also more informal ways women would have encountered the news. While cafés where newspapers were read aloud tended to be male-dominated spaces, women may have heard the headlines being read aloud by paper sellers while walking in the streets. Colonial surveillance reports also noted that Muslim domestic workers would listen to radio emissions playing as they cleaned European homes.

All Muslim publications were read closely by French colonial censors. They in turn created reports for superiors that would summarize their contents. They were especially concerned with tracking Algerian interest in Middle Eastern developments. The regime feared that news of anti-colonial revolt or pan-Arabism could inspire Algerian resistance, for example. At the same time, they monitored any supposed pro-French sentiment in a section of news surveillance reports titled "Evolution toward the Occident." As Asseraf has written, for the French colonial regime, "managing news was a form of managing space, and in particular, the distinction between 'Algeria' and 'abroad.'"[64]

The Woman Question Abroad

In the Middle East too, the press was an important outlet for discussions of women, and this is an important context for how these questions played out in Algeria. Discussions about women's place in society were part of the Nahda ("awakening"), a cultural and intellectual renaissance taking place across the region in the late nineteenth and early twentieth centuries. Early women's journals in Egypt included Hind Nawfal's *al-Fatat* ("The Young Woman"), published in Alexandria as early as 1892, and dozens that followed.[65] For elite women in Egypt, Palestine, Syria, and Lebanon, print culture was a mouthpiece for internal campaigns for women's rights, as well as a means of challenging external assumptions about Arab women. Within these spaces, efforts to push back against colonial intervention, to modernize, and to grant women rights reinforced each other. Some of these publications were quite long-lasting. The Egyptian Feminist Union's magazine *L'Égyptienne,* for example, was in print from 1925 to 1940. Others, of course, were more short-lived but still vibrant forums for women's issues.

Many of these publications were founded by elites, some with connections to the state. Mahmoud Zarrouk, a civil servant in Tunisia's Ministry of Justice, founded the Tunisian review *Leïla* in 1936. Zarrouk was from the wealthy coastal neighborhood of Tunis, Sidi Bou Said, and a member of a powerful family with direct ties to the bey of Tunis. These connections offered him and *Leïla* a certain degree of protection, although ultimately the publication was subject to censorship by the French in its later issues. *L'Égyptienne* (The Egyptian woman, 1925–40) was founded by Huda Sharawi, who was since 1923 the founder and head of the Egyptian Feminist Union. Sharawi's father was the president of the Egyptian Representative Council, the Egyptian parliament between 1881 and 1883, when the British disbanded it. Born into a wealthy family, Sharawi received the benefits of a privileged upbringing, including a multilingual private education. In 1910 she opened her own school for girls that taught academic subjects, as opposed to professional training, and in 1919 she organized the largest women's protest in support of the Nationalist Revolution. After her husband's death in 1922, she removed her face veil and eventually unveiled entirely. In addition to *L'Égyptienne*, she also founded its Arabic-language companion publication, *al-Masreyyah* (1937–40). Huda Sharawi's writings and other articles from *L'Égyptienne* were occasionally reprinted in Algeria.[66]

One theme that reappeared throughout the Middle Eastern women's press was Arab women's desire to challenge Orientalist assumptions about them. In *L'Égyptienne*'s first issue, the Egyptian Feminist Union's explanation of their decision to publish in French speaks to this agenda. They wrote that they intended to "introduce foreigners to the Egyptian Woman as she is nowadays—removing all the mystery and charm that her past reclusion carried to Occidental eyes—and to enlighten the European public opinion on the actual political and social state of Egypt."[67] Similarly, the editorial staff of the Palestinian journal *Filastin* wrote:

> It is gratifying to be able to inform the West and Westerners that an end is being put to their misconceptions of the Arab woman and her alleged slavish status. The Arab woman is not, as most Westerners think, a veiled creature hidden behind screens in voluptuous Hareems of wealthy Pashas and Beys. She is an enlightened

and free citizen enjoying equal rights and privileges as her mate and participating in his political activities.[68]

Both publications were motivated by a desire to write back against the stereotypes about them, including veiling, sequestrations, and harems.

Palestinian women described how they were confronted by these stereotypes even more because of the contact colonialism enabled between Palestinian elites and English people. A Palestinian women Matiel Mogannam wrote in 1936, "All English women think Arab women are uncultured. They believe they speak only Arabic, that they all wear veils and rush away at the sight of a man. How I wish I could take English women around to see my cultured Arab friends. How surprised they would be—European clothes, silk stockings, high-heeled shoes, permanently waved hair, manicured hands."[69] Elite Palestinian women's consumption of global fashion culture was a marker, according to Mogannam, of their emancipated status. These excerpts speak to Egyptian and Palestinian women's consciousness of how they were perceived as backward and oppressed by Europeans by virtue of their Arabness.

In Algeria, though, discussions focused on Algerians' Muslimness. Discussions in the Muslim press in Algeria about Islam's emancipatory potential for women were also directed at different audiences. Some French-language papers like those produced by the schoolteachers and the Fédération des élus (*La Voix des Humbles*, *La Voix Indigène*, and *L'Entente Franco-Musulmane*) sought to speak to Algeria's European settler population. They, more than other papers, were invested in educating the French about Islam. They used a variety of examples from Islamic history and the hadith literature to prove that Islam was not as misogynistic as French stereotypes insisted.

The reformist papers cited similar examples from Islamic knowledge and also argued that Islam was emancipatory for women, but to a different end. They sought not to convince Europeans but instead engage in an internal discussion with other Muslims, including Sufis, about Islamic ideals for women. The reformist position was that Muslim women's lack of education and strict sequestration was part of popular Sufi Islam's deviance from the "true Islam" of the time of the Prophet Muhammad and the Qur'an.

In the Muslim press in Algeria broadly, discussions about women were largely dominated by male voices. Yet when women were occasionally published in the Muslim press, they too, like their Middle Eastern counterparts, wrote fiery critiques of ignorant European attitudes toward Muslim women. They also directed their anger at Muslim men for not agitating for more rights for women and at the French colonial state for not providing more material resources to Muslim women.

Algeria's settler-colonial status set it apart from these other Middle Eastern contexts and gave Islam particular weight and meaning within discussions about women. As Muriam Haleh Davis has written, colonial Algeria enacted a "racial regime of religion" onto its colonial subjects.[70] In other words, racism against Muslims focused not on their Arabness or Algerianness but on their status as Muslims. Still, the stereotypes against Muslims, and the ways they were codified into colonial Algeria's legal and political apparatus, demonstrate that religion functioned as race would in other colonial contexts. French claims of Muslim misogyny were an important rationale that the French colonial regime used to legitimize their confiscation of Muslim land in Algeria toward their political and economic ends. So when Muslim commentators in the press insisted on Islam's feminist potential, they were challenging the very basis of the French colonial occupation.

Algerian Answers to the Woman Question

The debates about women in Algeria had different local stakes for each community. The schoolteachers sought to convince both Muslim society and the French colonial state that more schools for girls were necessary. For the Fédération des élus, Muslim women needed to be educated so that Muslim society could better assimilate to French norms. The Muslim reform movement saw women's education as necessary for a new generation of mothers to be able to instill in their children pride in their Muslim, Algerian identity. For the Alawiyya order, any new freedoms afforded to Muslim women were dangerous signs of Muslim identity being lost. Like other publications, *al-Najah* featured a wide range of perspectives on women's advancement but often described it as one avenue for Muslims in Algeria to enjoy the societal advancement of other modernizing Middle Eastern nations.

There was also a geographic story at play. While the schoolteachers who comprised the AIOIA were trained at the école normale in Bouzareah, a suburb of Algiers, the association itself operated out of Oran in the west of the country. While there were dozens of professional associations for European doctors, lawyers, and other professionals, the Association of Indigenous School Teachers was the first Muslim professional organization established in the image of its European counterparts.⁷¹ Oran was Algeria's most working-class city, as well as the city with the largest European population, many of whom were Spanish workers.⁷² Some of the schoolteachers, including the leadership of *La Voix des Humbles*, were also members of the socialist SFIO, active in Oran. Educated to be fluent in French cultural norms, the schoolteachers fit seamlessly into the predominantly European Oranais urban fabric. Constantine, on the other hand, in the east of the country, was a predominantly Muslim city, with a deeply rooted religious establishment. Constantine was home to a long-standing Sufi elite, including members of the family of El-Hachemi, and was where Ben Badis established his own mosque and school, out of which the Muslim reform movement grew. Constantine was also home to a sizable Jewish population. Jews in both Constantine and Algeria broadly maintained a "situational" relationship to their Muslim and settler counterparts, to borrow Ethan Katz's phrase about how different political and social circumstances resulted in different communal relations.⁷³ From the beginning of the French colonial presence in Algeria, Jews faced an antisemitism from Europeans so virulent that candidates who boasted being "antijuif" were particularly successful in local elections in the late 1890s.⁷⁴ Constantine was also the site of the 1934 riots in which right-wing extremists enflamed tensions between Jews and Muslims, resulting in twenty-eight deaths.⁷⁵ The Muslim publications that operated in these cities reflected each city's own ecosystem of public life, complete with their layered political and religious allegiances.

Sufism also played out in Algeria according to its own geography. Sufi power was more concentrated in Algeria's rural areas, which were peppered with important sites of Sufi power, *zawiyas* and shrines. Zawiyas were institutions that played a religious, educational, and charitable role. They offered a basic religious education as well as Maliki *fiqh* (jurisprudence) for future scholars. Zawiyas were usually led by a local saint or a *muqaddam* (leader) connected to the saint. Tombs and shrines devoted to saints and their families were also important centers where people made pilgrimage to pray for intercession. In the interwar years, as more Muslims migrated away from rural Algeria, first to France and then to Algerian cities, such centers lost many of their adherents and donors.⁷⁶ Yet the dominance of Sufi Islam in rural areas should not suggest that the reformist movement operated only in Algeria's urban centers. Courreye's work mapping reformist schools, for example, demonstrates their community's wide reach into rural areas as well.

Interestingly, while historians have stressed this shift in religious practice away from Sufi traditions with the arrival of the Muslim reform movement, these shifts were more subtle in people's lived realities. When asked about her family's religious practice, Dahbia Lounas, a woman was born in 1933, explained that "no one in my family or my region knew any Sufi practices."[77] She lived in the town of Mirabeau (today Draâ Ben Khedda) near Tizi Ouzou. For Lounas, the religious practices of her region were not "Sufi" but just broadly Islamic. This reflects how Charlotte Courreye has argued that there was much overlap between Sufi and reformist communities and scholars should be careful not to overstate their contrast.[78]

Muslim commentators made sense of their anxieties about women in Algeria by simultaneously looking outward to the Middle East and inward to their own society and their knowledge about Islam. The new technology of wire news granted Muslims in Algeria unprecedented, near immediate access to news from the rest of the world. The Muslim press in Algeria covered and commented on women's advancement projects happening across the Middle East, sometimes directly via women's publications, which suggests they had access to some. *La Voix des Humbles*, for example, reprinted articles from the Egyptian feminist publication *L'Égyptienne*. Muslim reformist publications reprinted articles from more religious Egyptian newspapers.

Interestingly, religious and secular Algerian Muslims alike saw themselves as part of this larger regional moment of rupture. They took pride in the successes of leaders like Mustafa Kemal Atatürk and interpreted his successes as shared victories for the Muslim world. As commentators in Algeria wrote about these projects, they were participating in a larger, transnational conversation about modernity. Indeed, as Marya Hannun has written about Afghanistan, "the very act of discussing women was cast as a central feature of modernity."[79] In Algeria too, these discussions about news from the Middle East, modernity, and women were a forum for commentators from multiple different social, political, and religious backgrounds to envision a feminist future Algeria that looked to the Middle East instead of Europe as a model.

The press offered commentators the space to offer their own interpretations of Islamic sources and map out their evidence for readers. Commentators in Algeria looked to the corpus of Islamic knowledge to make sense of their changing society and their changing ideas about women. The growing Muslim reform movement empowered average Muslims to read and interpret Islamic knowledge—a privilege previously limited to a select few—thereby chipping away at boundaries between Muslims and their religious leadership. Scholars had long arranged pieces of Islamic knowledge in the writing of fatwas, but in this period lay commentators took up the practice to construct arguments about women's lives and possibilities. They cited fragments from the same corpus of Islamic knowledge—the Qur'an, the hadith literature, and Islamic history—but the meaning of these fragments was never fixed. They interpreted the same verses in different ways and thus came to conflicting conclusions about contemporary women. Those engaged in this kind of work were not limited to reformist papers either. Even in more anticlerical papers, commentators would cite and rearrange Islamic knowledge in these ways. Commentators envisioned potentially feminist futures that did not shy away from Islam but reclaimed it as an emancipatory force for women that had been muddled by centuries of patriarchal tribalism and culture. Many publications, for example, either referenced or featured entire articles around the important women of early Islamic history, including Khadija, the businesswoman who married the Prophet Muhammad and became his first follower. While interwar commentators frequently referenced women from Islamic history, they notably did not mention Kahena, the seventh-century Amazigh warrior queen. This illustrates McDougall's argument about how interwar Muslim reformists sought to cement Algeria's Muslim identity over other forms of identity, including Amazigh, through their telling of history.

Writing about women offered interwar commentators in Algeria a forum to work through anxieties about the present and competing visions of the future. The numbers and diversity of individuals, including readers, who wrote about women in the press suggests the status of women was of critical importance to a broad segment of the population. In the present they observed a number of changes to Algerian society, many of them wrought by urbanization. These changes included changes in gender norms. Working women's new visibility, schoolgirls' limited access to education, and changing veil styles were all markers of present social upheaval, according to commentators. Muslims in Algeria described the Muslim world as in the midst of a transformation toward modernity—within which women's advancement was key. As commentators reflected on the present-day situation in Algeria, the changes in the Middle East, and Islam's emancipatory potential, they articulated visions of how women's advancement could create broader societal uplift in the future. While these commentators disagreed about the particulars of women's advancement and the ideal future Algeria, the path forward was articulated through aspirations of a future Algeria with women at the center of the process. Women performed—both rhetorically and through their lived realities—the symbolic labor of both Muslim society's decline and its aspiration.

Looking outward across the region and inward toward women in their society was a critical move through which Muslims imagined a better future. For schoolteachers educated within the French colonial system, women's limited possibilities signaled the failure of the French colonial state to live up to its values. Some among the growing class of Muslim bureaucrats and representatives saw Muslim women as the conduit through which they could slowly modernize the Algerian public through a French colonial model. They, like the schoolteachers, envisioned a future Algeria that while still under French colonial rule, was prosperous because of how women's advancement would uplift and modernize the entire society. For Muslim socialists, women's status represented the worst aspects of an entire political system designed to marginalize Muslims. For Muslim reformists, women's status reflected how Muslims had deviated from Islam's original reverence for women. They envisioned a future independent Algeria in which women played a critical role as guardians of Muslim Algerian identity in the next generation. For their Sufi adversaries, new forms of women's labor were alarming signs of a society losing its hold on what rendered it powerful: essentialist patriarchy. For them, a potentially feminist future represented the ongoing demise of Muslim society under colonialism. For all communities, change in women's status within Algerian society was a way forward out of the current crises and toward their vision of an ideal Algerian future.

Different religious communities envisioned different roles for women. In Sufi Islam as it was practiced in much of Algeria, women regularly visited saint shrines and cemeteries.[80] They prayed for themselves and their families, and on behalf of others for Sufi saints to intercede on their behalf with God. There were also cultural and religious rituals that accompanied marriages, childbirths, and deaths, carried out by women, among women. The scholarship on women's roles in colonial Algeria's Sufi communities remains underdeveloped. Still, some case studies of specific cases help illustrate what possibilities were available for women within Sufi communities. Julia Clancy-Smith, for example, has examined examples of female saints and leaders in nineteenth century colonial Algeria. She noted that women were of course adherents but also official members in the case of the Tijaniyya and Rahmaniyya orders. In areas where there were a large number of women members, like the commune of Akbou in Kabylie, there were women *muqaddamat* (circle leaders).[81] Women could also achieve sainthood, the most powerful position within the Sufi hierarchy, as did nineteenth-century saints Lalla Khadija and Lalla Zainab. Augustin Jomier has written about the educated Mzabi women who held multiple important roles within society, including preaching to other women, presiding over important events in women's lives, and washing women's dead bodies.[82] Jomier described a female literary culture among Mzabi women broadly in which many knew how to read Arabic. He analyzes how this particular form of female power declined alongside the rise of Muslim reform in the region.

Indeed, Muslim reformists had their own idea for Muslim women—sometimes articulated in direct opposition to the chaotic, unpredictability of typical Sufi practices. Muslim reformists in colonial Algeria, as in the rest of the Middle East, often wrote about women in terms of their responsibility to the nation as mothers. As he ushered Muslim reformism into Algeria, Ben Badis envisioned women's education as critical because of women's status as the custodians of the next generation. Reformist publications echoed this language. And yet, as he educated women and reformists opened schools for girls, they opened the doors to new forms of female power—both discursive and real. Later generations of women educated in reformist schools would themselves become teachers, and they would occasionally even clash with reformist leadership. Within the press too, some reformist commentators offered visions of women playing much greater public roles in society alongside men.

The Woman Question in Muslim Public Life

Print culture was one part of a larger ecosystem of an expanding Muslim public life in the interwar years. The woman question, a shorthand for concerns about women's status and rights, swept multiple interwar forums. Theater performances asked whether uneducated women could be equal partners to sophisticated male counterparts. Associations and charities banded together to address the scarcity of resources available to mothers. Conferences put on by Muslims and Europeans alike asked how best to help Muslim women.

Debates about women in the press reappeared on stage. Many plays circled around the questions of their lived realities—how Muslim women were forced to support their families in difficult economic times, their limited education opportunities, how they could find love in spite of generational differences in attitudes, how they could find good partners in the climate of alcoholism. Several of the plays of the era's most famous Muslim playwright, Mahieddine Bachtarzi, centered around issues surrounding working-class women's lives. His play *The Love of Women*, for example, reflected ongoing discussions in the press about women's lives.[83]

Bachtarzi attracted a wide audience. A surveillance report noted that in six months alone (September 1936 to February 1937), the Bachtarzi troupe performed nineteen shows of five different plays in twelve different cities, with one showing having up to two thousand Muslims in the audience. Women were among the crowds of spectators, sometimes in the thousands, who gathered to watch plays (figure 1.2). Within the theater audiences were also figures like Ben Badis and others from the AOMA, politicians, and schoolteachers, as well as editors and contributors to Muslim newspapers, such as Smaïl Mami, the editor of *al-Najah*.[84]

There were also dozens of smaller theater groups whose plays similarly reflected this interest in women.[85] In December 1936, for example, a local theater troupe performed a piece titled *Ya Baba Zouedjni* (Marry

FIGURE 1.2. Theater audience with women in haik visible, from *L'Afrique du Nord Illustrée*, 1933.
Source: BNF

me, father) to an audience of 250 in Skikda (then Philippeville), about a Muslim son who wanted his father's blessing to marry a young European woman, the daughter of a police officer. The play is largely a series of conversations between the young man and his parents. The turning point occurs in the third and final act, when the son reads about the modern, Muslim women of Egypt who were functionaries and doctors, drove cars, and flew planes. This new knowledge inspires the son to offer a speech about how Muslims need to elevate themselves through the education and emancipation of women. Just as in discourses in the press, the example of what Muslim women could achieve elsewhere served as a reminder of what was possible in Algeria. The valorization of the achievements of Egyptian women signaled the potential greatness of the working women of Algeria as well.

Women were also participants in interwar theater culture. While the stage was typically dominated by men, the Jewish actress Marie Soussan began acting on stage in 1925 at the Casino d'Alger.[86] Throughout the 1930s she appeared on stage in a variety of performances, many with the theater troupe of actor Rachid Ksentini, to whom she was also married. Women also attended theater performances. In 1933 *L'Afrique du Nord illustrée* published a photograph of a recent performance of Soussan and Ksentini in Blida, which shows several women dressed in haiks in the audience.[87] The quality of the photograph makes unveiled women more difficult to spot, though they may have been in attendance too.

Like theater, music was another domain of Muslim-Jewish collaboration in the interwar years. There too, concerns about women were the subject of many famous songs recorded, disseminated, and rerecorded by Jewish North African artists, sung in Arabic. Chris Silver has recently mapped the impact of four major Tunisian women singers of the era: Habiba Messika, Ratiba Chamia, Louisa Tounsia, and Dalila Taliana. They sang about love, sexuality, the challenges women faced, and their status as modern women, and like Bachtarzi, they were prolific. Silver noted that "between 1924 and 1930, Messika recorded close to one hundred records." Although they were Tunisian, their music was listened to across the region. In Algiers, Messika's performances had thousands in the audience.[88] Like theater, listening to music, through both live performances and records, was a popular art form enjoyed by men and women of all social classes in Algeria, which reflected the larger social questions swirling about women and their place in North African society.

Associations were another domain where the intellectual life of the Muslim press played out in public. The Muslim reformists had several important associations, including the Cercle du Progrès, which hosted conferences and speeches, and the Kheira mutual aid society. In 1940, when Kheira moved to a new location, they held a large celebration that featured speeches, a comedy theater performance from the Bachtarzi troupe, a sports drill, and a skit performed by young girls from the Shabiba school.[89] The range of these forms of entertainment speaks to the breadth of the networks through which Muslim reformist influence played out. When new Muslim reformist schools were inaugurated, they similarly held large public celebrations to foster community support.

Politics was another area in which Muslim women also participated alongside men in political rallies and protests. They crowded into stadiums alongside men to hear Messali Hadj, the leader of the nationalist and communist Étoile nord-africaine party, speak.[90] They also protested in the streets alongside men. In June 1936 women joined male workers to march in support of Messali Hadj's Étoile nord-africaine political party. Photographs of women protestors were published in multiple European publications, including *Liberté* and *L'Afrique française*.[91] In April 1939 around forty women were among the crowd of three thousand who marched in support of the Messali Hadj in Algiers.[92] During the national hymn, these women made their presence known by offering their *youyous*, an ululation offered by women across North Africa as a means of expressing support and cheer, often at weddings and celebrations. There was thus an entire ecosystem of intellectual energy devoted to Muslim women, the epicenter of which was the press, but which also included theaters, sports, associations, schools, and religious institutions.

CHAPTER 2

Domestic Workers in a Changing City

On a Sunday morning in May 1937, a young Muslim domestic worker named Rahma Ben Drahou traveled with a group of European communists from Nemours (Ghazaouet), a seaside town near the Moroccan border, to the city of Marnia (Maghnia), 50 kilometers south of Nemours.¹ In Marnia's city center, the group petitioned strangers for money to send to Bilbao for the children who survived the recent bombardment during the ongoing Spanish Civil War. When they returned to Nemours, the group had successfully raised the considerable sum of 516 francs. The local settler communist newspaper *Oran républicain* printed a letter about Ben Drahou's efforts alongside a photograph of her to commend her exceptional activism.²

Throughout the interwar period in Algeria, Muslim domestic workers provoked attention from settler and Muslim commentators alike because of their visibility and mobility. In the French imagination, Muslim women lived lives of total confinement with limited access to the outdoors or even sunlight. Nineteenth-century Orientalist European art depicted fantasies of the harem, the private area of Muslim homes reserved for family alone, in which naked Muslim women lounged around, prevented by the misogyny of Muslim society from being anything but sexual objects. Such ideas reappeared in official correspondence between colonial administrators as they explained how

Muslim women did not work. An administrator from Larbaâ wrote, for example, that administrators who wanted to offer schooling or work to Muslim girls and women were in a difficult position because Muslims were so "bridled with ancestral customs," like sequestration, and "this condition seems normal to them."[3] Yet urban, working-class Muslim women became increasingly mobile in the interwar period in ways that upended such long-standing Orientalist claims.

Muslim women's mobility depended on a variety of factors, including location and class. In rural areas of Algeria, women worked alongside men in the fields planting and harvesting a wide variety of crops.[4] Some maintained important positions within Sufi religious institutions, which involved a regular presence in shrines and cemeteries. In Algeria's cities, however, the women of elite urban families often led limited public lives. Poorer women took on various roles in public to earn money, including, for example, selling bundled herbs and other goods in marketplaces as well as working in European homes as domestic workers. This chapter focuses on the growing numbers of domestic workers and how others talked about them.

Oran républicain, which published the feature on Ben Drahou, occupied an important space in the settler intellectual landscape. As a communist paper, *Oran républicain* sought to foster understanding of Muslim society for their European audience, including through their women's page, which appeared on Saturdays. While the women's page was typically on the fourth or sixth page of the eight-page newspaper, in the issue with the feature of Ben Drahou, it was on the third page, with a single large illustration in the middle (other issues had smaller illustrations scattered on the page). Yvonne Mussot, the editor of *Oran républicain*'s women's page, published the letter she received about Ben Drahou in the middle of her own ongoing commentary about the emancipation of Muslim women. While her columns in other issues pointed to the need to improve the material conditions of Muslim lives, this column focused more on Islam. Mussot moved from the letter about Ben Drahou, published alongside a photograph of Ben Drahou in which she was unveiled (figure 2.1), to a discussion about the verse of the Qur'an that mandated hijab. This verse, she argued, was evidence that Islam required women only to cover their bodies and did not require them to veil.

As a domestic worker since the age of seven, Ben Drahou had spent considerable time in the company of Europeans. It was this repeated exposure to European culture, Mussot suggested, that emancipated

FIGURE 2.1. Rahma Ben Drahou, from *Oran Républicain*, June 12, 1937.
Source: BNF

her from the shackles of Muslim sequestration and veiling so that she could be unveiled, engage in such public activism, and model what an emancipated Muslim woman could look like. Rahma Ben Drahou's story affirmed another recurring fantasy for some settlers: that proximity to Europeans would encourage assimilation and thereby liberate Muslim women.[5] While the article, like the paper broadly, framed itself as in solidarity with Muslims, Mussot reproduced an idea also taken up by colonial administrators, that Muslim women's willingness to work outside the home, the resulting regular income they earned, and their proximity to Europeans were positive signs that the project to assimilate Muslim society was working. To Mussot and colonial administrators, the Muslim domestic worker was a liminal figure. As was the case with colonial soldiers, regular work and proximity to European norms could discipline women's bodies and thereby liberate them from the decadence of Muslim culture. Like the soldier who would return to his people reformed and assimilated, the domestic worker's body would carry Frenchness from her workplace to her society.

Domestic workers—many of them recent migrants from rural areas of Algeria—remade the norms for urban women's conduct in public.[6]

They crossed the boundaries of public space. They entered European intimate spaces. They uncovered their faces. They adopted manners of speech and self-fashioning in conversation with their European employers. They sometimes brought home more money than their husbands and fathers. They exerted more control over the family finances. The ways in which they reshaped urban life, in turn, reshaped Muslim families and communities.

As a result, domestic workers provoked alarm within the pages of the Muslim press. Some male, urban, elite commentators insisted that working women's mobility was a "catastrophe" that threatened the moral fiber of Muslim society.[7] To them these mobile, working women represented the beginnings of a seismic shift in Algerian society in which frivolous girls who could now earn an income would be more interested in buying makeup than starting a family, and more broadly, modernity would upend the dignity and sanctity of Algerian society. These concerns were not just static, timeless, patriarchal pushback. Instead, they reveal how urban elites were forced to reckon with the ways working-class migrant women were remaking their cities. As Hanan Hammad has written about urbanization in interwar Egypt, "By approaching gender as a primary way of signifying relationships of power and considering genders as temporal and spatial constructs rather than fixed categories, one realizes that ordinary life in the urban-industrial ethos could destabilize the female-male binary, to use Judith Butler's term."[8] Similarly, for this Muslim urban elite in Algeria, migrant women's new labor and mobility violated multiple social divisions at once—urban/rural, elite/working-class, male/female, and public/private. Inquiry into their concerns demonstrates how working women's mobility was at the intersection of these shifting divides.

Migration and the Colonial Economy

Economic crisis created the conditions for women's dramatic entry into the labor force in the interwar years. By the end of World War I, the Muslim middle and elite classes were small, with the overwhelming majority of the Muslim population struggling to eke out a living amid shrinking economic opportunities in both the Algerian countryside and cities. The settler economy produced an increasingly large gap between the modern, mechanized settler farms, which often operated on the most fertile land, and small family-run Muslim farms on less desirable land.[9] As large, European agricultural landholders, backed by the French colonial regime, continued to confiscate Algeria's best agricultural land, economic opportunity waned for rural Muslims. Muslims suffered famine-like conditions in 1912, 1920, and 1937 in particular, which led many families to abandon rural life altogether and migrate to nearby towns and cities. One noteworthy exception was how in this same period some former peasants bought back land from Europeans. They formed an emergent rural, mid-scale landholding class who would later comprise one of the social bases of the nationalist movement.

These conditions led many Muslims to migrate from rural to urban Algeria in the interwar years. In spite of the Great Depression, French settlers in Algeria fared better than those in the metropole, and European settler families enjoyed some upward mobility. Before the First World War, domestic workers in European homes were most often Spanish settlers.[10] As more Europeans experienced upward mobility, however, there was an increase in the demand for domestic workers as the pool of European domestic labor shrank. While some Muslim men did work as domestic workers, the roles were largely filled by Muslim women, who would accept lower wages and were perceived by Europeans to be less threatening than Muslim men.

The exponential growth in the numbers of women working in the interwar period was also due to the exacerbation of an existing phenomenon: a lack of male income providers. The death, illness, and migration facilitated by World War I left many interwar Muslim families without income earners. Large-scale male migration to France left many married Muslim women widowed or divorced, and unmarried Algerian women unable to depend on their brothers or fathers to support the family, although some of these men sent money home when they could. This outmigration from Algeria to France was legally facilitated by a 1914 law that authorized freedom of movement between Algeria and France for Muslims.[11] While scholars have emphasized the flows of migration facilitated by colonialism, including of soldiers and workers between Algeria and France, between 1911 and 1921 two hundred thousand Muslims left Algeria for places other than France, most often the Middle East.[12] The Muslim men who stayed in Algeria struggled to find work. Many were only able to find sporadic employment as day laborers.

Many migrated en masse to Algeria's urban centers. The urban Muslim population increased from 558,000 in 1926 to 819,500 in 1936.[13] Between 1926 and 1936, then, Algerian cities were populated with 261,500 recent arrivals from the countryside.[14] This trend continued with the urban Muslim population reaching 1,642,000 by 1954.¹⁵ The informal segregation of colonial life, under which Muslims were often relegated to particular neighborhoods, meant that this urban population was often concentrated in cramped quarters.¹⁶ Algiers's working-class Muslim population was largely concentrated within the boundaries of the casbah, which was composed predominantly of a series of Ottoman-era constructions, with a small number of European buildings around the perimeter. The casbah was not only marked by its historical architecture but also delineated by very specific cartographical boundaries: the Rampe Vallée, the Guillemin boulevard, and the Militaire du Nord boulevard.¹⁷ While the ancient walls that once marked the limits of the city no longer stood, Muslim inhabitants largely remained within their boundaries.¹⁸ As the population of the casbah grew exponentially throughout the first half of the twentieth century, its limited space became increasingly densely inhabited. Between 1881 and 1931 the population density of the casbah of Algiers more than doubled, from 1,436 to 2,984 inhabitants per square hectare.¹⁹ In 1931 alone, of the 53,517 inhabitants of the casbah of Algiers, 87 percent were recent migrants to the capital city from rural Algeria.²⁰ Many of these recent arrivals struggled economically. Kabyle men mostly worked as day laborers, while their wives worked as domestic workers.²¹ Yet despite continued economic hardship, these recent migrants and working-class men and women of the casbah left their mark on the booming urban culture.

The geography of the casbah also allowed for an alternate sphere of circulation for all Muslim women: rooftops. Women could move through the city in semi-privacy through the rooftops and still avoid the casbah's crowded streets.²² The rooftops also offered women the space to escape the heat of their apartments, entertain friends, and enjoy the view of the Mediterranean.²³ In the 1937 film *Pépé le Moko*, shot in Algiers, the protagonist Pépé escapes from the police via rooftops to return to his hiding place. As he moves across the rooftops, veiled women stand and stare, unused to the presence of a man in their otherwise female domain.

While the data about women's work is often sparse, some statistics offer a few broad strokes of the landscape of women's work in the early twentieth century. In 1911, for example, women were most often employed within the clothing industry, including sorting secondhand clothes to be resold. Broadly, there was an exponential increase in recorded numbers of Muslim women working in the early twentieth century, from 1,520 in 1902 to 25,821 by 1924. Before the interwar period, the most dominant forms of work for Muslim women were agricultural labor (largely underreported) and work in the clothing industry as seamstresses, weavers, embroiderers, and lace makers.

Table 2.1 Total Muslim women workers, by year

YEAR	WOMEN WORKERS
1902	1,520
1905	7,533
1911	21,397
1924	25,821

Source: Ageron, *Les Algériens musulmans et la France*, 849

Table 2.2 Types of Muslim women's work in 1911

TYPE OF WORK	WORKERS
Workers in the food industry	710
Workers in the clothing industry	18,903
Construction workers	66
Other workers	605
Other types of employment	1,113
Domestic workers	4,655

Source: Ageron, *Les Algériens musulmans et la France*, 850

Table 2.3 Types of Muslim women's work

	1911	1954
Domestic workers	4,655	23,511
Industrial workers	19,613*	5,635
Agricultural workers		7,036

* Here I am combining the numbers of women who worked in clothing and food industries in 1911, according to Ageron, 850. Sources: Kateb, *Européens, "Indigènes" et Juifs en Algérie*; Ageron, *Les Algériens musulmans et la France*, 850

Table 2.4 Domestic work by sex in 1911 and 1954

	1911	1954
Male domestic workers	19,074	970
Female domestic workers	4,655	23,511

Source: Kateb, *Européens, "Indigènes" et Juifs en Algérie*, 255

Table 2.5 Muslim women's labor according to the 1936 Census

Industries extractives	18
Industries mal désignées	11
Industries alimentaires	195
Industries chimiques	71
Industries textiles	1,425
Travail des étoffes	1,010
Manutention	2,128
Commerce, banques, assurances	269
Professions libérales	112
Soins personnels, domestiques	14,530
Services publics privés	37

Source: Archives nationales d'outre-mer

What is noticeable from these statistics is not only that women's labor in domestic work increased rapidly between 1911 and 1954 but also that it bore an inverse relationship to men's employment in domestic work. In other words, between 1911 and 1954 Muslim women replaced Muslim men as domestic workers. Of the total population of Muslim women in 1954, 2,236,950, only 2 percent were employed at all and 1 percent as domestic workers. So the number of domestic workers with respect to the overall population of women remained small but still significant, particularly considering its dramatic increase over the interwar years. Other qualitative sources suggest that women also took up other forms of work, including embroidery, shoemaking, weaving, and cigarette manufacturing, among others, which are not reflected in these statistics. In the Arab world broadly, as Nadia Hijab has argued, despite claims that Arab women do not work, they are often central actors in national economies, although generally in less visible sectors, including agriculture and the domestic economy.[24]

While many rural women were skilled in artisanal crafts, including spinning wool, weaving, and sometimes pottery, rural and urban women earned more from domestic service. In Algiers, after domestic work, artisanal work completed within the home or in workshops was the second most dominant form of work. In general, there was great diversity in the reported wages for women's work. One administrative memo claimed that domestic workers in Algiers earned between thirty and forty francs per hour. This figure may have been exaggerated since a range of documents and memos suggest that in other cities, domestic workers made thirty to sixty francs per month.[25] In most industrial settings, administrators reported that women were paid between four to ten francs/day depending on their age and skill. The form of most profitable work was not the same across all Algerian cities. Constantine, for example, had a smaller population of European settlers and a larger existing market for gold and silver thread work, so there more women earned income from craftwork than domestic service.[26]

In colonial Algeria domestic work arrangements were often informal and underreported, so official statistics offer only a partial view. While urbanization was underway across Algeria, the archival record is particularly fruitful for the city of Algiers. In May 1929 the mayor of Algiers counted 1,430 women (980 women and 450 "young women") who worked as domestic workers in Algiers alone.[27] He noted that the hours of employment for domestic workers were "very variable." This statistic was likely on the lower end of the actual number, considering that other sources suggest the total number of Muslim women domestic workers in Algeria was already at 4,655 in 1911.[28]

Within the family space, women's earning power changed how families operated. Marie Baroy, a master's student, conducted interviews with Muslim families to better understand women's labor.[29] She described the change within the family space provoked by women's earning power as a "revolution." Since women who secured domestic work were more likely to bring in regular income than their husbands, women exerted greater control over the family's budgeting. Men began submitting their entire paychecks to the woman of the household, with the exception of a few francs men might keep for cigarettes. According to Baroy's interviews, it was the woman of the house who decided whether there was enough extra money for a man to visit the cafés—a key space of male sociability. Since women maintained more regular hours, men were more often primarily responsible for taking care of the children while she was at work. Finally, before and during the interwar period, it was often the men who would complete any shopping for the home, including groceries. Baroy reported, however, that many of the casbah women she interviewed completed the shopping for the home themselves, further expanding the visibility and mobility their employment already granted them. While it is difficult to determine how representative Baroy's interviews were, they speak to what was newly possible for some Muslim women because of their new income from domestic work.

Women's work transformed not only family life but the optics and dynamics of urban life as well. As rural populations flocked to nearby cities in the early twentieth century, they brought with them their own norms and attitudes about gender. The status of women in rural Algeria varied widely, dependent on the particularities of their region and sometimes their tribal affiliation. Rural women may have covered their hair, but they often did not don the haik with its face veil more common in Algerian cities. Some tribes, including the Ouled Nail and their neighboring tribes in the South and the Azriyat in the Eastern Aures Mountains, allowed remarkable sexual freedom for women.[30] In rural Algerian villages, women and girls contributed to the economic life of the family, through picking fruits and vegetables and preserving them, pressing olives into oil, and weaving carpets and other textiles. Indeed, across North Africa, as Julia Clancy-Smith has written, women have always "played a significant role in the service sectors of the region's economies, acting as religious agents, healers, marriage brokers, midwives, laundresses, cooks, prostitutes, servants, musicians, and entertainers—in addition to toiling long and hard as agriculturalists, pastoralists, and traders."[31]

However, as rural populations migrated to Algerian cities, they came into closer proximity with not only European settlers but also urban Muslims, for whom women's participation in public life was rarer. Algeria was not unique in the different attitudes about women's presence in public life between rural and urban populations. Judith Tucker has shown that in Egypt and Palestine too, lower-class women enjoyed less sequestration, more mobility, and more decision-making power with regard to their marriage and property.[32] In Algeria these regional class tensions intersected with the particularities of the colonial economy and the pressure it placed on Muslim men and women. These rural women's migration to Algeria's cities and their daily movements through urban space embodied the social upheaval caused by the colonial economy. The discussions that ensued illustrate that the woman question was also, inextricably, a class question.

Working Women on the Move

Domestic workers were not the only Muslim women who were mobile in the interwar years. Some rural women, for example, would travel to small towns to sell jewelry, clothes, home goods, and artisanal goods. Yet domestic workers were a noteworthy group, both because of their scale and because most of them lived and worked in Algeria's urban centers, where previously women were less visible and mobile. Employment in domestic service drastically transformed women's "constellations of mobility," to borrow Tim Cresswell's term, in ways that changed the optics of Algerian urban space.[33] Both Muslims and settlers wrote about the "processions of veiled women" who left the casbah every morning to work in European neighborhoods.[34] It was not only in the streets that one more often saw Muslim women. One Muslim man complained that "now women are everywhere: factories, stores, and administration."[35]

Domestic workers were exceptionally mobile Muslim women. They not only left their homes but moved from Muslim neighborhoods into European neighborhoods. In his study of how color lines operated in multiple colonial spaces, Carl Nightingale argues that the maintenance of colonial power required "keeping color lines semiporous... by authorizing very specific forms of urban boundary-crossing," including domestic workers. He asserts that certain social actors like domestic workers could cross color lines without disrupting the fundamental power relations between colonizer and colonized. He continues, "Gendered interests matter too: white people, typically men, always have tacit permission to cross color lines in search of sex."[36] In interwar Algeria too, while domestic workers' mobility did not disrupt power dynamics between European settlers and Muslims, it reflected an important reversal of earlier patterns of gendered movement.

As domestic workers crossed into European neighborhoods and intimate spaces in the interwar years, they broke older patterns of gendered movement where the only figures authorized to cross color lines were European men in search of sex.[37] From the start of the French colonial experiment in Algeria in 1830, the casbah was where European men would come to purchase sex from Muslim women. For many settlers, the entire casbah was coded as a space of licentious possibility. As one settler wrote in 1939, "For the Algerois [the settler population of Algiers], the popular expression 'going to the Casbah' means to debase oneself [through the purchase of sex]." Domestic workers' regular daily movement across these neighborhood bounds then broke long-standing patterns of who was authorized to move where in Algeria's cities. Many of them were permanent migrants. An administrator noted that women who left rural areas to work as domestic workers in Algiers and Berrouaghia (a town 100 km south of Algiers) rarely returned to their families.[38]

While their work enabled mobility between their homes and their places of work, some domestic workers also took on greater public roles. The public lives of two domestic workers in particular, the aforementioned Rahma Ben Drahou and her contemporary Melika Douifi, although not representative, offer more details about what was newly possible in the interwar years for some domestic workers. Rahma Ben Drahou was the daughter of the local sheikh and teacher at a Qur'anic school in a village just outside of Nemours.[39] Since she was seven years old, Ben Drahou had worked as a domestic worker for multiple families in Nemours, and her income helped support her entire family. This suggests that even though the pay for domestic work was often meager, it could still bring some material stability to families. *Oran républicain* published a letter from a Muslim woman ("B.") who wrote to the publication to share Ben Drahou's story. She reported that Ben Drahou "enjoyed great popularity" in the town of Nemours for her activism and suggested that Ben Drahou could serve as a model of Muslim women's emancipation. While her story may have been exceptional, her activism and popularity demonstrate that despite their absences in the archival record, domestic workers were not marginal or invisible actors in interwar public life.

Melika Douifi was a domestic worker who also acted on stage as part of the Alif-Ba theater troupe.[40] She had moved from Blida to work as a domestic worker in Algiers. Of the six actors in the troupe, some worked for the French colonial regime as interpreters or in the Tribune de Commerce courts, and others were unemployed. Among them, Douifi was the only woman. The troupe performed classic French theater pieces in Arabic. A colonial surveillance report noted that in April 1941, Douifi would be on stage performing in one of the city's largest venues. In celebration of the Mawlid holiday, which celebrates the Prophet Muhammad's birthday, the troupe would perform Chateaubriand's *The Last of the Abencerrajes* either at the Algiers Opera House or the Majestic Theater.

Douifi's presence on stage as a woman was exceptional. Muslim women performed as singers or dancers in private gatherings such as weddings, but in many of Algeria's bigger Muslim theater troupes, the parts of women were played either by Egyptian actresses or by men. Marie Soussan, a Jewish singer and actress who was the most important female performer of the interwar years, was a notable exception.[41] Scholars had long thought Soussan was the only non-European woman of her time to appear on stage, but they have now identified at least three Muslim women who also appeared on stage in the 1930s. Still, although she only appears briefly in a surveillance report about Muslim theater, the life of Melika Douifi, recent migrant, domestic worker, and theater performer, modeled newly possible transformations. Although she was a new arrival in Algiers, her unlikely presence as a domestic worker on stage in Algiers's biggest venues illustrates how women like her left their mark on the city despite their gender and class position.

Both Ben Drahou and Douifi were not only highly mobile women—moving from city to city—but also particularly comfortable in public. Ben Drahou engaged in public activism, while Douifi was willing to act on stage—the only woman in an otherwise all-male acting troupe and one of the few Muslim Algerian women on stage at all in the interwar years. While all domestic workers likely did not share Ben Drahou's and Douifi's independence and confidence, they remained objects of inquiry for a broad range of commentators preoccupied with Muslim women's bodies. Commentators were concerned with not just how such women moved (out of their homes, into European neighborhoods and homes) but also how they dressed (unveiled, wearing makeup). Onto these bodies, each group asserted their own vision of Muslim society's evolution or descent.

En Route to Assimilation

In May 1929 the mayor of Algiers reported to the prefect of the Department of Algiers that the "indigenous female workforce" was growing "rather rapidly."[42] In Algiers alone this workforce had now reached 5,460 women and girls. He noted that of this number, 3,510 (or 64 percent) worked outside the home, the vast majority as domestic workers in European homes. The mayor interpreted these figures as a victory for the project of assimilating Muslims to French culture.

European officials such as the mayor presumed that, if given a chance, Muslim women would model themselves on European women. The growing number of women working, from this perspective, reflected, according to the mayor, "a real progression in the evolution toward the assimilation to European customs." For the mayor, women's movement outside of the home indicated this "progression." For others in the French colonial administration, proximity to Europeans was the factor that would transform the Muslim domestic worker. An administrator from the town of Ksar Boukhari wrote that through domestic service, Muslim women "familiarized themselves with our way of life," which in turn "quickly transformed their manners and personal customs."[43] What prevented the assimilation process from becoming even more "accentuated," the mayor wrote, was "Muslim husbands [who] forbid their wives and daughters from going to work outside [the home]." In other words, according to the mayor, this uptick in women working outside the home was an important step toward assimilation and progress, but the project of assimilation still clearly had ground to cover, given the intractability of women's sequestration.

Muslim writers marveled that, despite the dramatic evidence offered by the sight of domestics en route to work every morning, Europeans clung to their stereotypes about women's sequestration. One author, al-Gharbi, suggested that Muslim women's sequestration was an "illusion."[44] With "a little more attention," he wrote, Europeans would certainly notice working Muslim women moving through the city, traversing neighborhood boundaries daily. He asked, "Don't you see every day, in Algiers without going too far, all the poor Muslim women . . . going early in the morning to work, where they are employed in certain factories, or as cleaning ladies, washers, sweepers of stairs and hallways in European homes . . . [or] servants at the homes of European men?" Al-Gharbi's description emphasized the unmistakable visual spectacle of masses of Muslim women traversing neighborhood boundaries to work in European neighborhoods. Working-class Muslim women's movement was regular, predictable, and clear evidence, according to al-Gharbi, that Muslim women were not strictly sequestered. Instead, al-Gharbi wrote that those interested in the Muslim woman's emancipation needed to shift their focus from her supposed sequestration and veiling to the larger questions of political rights and education, because those alone could elevate Muslim women and society.

Yet the focus on sequestration, like that of the veil, persisted. Like the mayor of Algiers, Mussot read Ben Drahou's story as evidence of the transformative possibility of domestic service. Alongside the letter and Mussot's commentary, the newspaper published a picture of Ben Drahou unveiled but wearing a beret. For Mussot, Ben Drahou's unveiled body was another marker of her emancipation.[45] On one hand, Mussot introduced her column on Ben Drahou with a mention of how little the French colonial state and settler society had done for "the emancipation of the Muslim woman." Yet her analysis returned to stagnant Muslim customs like sequestration and veiling as the most central impediments to women's advancement.[46] Like the mayor's commentary, Mussot's suggests that stereotypes about Muslim women did not lose their explanatory power, even as they were complicated by the realities of domestic workers' mobility.

Featured alongside the column was an illustration (figure 2.2), signed by Mussot, and its caption, presented without commentary or

Figure 2.2. Illustration of Muslim women in *Oran Républicain*, 1937.
Source: BNF

elaboration. The image depicts a veiled Muslim woman with only a single eye uncovered in the Mzabi Ibadite style to represent the past, an unveiled woman in makeup to represent the present, and a woman with popular, flapper-style hair, makeup, and jewelry to represent the future. The caption reads, "The past is no longer. The present has already passed. Only the future is ours." The image and caption present the fashionable, European young woman as the model of emancipation for Muslim women. The unveiled Muslim domestic worker like Ben Drahou, then, was a step toward assimilation. Here the Muslim woman's body and its modes of comportment were something to be conquered by French society in order to be able to claim ownership over a future Algeria that would be under French domination culturally.

Some Muslims also celebrated working women's mobility and the increased public presence of women broadly. The pro-assimilation editor of *La Voix Indigène*, Rabah Zenati, wrote in 1932 that "the modern young Muslim woman no longer accepts" sequestration.[47] For Mussot and colonial administrators, Muslim women's visibility was not a negotiation of customs but rather a consequence of the French colonial project to assimilate Muslims. Yet sequestration in Zenati's estimation was not a static Muslim custom or something unwaveringly enforced by Muslim men but rather something that Muslim women were empowered enough to negotiate or shrug off. He remarked that one could regularly now observe "some young girls, veiled and not alone of course . . . in the stores going shopping, taking a walk in the sun which they love, and going to the cinema and even the theater." Zenati celebrated women's new, active presence in public life. His note that young women engaged in these activities in groups suggests that women adopted strategies, such as being in public in groups, to avoid presumptions of impropriety and harassment.

Social Upheaval and the Woman Question at the Intersection of Class and Gender

The Muslim press featured a wide range of opinions on working women's mobility and the increased public presence of women broadly. Unlike Zenati, some were alarmed. Commentators panicked about how women's greater public presence changed urban space. As they debated whether women should be able to go to the mosque alone at night, for example, commentators recoded urban space into appropriate and inappropriate spaces for women.[48] Some emphasized sexual danger and framed the question of women's mobility as a public safety concern.[49]

Concerns about women's movement were not limited to where women were going and why, however. Commentators pored over the details of how women moved. They questioned whether colorful fabrics, perfume, and noisy jewelry were appropriate. Every aspect of a Muslim woman's comportment, including the degree to which she was covered, the ornamentation on her clothes, her style of walking, her scent, or the noise her body made when walking, could render her public presence inappropriate. In such discussions, the concern was not women's safety but rather their naturally cunning and deceitful nature, which required strict control from men. In this climate of urban danger and unrestrained women, some commentators urged men to take on a disciplinary role with the women in their lives, limit women's mobility, and reassert their own power. They suggested the greater women's access to public life, the greater the risk of sexual impropriety and moral damage to both man and wife.

Some of these commentaries used pieces of Islamic knowledge to urge men to take on a disciplinary role with the women in their lives and frame masculine control as a religious obligation. In *al-Najah*, Sheikh Yahya bin Muhammad al-Darraji wrote that the risk of sexual impropriety was so high "in our current time" that men should not allow the women in their lives to visit the mosque alone at night.[50] He described the potential sexual impropriety as the "risk of *fitna*" (a trial). This alluded to a larger canon of conservative religious interpretations that described women themselves as *fitna*, for being temptresses who create disaster for the men they seduce, a concept which feminist sociologist Fatima Mernissi has mapped.[51] He then turned to a hadith that stated God would curse both the woman who left her house in perfume and makeup with the intention of attracting men and her husband. He also cited another hadith stating that women were the most potentially "harmful" test from God. These references to hadith functioned to remind men it was their Islamic duty to control their wives' mobility and comportment, since their own standing with God was at stake. His emphasis on how such actions were necessary in "our current time" illustrates that such commentaries were not simply timeless critiques of women's mobility but rather specific critiques rooted in the particularities of women's increased mobility and visibility in the interwar moment.

In contrast to the lack of sources on domestic workers' lives, a plethora of published sources feature Muslim men's anxiety about working women and their mobility. At first glance, many of these responses conform to the broader model of conservative backlash in the interwar years. As women across the world participated in public life in unprecedented ways, men's complaints illustrated simultaneous misogynist desires to curtail women's freedom, as well as a wariness of modernity writ large and how it would disrupt power dynamics. A closer look at the commentaries of three authors in particular—Abdelhafidh ben El-Hachemi, an anonymous writer, and Ali bin Ahmad bin Muhammad al-Namri—illustrate more complex local critiques at play.

Abdelhafidh ben El-Hachemi, the co-owner of *al-Najah*, the largest Muslim newspaper in Algeria, warned in 1927 that a "catastrophe" had taken place.[52] The recent entry of thousands of women into the labor force as domestic workers had changed Algeria's public spaces. One could regularly observe "servant girls walking in the road[s]." It wasn't just these women's movement that troubled him but *how* they moved. These women walked with their "faces uncovered, flirting with storekeepers, and talking with passersby for no reason." To El-Hachemi, the bodies of this new class of Muslim women domestic workers and their movement represented everything that urbanization enabled: assimilation to European norms, sexual impropriety, and potential frivolity.

Class tensions help explain his concerns. As Muslim commentators—many of them members of the small Muslim elite—disparaged the mobility of working women in Algerian cities, many of them also contested the imposition of these women's working-class, migrant norms onto urban public life. El-Hachemi closed his lament about domestics flirting in the street with, "I am sorry that giving this [article] to women servants will not work because they cannot read and they are not in our world, they are in a different world." He set up a contrast between "our world," shared by his largely elite male readership, and the "different world" of domestic workers. This "different world" was made possible by urbanization and blurred lines between middle- and working-class Muslims, as well as European and Muslim women. His disgust for these working-class women was palpable.

Like other interwar Muslim commentators, El-Hachemi took issue with domestic workers wearing makeup. He wrote that Muslim women were "absolutely not ready to wear makeup." He set up a contrast between worldly and sophisticated European women on one hand and Muslim women on the other, who had "never been to an office or seen a store." The "office" or "store" here functioned as sites of elite and European sociability. While certain Muslims, like elite Muslim men, may have been permitted entry into some such spaces, Muslim women clearly did not belong. Since El-Hachemi's account stressed the "catastrophic" nature of the present moment, there was also a contrast implicitly established with an earlier, less salacious time. Then, urban Muslim women respected the lines that divided elite and non-elite society, whereas now Muslim women self-fashioned in ways that, according to him, betrayed a desire to appear more European or more sophisticated.

Alongside these concerns about class, writers identified women's comportment outside the home as a marker of the honor of all of Muslim society, not just a family affair. When El-Hachemi chastised "servant girls" for their makeup, he wrote that they needed to "go back to [their] homes" because they "have dirtied the honor of Muslims with this shame." The home was thus coded as a space of safety and protection, while it was these women's comportment in public that polluted communal honor. El-Hachemi framed his commentary as a response to women's mobility, but what his hysteria revealed was how women were transforming urban space.

For the author, likely El-Hachemi or the paper's editor, Smaïl Mami, of an unsigned 1926 editorial in *al-Najah* titled "The Danger of Women," the issue was the growing threat of female control. He wrote that because of "civilization . . . now women are everywhere: factories, stores, and administration."[53] The critique of modern, urban life is evident from his connection between "civilization" and women's greater public presence. The inversion of traditional gender dynamics threatened male domination. The author lamented that since women had assumed these new positions in labor, "she is trying to be better than him and trying to . . . control him as he controlled her before." This author suggested women's goal was the total domination of men, including within the realms of government and labor. He wrote that if men were not careful, all of "commerce will be in the hands of women in twenty years." All of this concern over economic control reflected anxiety about the economic vulnerability of Muslim men within the colonial economy. While women were able to secure steady, regular employment as domestic workers, urban men were often limited to sporadic forms of work, as day laborers, for example.

The unsigned author of "The Danger of Women" closed his editorial with a set of commandments for men: "Women should do the housework, and make the food and clothing. She should be taught [only] religious material and she should not mix with strangers. And she should be kept away from politics and poetry." This author's inclusion of heterosocial interaction also suggests a concern with the danger of women's public presence. His reminder about housework functioned to reinscribe domestic duties onto women's increasingly visible and mobile bodies. Like El-Hachemi's call for women to "go back to [their] homes," this author similarly closed his account with an attempt to reinscribe domestic duties onto urban women's newly mobile bodies.

Elite Muslim men like this author saw themselves under siege—by a colonial economy that denied many men the opportunity to work, by calls for assimilation that stressed their cultural and religious inferiority, and by their potentially deceptive wives. While elsewhere sex was alluded to, when it came to the threat posed by Muslim women's labor, commentators were willing to talk openly. In between the lines of conservative responses to women's entry into the labor force was a critique of how urbanization had led to the erosion of multiple boundaries— between Europeans and Muslims, between public and private space, and between men and women. As they sought to reinscribe women's subordinate status onto them, male commentators also sought to reclaim patriarchy as a source of Muslim society's strength—a rebuttal of French colonial claims that it was the root of their inferiority.

The final article that illustrates these tensions appeared in the anti-French, anti-reformist newspaper *al-Balagh al-Jazairi*. While its focus was on educated women, its concern with the effect of women's advancement on Muslim society reveals the sexual concerns that undergirded commentaries about women's mobility. Ali bin Ahmad bin Muhammad al-Namri affirmed that any education beyond what was necessary for basic literacy, religious education, and domestic training would lead to promiscuity.[54] He wrote that the educated woman would "play, have fun, and caress whoever she wants, whenever she wants." The "whoever" and "whenever" here emphasized the erosion of boundaries that previously constrained women. His depiction of a sexually promiscuous wife was intended to remind men that the education of their daughters or wives could lead not only to deviousness but also to emasculation. Women's inherently promiscuous nature, al-Namri argued, would be exacerbated by the increased opportunities education offered her. His language stressed the need for men to retain strict control over women's possibilities and to limit women's access to education and mobility.

Women's unhinged promiscuity became a metaphor for al-Namri to critique "modern civilization," which imposed and facilitated the education of women. He described modernity's potentially devastating effects for Muslim men. He wrote, "Thanks to modern civilization, he [the husband] has lost his dignity and honor . . . [and] has become a slave to her desires. . . . Is there any Arab among us who would not be jealous to see his wife pulled in close by another man?" He contrasted natural Arab dignity and jealousy with "modern civilization." "Modern civilization" then would only further enable women's inherent promiscuity, rendering Arab men cuckolded, emasculated, and powerless. Women's education was the doorway to men's loss of control over the sexual integrity of their households. In al-Namri's estimation, Arab culture and modern civilization were incompatible. He posited masculine control as an important facet of an Arab man's very Arabness. He wrote that "modern civilization" would make men "a slave to [women's] desires." A woman's potential control over her husband was an even bigger concern than promiscuity. His article can also be read as a response to not only women's expanded visibility and mobility but also their new access to decision-making power within families, which compromised male control. Inherent in this discourse of sexual danger and impropriety was a critique not only of working and educated women but also of urbanization and modernity.

Within these commentaries, Europe served as a powerful anti-model where women's education and entry into the labor force had violated the ideals of femininity. Al-Namri wrote, "The intelligent of [the Westerners] say that we now have a female doctor and a female engineer and a female lawyer, but when will we have a female woman?" Women's entry into the labor force, he argued, compromised women's essential womanhood. The reformist poet Mohamed Saleh Ramdane similarly stated that it was important that both men and women "not exceed their limits" by going "against their nature" and moving outside of their designated realms of gendered labor.[55] If social developments violated natural limits on men and women's functions, he wrote, the result would be "a masculine woman or a feminine man."

These articles critiqued gender relations in Europe and reveal anxiety about Muslim women becoming more like "Western" women. Al-Namri wrote that in the West one could see not only a woman's "equality to man but even her superiority in some matters."[56] He wrote that the men of the West clearly "believe they were mistaken and wish they could take the woman back [in terms of progress] so she would respect her limits." In a letter to the editor published in *L'Entente franco-musulmane*, a reader wrote that those who called for Muslim women's advancement should not forget "the question of the too-free woman," whom one could see on display in France.[57] Women's excessive liberty, he wrote, was the cause of "the complex problems of declining birth rate, of unemployment, of the physical and moral health of individuals and the nation."

These critiques of France leveled by al-Namri and others inverted colonial attacks on Muslim patriarchy.[58] They argued that Muslim society's adherence to essentialist patriarchy was the source not of its inferiority but its superiority. By permitting European women to enter the labor force and maintain public positions, European men had upended the basic principles of patriarchy and thus destabilized European society. The signs of this destabilization were precisely the pronatalist concerns that captivated both metropolitan and settler French publics in the interwar years, including the declining French birth rate.[59]

Other commentators also used news from Europe to legitimize similar concerns. One article in *al-Najah*, likely written by El-Hachemi or Mami, reported on a recently discovered "evil" gang of violent women thieves in London.[60] The article reported with horror that the women had "huge bodies" and "strong arms," which they used alongside guns and knives. The article likely referring to the Forty Elephants, an all-female crime syndicate in existence in London from the late nineteenth century to the mid-twentieth century who were particularly powerful in the interwar period.[61] The article's critique was rooted in not only these women's violation of gender norms but the entire society's violation of normative gender labor. It stated plainly that "thievery is not a job for the gentler sex." Moreover, the article argued the British government paved the way for this female gang when they allowed women to join the police force, a form of labor that should be "just for men." These women, with their abnormally masculine bodies, embodied an entire society in chaos because of violations to the normative gender labor supposedly intended by nature. The article implied that Muslims in Algeria too needed to be careful not to encourage such violations to normative gender labor because "we do not want to see theft or thievery gangs happen." Women should "do no job in the world but managing the house," the article stated, to ensure the peaceful stability of the society as a whole. Such implicit threats illustrate how interwar commentators envisioned their society as on the precipice because of women's changing mobility, visibility, and labor. Algerian society could, according to such concerned commentators, either limit women's labor to the home or allow women to complete more diverse forms of labor, advance in the way of Europe, and suffer chaos.

News from the Middle East also offered commentators material for lamenting how societies changed as a result of women's changing labor. One 1924 article in *al-Najah* lamented that since urban women joined the workforce in larger numbers in Turkey, they began also frequenting heterosocial places, like "bars and clubs."[62] Village women, on the other hand, merited praise according to the author because they worked alongside men completing agricultural work, but they did "not go with him to the café in the evening." Inherent in this comparison was a critique of the kinds of gender upheaval modern urban life facilitated. Cafés played a particularly important role within Algerian society.[63] Typically an exclusively masculine space, cafés fostered community social and intellectual exchange. Women's potential entry into this space, then, represented more than just movement into a masculine space. It also signified entry into Muslim public life.

Sometimes such claims that mobile women could create societal chaos were encapsulated in brief maxims, published without commentary. A set of sayings published in the reformist *al-Shihab* stated, "The women and the microbe should stay isolated from people to prevent their damage and their evil. The more you give them freedom, the more they create damage and create evil."[64] The link to women's greater independence was clear: the greater women's access to public life, the greater the risk of sexual impropriety and moral damage to both man and wife.

The Safety and Shame of Domestic Work

Other commentators in the Muslim press also questioned whether domestic service was safe for Muslim women. On a rhetorical level, many authors referred to domestic workers in ways that evoked sympathy for the humiliation of their work. In *La Défense* al-Gharbi referred to the domestics in the streets every morning with sympathy as "poor Muslim women." Abdelhafidh ben El-Hachemi wrote that the term "service . . . talks to the heart and melts it."[65] An author, Sayyid ʿAbd al-Qadir bin Si Ahmad, wrote in to *al-Bassair* from Aïn Beïda to complain that something needed to be done about "our ignorant girls . . . working as maids and servants for people who do not respect their religion or their purity."[66] In her letter to *La Défense*, a woman who signed her letter "Séti B. M." complained that so many "poor girls are working at the age of fourteen or earlier in European homes . . . and not even [employed] by a single family, but by multiple ones."[67] She urged the Muslim elite to fight harder for women's education so that women could have other opportunities for income beyond domestic service.

Muslim commentators in the press emphasized the vulnerability of domestics at work, where they were at risk for sexual attack by their European bosses or fellow male servants. It bears noting that women's safety at work was a concern in other contexts as well. The Algerian Office of Familial Action, which focused on European settlers in Algeria, released a pamphlet from their French counterparts on "the fight against public immorality," which targeted cinemas and places of work as potential sites of immoral behavior.[68] It discussed how women were often the targets of harassment while at work. They recommended severe punishment for any men who abused their power, reminded people of their responsibility to be respectful, and advocated keeping children out of factories and other potentially immoral spaces. This demonstrates that while there was a particular concern for domestic workers in the Muslim press because of the privacy of their workplace, to some extent these concerns were shared by some members of settler society for women even in industrial workplace settings.

Newspapers occasionally reported on the sexual violence Muslim domestic workers faced. In 1928, for example, *al-Najah* reported that a Muslim male domestic worker had raped a Muslim female domestic worker in a European home in Tlemcen where they both worked.[69] While the matter was initially headed to court, the homeowner convinced the Muslim woman to marry her rapist. The newspaper applauded the Muslim woman for practicing "forgiveness" but presented the story as a troubling warning of what could happen when men and women worked side by side, and as a reminder of the vulnerable position of women who worked in service. They feared the story would "encourage other people to rape the local servants," since the rapist was ultimately unpunished. This type of reporting about shocking sex crimes functioned to create a climate of fear around women's new employment.[70]

Oral interviews suggest that attitudes about domestic work varied between urban and rural peoples. Fatma Zohra Benaik, who was born in 1932 and grew up in Algiers, noted that domestic work was so common in the city by the 1940s that it was not at all seen as concerning, although she suggested that Muslims in smaller "villages tended to look down on" domestic work.[71] Dahbia Lounas was born in 1933 and spent much of her life in the rural town of Mirabeau (today Draâ Ben Khedda) near Tizi Ouzou. She described how many women from her town worked as domestic workers in the 1930s and 1940s "despite the shame."[72]

Commentators questioned why women had to turn to such degrading work in the first place. Their answer was a failure of resources—both those designated by the family and those allocated by society or the French colonial state. At the familial level, blame was placed with fathers who had disinherited their daughters, particularly common in Kabyle families.[73] This idea of women as economically vulnerable was not entirely limited to domestic workers. The prominent interwar Moroccan reformist scholar al-Mahdi al-Wazzani described women as "poor by nature" and thus in need of financial security from their male dependents to ensure their well-being.[74] He argued, and many in Algeria echoed, that fathers needed to ensure that an appropriate portion of their inheritance was assigned to their daughters. In Algeria this lack of economic security from inheritance was then directly tied to women's labor as domestic workers. An unsigned editorial in *al-Najah* chastised Muslim fathers "in so many cities and villages" who disobeyed the mandates of the Qur'an by leaving their inheritance only to their sons.[75] The author wrote that these fathers' neglect for their daughters "forced [them] to work as a housemaid and to live in humiliation." The state too, many argued, had failed to offer Muslim women education or skills training that would offer them another way to earn income. In 1928 *al-Najah* reported that the state had established a training factory for women in Ouargla, a Saharan town 600 kilometers south of Constantine. The editorial praised the factory for offering work to "poor women" so they would not be forced "to work as maids in European" homes.[76] Although the press depicted the Muslim domestic as small, desperate, and vulnerable, her mobility and the anxiety it provoked also suggest she should not be overlooked as an important social actor in the interwar landscape.

Women's Growing Presence in the Changing City: A Conclusion

Urbanization created the conditions for domestic workers to step into public life in an unprecedented way. Yet domestic workers' power in society was constrained in significant ways, including that they earned little pay, had little job security, were subject to harassment from their employers or other Muslim men at work, had limited power within their families, and lacked the respectability of other positions. For most Muslim women, the colonial economy and restrictions of life in a settler colony continued to stifle their daily lives despite their paid labor—as it stifled most opportunities for Muslim uplift.

Despite the plethora of literature that focuses on their silences, women, and domestics in particular, were not marginal in interwar Algerian society. Some, like Ben Drahou, engaged in public activism. Others collaborated on projects like the construction of new schools. A few acted on theater stages. Many frequented spaces like cinemas and music performances. Some of them were mothers to future leaders. The nationalist fighter Baya Hocine, for example, was born in 1940 in the casbah of Algiers. Her parents had recently migrated to Algiers from the Kabyle village Ighil Imoula. While her father worked a variety of inconsistent jobs, her mother brought in steady income as a domestic worker.[77] Muslim women participated en masse in demonstrations, like those in support of the Popular Front, a coalition of political parties on the Left including the SFIO and the Parti communiste français (French Communist Party). Photographs from June 1936 Popular Front protests show Muslim women dressed in haiks, with their long white veils, in a women's section of the protests with fists raised (figures 2.3 and 2.4).

Figure 2.3. Muslim women in Popular Front protest, 1936.
Source: BNF

Figure 2.4. Muslim women in Popular Front protest, 1936.
Source: BNF

Muslim women broadly and domestic workers in particular also contributed in meaningful ways to the anti-colonial struggle throughout the War of Independence, as Caroline de la Brac Perrière has shown in one of the only studies of domestic workers in Algeria.[78]

When we hold these perspectives together—women like Rahma ben Drahou who worked as domestics and also engaged in public life in novel ways; French commentators insisting that Muslim women's labor was a path to assimilation; and Muslim elites who struggled to make sense of their changing cities—we can see more clearly the tensions urbanization provoked. Scholars have described interwar urban life in Algeria as a bustling public environment on the eve of the rise of nationalism. Although not wholly inaccurate, this perspective leaves out the ways urban space was a contested terrain in which women's bodies occupied an important position both for how they actually moved and what this movement represented to various communities. When we instead attend to those who questioned what would be lost because of women's mobility, rather than only those who celebrated it, the heated debates that urbanization precipitated come more clearly into view.

In between the lines of commentators' warnings about the danger of urban space were masculine anxieties about growing female power. This fear of women's expanding power was not entirely imagined. While employment was difficult to find, sporadic, and low-earning for Muslim men, Muslim women earned more consistent income from their work as domestic workers. Their status as consistent wage earners in turn earned them the right to manage the family finances and complete the shopping for the home. Domestic workers' movements to and from work also changed the optics of urban space and provoked anxiety within the press. Elite Muslim men were threatened enough by them that they wrote diatribes in the press railing against these women's mobility and growing public presence.

Histories of interwar Algeria have rightly mapped how the period saw an enormous expansion in association life, café culture, and access to international news and cinema. Yet not all Algerians were enamored with these changes to their cities and public life. The scholarship on "new women" or the "modern girl" globally has focused on the transformative progress of the interwar years. Yet in Algeria the women in question who were newly mobile—domestic workers and a small number of students—did not have the buying power to grant them access to the new consumption patterns characteristic of the "modern girl."[79] There is not enough evidence to suggest whether these women were also organizing themselves into the social or political movements of "new women" elsewhere. Still, their contested movement changes our view of a Muslim society in flux after urbanization in multiple ways.

Too disproportionate an attention to women's growing power risks both too hastily characterizing women's lives before the interwar years as entirely constrained and reproducing the colonial idea that the waged labor of domestic service was salvation from the incessant misery of Muslim patriarchy. Yet to dismiss these women as marginal further silences their impact on public life and the anxiety they provoked for what they represented: a rapidly changing Algeria. The story of how domestic workers transformed the cities around them is a story about urban space. Working-class Muslim women transgressed the boundaries of their homes and neighborhoods en masse daily. As they did so, they broke with the norms for urban women. But this is also a story about the social friction and masculine anxiety that unfolded because of these women's mobility. In between the lines of elite urban male commentators' complaints about domestic service in the press was fear about how their cities were being remade by domestic workers. For them, women's mobility was a troubling sign of how Algeria's social fabric was beginning to unravel.[80] Of course, women's labor and mobility were not the only sources of Muslim men's anxiety. As the next two chapters illustrate, Muslim men were equally concerned about women's limited access to education and dress, both of which, like labor, became discussions about larger issues relating to Muslim society and Algeria's place in the world.

CHAPTER 3

The Educated Muslim Woman and Algeria's Path to Progress

On May 23, 1937, Muslim families piled into one of the oldest mosques in Blida to celebrate one of the most important Muslim holidays, al-mawlid al-nabawi al-sharif, the birthday of the Prophet Muhammad. Amid the celebrations, a small girl came forward to speak in front of the crowd. Her family had immigrated to Blida from the Mzab, a desert region of Algeria on the northern Sahara, in order for her father, a merchant, to secure work. She attended one of Blida's first Muslim reformist schools. Though she was not even ten years old, this girl delivered a moving speech that amazed the crowd. She proclaimed, "If you had never dreamed before today that an honorable girl from the great Mozabite nation would advise her fathers, I stand before you to set a good precedent."[1] She pleaded with them to take seriously the plight of Muslim girls and to support efforts to educate Muslim girls.

The Mozabite girl's migration to Blida, her public speech, and the contents of her speech stunned her audience. Local Ibadi law, the school of Islamic thought followed in the Mzab, prohibited men from allowing women to leave the region.[2] Men who violated this law would be excommunicated socially, legally, and commercially. That the Mozabite girl's family migrated together in spite of these strict laws reflects the strength of the rural-to-urban pull in the interwar years. The Mzab's uniquely strict gender norms also constrained women's participation in public life, so her willingness to deliver a speech publicly was also exceptional. Finally, the contents of her speech likely fascinated her audience. She used her knowledge of the Qur'an and Hadith literature to insist that Islam mandated education for women. She cited a hadith from the Prophet Muhammad: "The [Qur'anic] demand for knowledge is a requirement for all Muslim men and women," and she noted that this proved "the requirement was for both sexes without distinction."

The communist Muslim newspaper *La Lutte Sociale* reported on her speech. Impressed by her ability to deliver such a powerful message to the large crowd at her age, they noted how she employed "good language," which strengthened her delivery. In between the lines of their abundant praise, however, lay another set of concerns. Twice within the article, the newspaper described her as "chaste" (*masuna*). Alongside the praise for the girl, this descriptor hints at the existence of an audience who would fear that this young girl's sophistication perhaps signaled compromised virtue. The newspaper commended both her impassioned plea for better access to education for girls and her ability to deliver such a speech at her young age. Yet language like "chaste" reveals the lurking concern that education for girls and women's advancement could bring impropriety. Like domestic workers, educated Muslim girls symbolized both the changing times and the growing risk of sexual impropriety.

The Mozabite girl's speech and *La Lutte Sociale*'s article about it reflect both the excitement and the anxiety about women's education in interwar Algeria. The Muslim press devoted enormous intellectual energy to discussions about women's education across the interwar years. In the early 1920s a group of the French-educated Muslim middle class schoolteachers in French colonial schools initiated these discussions, publishing regular commentary in *La Voix des Humbles*, the official organ of the Association of Schoolteachers of Indigenous Origin, and then in *La Voix Indigène*. In publications such as *al-Bassair* and *al-Shihab*, the growing Muslim reform movement offered another frame to discussions about women's education in Algeria: a return to former Muslim glory. The Arabic-language journal of the conservative 'Alawiyya Sufi zawiya, *al-Balagh al-Jazairi*, was firmly against any sort of assimilation or cooperation with the French colonial regime, the Muslim reformist movement, and any change to patriarchal gender norms.[3] Algeria's largest Muslim newspaper, *al-Najah*, offered regular news coverage of developments in other Muslim countries in the region, including advances in women's education. These papers were sites of debates about women's education and its potential to chart a new path forward for Muslim girls, whose status was inextricably linked to Muslim society writ large.

The calls for women's education spoke directly to French colonial stereotypes about Muslim misogyny. In *Sex, Law, and Sovereignty in French Algeria, 1830–1930,* Judith Surkis demonstrates that ideas about Muslim misogyny were not simply ideologies that ran in the background of the colonial project on display in postcards and expositions. To the contrary, she illustrates how claims about the intractability of Muslim misogyny were fundamental to the state's legal apparatus since the beginning of the colonial project. Administrators and lawmakers relied on such claims to confiscate Muslim land, dismantle Muslim institutions, and exclude Muslims from political rights. Colonial authorities specifically cast intractable Muslim misogyny as a legal matter: Muslims loved their supposedly misogynistic Islamic law, so they required their separate legal system—a system that conveniently excluded Muslims from French civil law. The discourses about Muslim inheritance and property rights raised by Muslim commentators in discussions about education, then, were a challenge about not just Muslim misogyny generally as a matter of reputation but also the precise legal basis of the dual-law system that facilitated Muslim disenfranchisement and dispossession.

These dialogues overlapped with campaigns for women's education elsewhere. As Shenila Khoja-Moolji has written about South Asia, "Oftentimes, the composite figure of the Muslim woman/girl emerges as an example par excellence of this backward femininity—she is threatened by religion, tradition, patriarchy, and local customs, is ill-equipped to survive in the modern social order, and is thus unable to fulfill her potential."[4] In Algeria too, colonial officials and Muslim press commentators alike echoed such claims. Yet in the analysis that follows, I have focused on how these Algerian discourses were shaped by local dynamics, including a response to the French colonial characterization of Muslim misogyny, internal Muslim discussions about Muslim reform, and an engagement with regional news shaped by Algeria's status as a settler colony.

These discussions illustrate both external concerns about Algeria's place in the region and internal concerns about ideals for Muslim women in Algeria. Rather than advocate for women's education within a framework of national uplift, most Algerian Muslim educators and commentators looked east to other Muslim-majority countries in the region and to Islam's own history of feminist reform to assert Algerian

Muslim belonging in the modern world. These discussions of women's education render visible the interwar social tension between the assimilationist schoolteachers in the western city of Oran, the more conservative existent urban elite in the eastern city of Constantine, and, also in Constantine, the emergent Muslim reform movement—each of whom proposed their own vision of women's role in elevating Muslim society within Algeria. Interestingly, however, while these three groups often disagreed about political and religious matters, there was remarkable compatibility between their calls for women's education.

A Colonial Education

Some French administrators and settlers claimed education in Algeria began with French colonialism. The Constantine-born ethnographer and lawyer Mathéa Gaudry, for example, wrote in 1935 that there was no education system in Algeria at the start of the French colonial project in Algeria in 1830.[5] Such claims ignore how over the course of the nineteenth century, the French colonial state dismantled precolonial education systems, and since the 1905 metropolitan law that separated church from state in particular, the state continued to dismantle the Qur'anic education system, limited the numbers of Qur'anic schools open, and kept Sufi zawiyas under strict surveillance.[6]

In the interwar years, access to French colonial schools remained extremely limited for Muslim boys and girls alike. The proportion of school-age children enrolled in French colonial schools rose slowly in the first half of the twentieth century from "under 2% in 1890, not quite 6% in 1918, almost 9% in 1944, and nearly 13% in 1954."[7] In much of the Middle East too, widespread multidisciplinary, public education was only available from the late 1940s onward.[8] While all Muslim children suffered from the limited numbers of schools open to Muslims, the problem was exacerbated for Muslim girls. In 1921 only 4,455 school-age Muslim girls were enrolled in French colonial schools. This number rose to 15,736 in 1936, but that was still only 2.7 percent of the total population of school-age Muslim girls, as compared to 12 percent of Muslim boys or 68.7 percent of settler girls.[9] The numbers of schools for Muslim girls across Algeria slowly increased from four in 1892 to twenty-three by 1929, twenty-six in 1930, thirty-six in 1933, and forty-eight in 1934. Of the 851 young girls who attended the two schools for girls in Algiers, 19 percent were from middle-class or

Table 3.1 Muslim women and French in 1936

	TOTAL NUMBER OF MUSLIM WOMEN	FRANCOPHONE MUSLIM WOMEN	MUSLIM WOMEN LITERATE IN FRENCH
Algiers	44,102	4,227	808
Oran	14,344	2,475	24
Constantine	22,226	217	61

Source: BNF

Table 3.2 Number of Muslim girls in different schools in 1933

Public indigenous schools	5,741
Private indigenous schools	224
European schools	0
Kindergarten	630
Primary elementary classes	4,322
Complementary courses	17
Private European schools	84
Total in all schools	11,018

Source: BNF

Table 3.3 Number of Muslim girls admitted to Ecoles Primares Supérieurs

1929	8
1930	9
1931	8
1932	16
1933	17
1934	34

Source: BNF

Table 3.4 Number of Muslims in all schools

	MUSLIM GIRLS	MUSLIM BOYS
1892	1,132	10,277
1929	6,712	Unknown
1933	11,018	74,002

Source: BNF

Table 3.5 School-age Muslim children enrolled in primary schools

	NUMBER OF STUDENTS	PERCENTAGE
1908	33,397	4.3
1914	47,263	5
1930	68,000	5
1944	111,000	8.8
1954	302,000	14

Source: Ageron, *Modern Algeria*, 76

Table 3.6 Education of Muslim girls, ages 6 to 14 (255)

YEAR	NUMBER OF GIRLS	% OF THE SCHOOL-AGE FEMALE POPULATION
1901	1,409	
1911	3,084	0.6
1921	4,455	
1936	17,286	3.0
1948	42,103	4.5
1954	73,685	8.4

Source: Kateb, *Européens, "Indigènes" et Juifs en Algérie*, 255

elite families, while the majority (81 percent) were from poorer families. The number of girls who continued on to French colonial secondary education was very limited. In 1934 in Algiers, for example, the Lycée for Girls admitted fifteen Muslim girls, five of them from mixed Muslim/European families.[10]

Within the French colonial education system existed two separate tracks, one for settlers and one for Muslims, which primarily offered professional training. While some metropolitan officials argued that Muslim boys should receive a multidisciplinary education similar to that of settlers, the settler lobby insisted that Muslim boys should strictly receive professional training, which would enable them to either work as translators within the French colonial bureaucracy or legal system, or perform agricultural work.[11] For Muslim girls, French colonial schools taught solely artisanal training, most often carpet weaving. The colonial education system thus worked to produce stratified laborers for the Algerian economy and maintain settler dominance. Indeed, in his memoir former governor-general Maurice Viollette lamented that schools for Algerian girls offered no real instruction. "In reality," he wrote, "they function more like workshops than schools."[12] Although technical, schools for Muslim boys and girls still sought to inculcate Muslim boys and girls with French culture. As in other colonial spaces, administrators described French colonial schools for girls as conduits through which the French colonial project could penetrate Algerian homes. The superintendent of the schools of Algiers, Georges Hardy, stated, "When we bring a boy to a French school, we gain unity. When we bring a girl, that unity is multiplied by the number of children she will have."[13]

The benefits of women's artisanal training were twofold: the workshop would be a place where Muslim women could gently learn new skills and French norms, and in return the state would benefit from the eventual labor of a new workforce of Muslim women who would contribute to the economic progress of Algeria.[14] Administrators envisioned that artisanal training was ideal because it could be described as emancipatory in a gentle way, but it would not be too disruptive to Muslim family dynamics because ultimately it would not radically transform women's possibilities.[15] Artisanal work could also be taught in ways that would not disrupt class, so the particular crafts taught were oriented toward the girls' class, embroidery for richer girls and carpet weaving for poorer girls, with sometimes both offered in the same workshop.[16] These distinctions often also mapped onto rural/urban divisions, in which urban students worked with linen, silk, and precious metals, while rural students worked with wool. While urban students made luxury items like lace, rural students often wove objects of necessity like tents, haiks, or burnouses.[17]

Many French administrators envisioned women's artisanal training as an avenue through which Algerian women's labor could be standardized and captured for the benefit of the colonial state, producing both a new class of workers and a new market of goods. This was seen as benefiting the colonial economy, while also offering supposedly lazy and oppressed Algerian women the emancipatory opportunity to work and thus be transformed into modern workers. Incapable or unwilling to penetrate the Algerian domestic sphere out of concern for male reactions, colonial administrators landed on artisanal workshops in an attempt to expand both the colonial economy and the sociocultural reach of the colonial state.

Despite critiques from Muslims and settlers alike, Muslim families took advantage of these schools. In 1925 *al-Najah* reported, for example, that "the girls of Ouargla have achieved the maximum degree of artistry in . . . weaving, chic embroidery, [and] lacemaking, and all locals confidently and eagerly send their daughters."[18] For the author, these girls' training was salvation from a life of poverty and potential vice. Articles in *al-Najah* and other publications also defended the schools against concerns that attendance in French colonial schools may corrupt girls. Expressing that they "disapproved" of such fears, the newspaper insisted that such ideas were "holding us back from a great personal and national benefit."[19] This position was Islamically framed and tied back to the flexibility of sharia. They wrote, "The Islamic sharia does not forbid girls from industrial [artisanal] education. . . . To forbid her from her education is an injustice!" Another article in the reformist *al-Shihab* similarly urged readers to send their daughters to French schools with a reference to sharia.[20] They reminded readers that any fear of Muslim girls being corrupted by the time they spent with their French teachers was unfounded and had no religious basis, since "the Islamic sharia is a sharia of advancement, fraternity, and humanity." Because of its values of "fraternity and humanity," the sharia was open to women's education, necessary for "advancement," even in French colonial schools.

By 1926, however, *al-Najah* was complaining that while Muslim girls were supposed to earn income from the sale of the goods they made in school, "no matter how fast [they] work[ed]" they earned only "one franc per day." Others critiqued the schools' limited focus. Administrators and settlers lamented that such schools did not teach women the necessary skills to make good homemakers, such as basic sewing and ironing.[21] Critiques from the Muslim community became more vocal and regular with the appearance in 1922 of the journal *La Voix des Humbles*, published by the Association of Schoolteachers of Indigenous Origin as part of its attempt to speak directly to the French colonial state and settler society, and to challenge the state's excuses—namely, limited budget and Muslim misogyny—for not opening more interdisciplinary schools for Muslim girls. Some commentators in the press worried that Muslim youth internalized shame about their culture, religion, and identity. These editorialists warned that the pressure to assimilate to French norms would erode and erase Muslim culture over time.

In Tunisia, a French protectorate between 1881 and 1956, education for women also remained limited in terms of both numbers of schools and curriculum. The resident-general's wife was envisioned as an emissary between the French colonial regime and Tunisian women. In 1900 the wife of Resident-General René Millet founded a school exclusively for Tunisian girls that would teach the French language and domestic tasks.²² Tunisians distrusted this school, and many wanted their daughters to receive the multidisciplinary education offered in French schools.²³ It initially only had twelve pupils enrolled and maintained a majority French student body for most of its existence into the 1940s. By 1920 there were fourteen French-run primary schools exclusively for girls across Tunisia, although until 1945 Tunisian girls had no access to female-only secondary education. There too, elites took to the press to express their frustration with the lack of access to education for Tunisian girls.

The Schoolteachers of Oran and the Fight for Women's Access to Education

The most vocal group who initiated consistent calls for Muslim women's education were the French-educated schoolteachers. They were predominantly concerned with the material aspects of women's education—the limited number of schools open to Muslim girls and the fact that they taught only artisanal training. Publishing in French meant that *La Voix des Humbles* and *La Voix Indigène* could direct their critiques directly to settler society and the administration. They challenged the excuses of French colonial administrators for not building more schools for girls, and they occasionally marshaled the rhetoric of the colonial project itself. An unsigned editorial in *La Voix des Humbles* titled "Schools for Our Girls" claimed that French inaction on the issue of girls' schooling did not reflect the spirit of "French generosity." They challenged the words of the French deputy, "Ch. Damas," who had said, "A race will not emancipate itself when it condemns half of itself to eternal servitude."²⁴ Damas repeated a long-standing claim of state officials since the nineteenth century that Muslims' intransigent misogyny rendered their advancement impossible. *La Voix des Humbles* labeled this a "sterilizing theory," since the state refused to endow Muslim society with the means (schools) to enact this emancipation. In another article, Mohand Lechani critiqued French claims that they could not offer girls a multidisciplinary education because of the risk of upsetting the gender balance of Muslim households. He wrote that the ongoing petitions by Muslim men to build more schools for girls rendered such claims "a fallacious pretext."²⁵ In the face of such demands, he said, the state had redirected their excuse to limited budget.

Many publications frequently called for women's education broadly without specification about the parameters or curriculum of such an education. In October 1929, for example, *al-Najah* reprinted an article from *La Voix Indigène* called "The Kabyle Woman and Marriage," which called for her to be educated. In the following issue they wrote, "The article that we reprinted in our last issue is from our colleague, *La Voix Indigène*. We share their opinion on [the need for] education for the Kabyle woman, on the condition that it conforms with Islamic principles."[26] Even among schoolteachers, despite the continued calls for women's education in schoolteacher publications, the topic of women's advancement broadly remained contentious. At their annual conference in Tlemcen in 1934, when a speaker raised the topic of "the emancipation of the Muslim woman," audible protest was heard from the audience.[27]

There were a few moments where women contributed to the discussion about women's education initiated by schoolteacher publications. In 1929 *La Voix Indigène* reprinted an editorial by Houria Ameur, the first Muslim woman to attend the Algiers Law School and daughter of Tahar Ameur, the *conseiller général* of Fort National (Larbaâ Nath Irathen) with Sufi lineage.[28] She wrote that most Muslim girls "have an ardent desire to go to French schools, and their mothers" support them. The obstacles standing in women's way were twofold: the insufficient number of schools and "eternal masculine pride, common among all races." Ameur's claim that this pride was shared "among all races" allowed her to challenge Muslim men while not giving weight to French colonial stereotypes that Muslim men were particularly misogynistic. Ameur's attention to Muslim men is also a reminder that while men may have rhetorically proclaimed their support for women's education, many still discouraged the girls in their own lives from attending school. An administrator from Philippeville (Skikda) explained that a Muslim qadi, Hadj Youcef Bouhedja, had initially wanted to send his daughter to be educated at the Legion of Honor's *maison d'éducation*, but his family eventually pressured him that it was inappropriate.[29] If true, this suggests that even more assimilated men who were part of the French colonial legal apparatus faced social pressure around educating their daughters.

The Muslim Reformists and Women's Uplift of the *Umma*

Calls for women's education were also taken up by the increasingly popular Muslim reform movement. Like the schoolteachers, Muslim reformist thinkers envisioned themselves as educators of the broader

Muslim public who needed to learn about the compatibility between Islam and a modern education for Muslim girls. For the reform movement, the education of Muslim women was an integral part of a return to Islam's true principles, a turn away from the Sufi Islam practiced in Algeria, which had deviated from these true principles, and a revival of past Islamic glory through education and uplift. Some Sufi voices, like those published in *al-Balagh al-Jazairi*, on the other hand, were wary that women's education beyond childhood Qur'anic memorization may lead to licentious behavior.

Women's education was an important pillar of the Muslim reform movement since its inception in Algeria. The reformist movement empowered lay people to read the Qur'an themselves, unmediated by an overreliance on local Sufi scholars. In 1913 Ben Badis returned to Algeria after five years in Tunis at Zeitouna University and began teaching at Constantine's Djamâa El Akhdar, or Green Mosque. In the 1910s Ben Badis himself offered a weekly night course for women in the Green Mosque, where he taught about important women in early Islamic history and their example.[30] Men were asked to wait outside, and the lights were turned low so women could unveil if they wanted.

This attention paid to an Islamic education for women adhered to the ideas of Egyptian reformist thinkers like Muhammad Abduh, who described the equality between men and women as one of Islam's foundational principles (albeit with the caveat that the family still needed a leader, the husband).[31] Similarly, Rashid Rida wrote that he agreed with feminists that women had the right to pursue education, to own property, and to hold certain public roles.[32] Ben Badis agreed too on these points and argued that educated mothers would be critically important actors in the struggle to raise a future generation with Islamic values and identity—a matter of particular importance in a settler colony where settlers denigrated Islam and Algerian identity. Reformist thinkers repeated the claim that woman was man's first school, and thus her education was critical in order to establish a foundational Islamic education in the population writ large. Sheikhs from various local Sufi tariqas (brotherhoods) harshly criticized Ben Badis's ideas about women's education and courses for women as inappropriate.

Reformist discussions about women were shaped by the reform movement's call for laypeople to engage with Islamic knowledge unmediated by scholars. Muslim scholars or judges had long issued fatwas, or rulings, in which they arranged various pieces of Islamic knowledge (taken from the Qur'an, hadith, or Sunna) to argue for a particular interpretation or rule. Empowered by the Muslim reformist call for lay Muslims to read the Qur'an themselves and not rely too heavily on scholars for interpretation, interwar commentators in both the French- and Arabic-language press cited the corpus of Islamic knowledge—Islamic history, the Qur'an, Sunna, and the Hadith literature—to support their calls for women's education and advancement. They celebrated the rights Islam granted women, which included education for both sexes, a marriage contract that ensured women's consent, the payment of a dowry from the groom's family, and women's right to divorce and to inherit.

This discussion of Islamic knowledge within the debates about women's education added another dimension to the Muslim press's project to educate its readers. Through references to Islamic knowledge, authors worked simultaneously to challenge both French colonial claims about Muslim misogyny and long-standing arguments from some Sufi communities that women's education in anything beyond the Qur'an was dangerous. Both sets of ideologies needed to be dismantled, they argued, for Muslim society to enjoy a prosperous, modern future.

Muslim reformist commentators positioned themselves against such Sufi voices both theologically and in terms of women's advancement. They reminded Muslim readers that there was a host of evidence from Islamic knowledge that proved women's education was an integral part of the Islamic tradition since its inception. As one unsigned editorial stated, Islam "does not forbid women from learning or being educated, but the opposite! And this is what we must write and talk about with a loud voice so all the people will hear and learn."[33] Examples from Islamic history also supported such claims. In 1935 Ben Badis wrote in *al-Shihab* about how the Virgin Mary, Moses's mother, and the Prophet Muhammad's wife Aisha were examples of feminine perfection for not only their morality but also their intellect.[34] Later, in 1939, he wrote that the many women in Islamic history celebrated for their scientific and literary knowledge should inspire Muslims to work toward education for both sexes "on the basis of our religious and national identity" so that Algeria can take "a dignified place among nations."[35] He saw "religious and national identity," women's advancement, and Algeria's global standing as intertwined.

A key ideological commitment of the Muslim reformist movement was the idea of Islamic renaissance in the present that would revive a lost former Islamic glory.[36] The movement argued that if Muslims could return to Islam's true principles and focus on education, the entire *umma*, or global community of Muslims, would be uplifted out of the stagnation and poverty of their current situation, including the harsh realities of much of North Africa and the Middle East under European colonial domination. Muslim reform offered Muslims a path forward out of the stifling realities of colonial domination in which a new emphasis on their own faith could produce communal uplift.

Such reformist ideas about how Islam was emancipatory for women had such currency in the interwar years that they reappeared in schoolteacher publications as well, as in the coverage of the 1932 International Congress of Mediterranean Women in Constantine. The congress in Constantine was organized by metropolitan French and settler women. They invited participants from various Mediterranean countries and asked each representative to offer a thirty-minute presentation about the status of women in their country, including both their rights and the challenges they faced. This congress was one of several women's conferences held in Beirut, Baghdad, Cairo, Constantine, Damascus, Istanbul, and Tehran between 1928 and 1938.[37] Unlike the other women's conferences in the region, the Constantine congress did not connect the challenges women faced to the constraints imposed by colonialism, likely because of its European organizers. *La Voix Indigène* published coverage of the conference and a series of editorials directed at the congress's attendees. In advance of the congress, *La Voix Indigène* published an "open letter" to the French women attending the conference asking them to lobby the state to build more schools for girls.[38] The editorial reminded French women that the Muslim people would not evolve because of a "more or less sincere discourse or under the effect of a magic wand."[39] In other words, speeches and congresses alone were insufficient. Instead, they urged European women to intervene on their behalf in favor of a multidisciplinary, "general, [and] rational" education for Muslim girls, equal to that of French girls.

At the congress itself, Hamed Largueche spoke on behalf of Algerian women. His speech, which was later reprinted in *La Voix Indigène*, illustrates how some contributors wanted to depict early Islamic history as emancipatory for women to push back against French colonial stereotypes that equated Islam with misogyny. Such commentators cited the important roles Muslim women occupied in early Islamic societies, including as poets, writers, teachers, and jurists.[40] Largueche explained the Prophet Muhammad's role in ushering in a series of reforms that elevated both Muslim women and society as a whole. He described a rich intellectual life in which women participated as equals. This depiction of early Islamic history evoked modern ideas about enlightenment, including an active print culture, educated women who held prominent public roles, and intellectual freedom. He reframed Islam as emancipatory in terms his audience of European women would understand.

In the following month after the congress, on its front page *La Voix Indigène* published a Muslim woman's response to the congress. Madame Seghir Hacène was the wife of the caid of Sigus, a small town 20 miles south of Constantine.[41] Hacène angrily argued that the feminists' perspective was clouded by their stereotypes about Muslims. She wrote that the attendees "ignore[d] everything or almost everything about the life of my sisters," whom the attendees saw as "savages, resistant to civilization and progress." Like Ameur, Hacène wrote that Muslim women suffered not because of an oppressive religion that rejected their education but rather because of the same problem that plagued people globally: the persistence of misogynistic customs and limited access to education. She stated that while Islam itself respected women and mandated education for women, the Muslims of Algeria "did not observe the Qur'anic prescriptions," and instead subjected Muslim women "to an arbitrary regime . . . [of] egoism."

Hacène sought to shift the discussion away from Islam's supposed backwardness and instead to the question of access. She wrote that the feminists ignored that education alone was "the magic key to the emancipation [of all] human being[s], men or women." Like Ameur, she worked to deracialize Muslims through her use of "human beings." For Muslim women to advance, they, like all peoples, required access to schools. She urged French women to push the state to build "schools, many schools, many schools, for all the indigenous girls with obligatory attendance." While the French feminist publication *La Française* occasionally reprinted articles from *La Voix Indigène*, they neither reprinted nor responded to Hacène's letter. Seghir Hacène never reappeared in the interwar press, although she may have been related to Ali Hacène, a judicial interpreter within the French colonial courts, who published several legal manuals as well as an article about the challenges Kabyle women faced in *L'Echo Indigène*. Seghir Hacène's choice to publish her commentary in *La Voix Indigène* suggests that she read it and may indicate she was ideologically aligned with Zenati and other schoolteachers. It may have also been a pragmatic choice since the conference attendees would be more likely to read a response published in a French-language publication. Despite Zenati's overall assimilationist tendencies, he was willing to publish Hacène's critique of the congress and the French colonial state's failure to educate Muslim women, which reflects how assimilationists too issued critiques of the state, particularly around questions relating to women.

These claims echoed regional feminist discussions. In contemporaneous Tunisian and Egyptian publications, women also stressed that education was the most important factor that would transform women's possibilities and lives. While the French colonial regime focused on the veil as an impediment to women's advancement, Tunisian women took to the women's review *Leïla* to insist that education was most important in improving women's social standing. They insisted that unveiling was more of an ideological gesture than a marker of real reform. Instead, they used forums like *Leïla* to make direct, specific demands of both French and Tunisian society at large for education. Speaking to Tunisian socialists who insisted on the importance of unveiling above all else, *Leïla* contributor Bahri Guiga "explained sarcastically that the elimination of the hijab would not reduce infant mortality, ameliorate general hygiene, or [offer] education." Similarly, female contributor Essaida Foudhaili wrote that even if all Tunisian women stopped veiling immediately, they would continue to be unequipped to participate in Tunisian society as equals to their male counterparts because of their lack of education. Like Hacène, some Tunisian commentators also critiqued Tunisian men for not doing more for women. A contributor, Mademoiselle Radhia, for example, wrote that the responsibility lay with men to encourage change in their own families by insisting their own sisters and daughters receive an education. She insisted as well that women be strong in standing up to their husbands and fathers, reminding them that "men are not God."[42]

In Algeria, commentators in *La Voix des Humbles* and *La Voix Indigène* echoed Largueche's and Seghir Hacène's insistence that Islam was emancipatory for women. Some even attached the term "feminist" to the possibilities for change they saw in Islamic history. In *La Voix Indigène*, Chérif bin Larbi Cadi described Muhammad as "the first Arab feminist" because "he, inspired by God, recommended treating women equitably."[43] Cadi was particularly committed to spreading the message that Islam was progress-oriented. He wrote that some Muslim elites were "too assimilated . . . with regard to religious practice and alcohol to be effective links" between Muslim and settler communities.[44] While he was critical of what he described as the excessively assimilationist tendencies of the schoolteachers, he published in their publications such as *La Voix Indigène*. He himself was a naturalized French citizen and lieutenant colonel, and he came from an elite family, in which three out of his four brothers were knights or officers of the Legion of Honor, and all four were qadis, Muslim judges within the French colonial system.[45] His family's connections enabled him to be educated in French schools in Constantine and Algiers, and eventually Paris. He was naturalized as a French citizen at the age of twenty-two in 1889 and later became one of the few Muslims to become an officer in the French army. Cadi was also married to settler Jeanne Dupré until she passed away in 1913, and in 1918 he remarried Cyprienne Bertrand from the metropole. Many of Algeria's elite Muslim families maintained ties to the Muslim side of the French colonial legal system, yet his position as an officer in the French army and his naturalized citizenship rendered Cadi unique. Yet at age sixty-seven, despite his own complicated allegiances, he contended in *La Voix Indigène* that it was important elite Muslims retain their ability to connect and speak to average Muslims by not assimilating too much, indicating how nuanced elite Muslim self-identification was in this period.

Cadi was not alone in his use of the term "feminism" in his 1932 discussion of Islam's compatibility with feminism. In the 1934 wedding speech reprinted in *La Voix Indigène*, Abou-Ezzohra similarly described "the feminist movement gaining terrain every day" in the Middle East as a "completely Islamic movement."[46] The education and leadership of "our Muslim sisters" in the Middle East, he contended, was "the foundation" of the "renaissance of Islam." While Cadi and Abou-Ezzohra were published in schoolteacher newspapers, they agreed with Muslim reformists that while local Sufi practices had allowed misogyny and tribalism to reign, a return to Islam's true feminist principles would allow for a truly modern future Muslim society. Indeed, in the 1930s, as the Muslim reformist movement grew across Algeria, the discussion of women's education shifted from a focus on French schools to calls for a more hybrid Islamic education.

Reformist discussions similarly presented women's education as a path to future renaissance. In November 1937 Mohamed Saleh Ramdane, a twenty-four-year-old poet from the rural town of El Kantara, penned a commentary titled "The Education of Women" in the Muslim reformist *al-Bassair*.[47] For Ramdane, the lamentable plight of the "poor, ignorant [Algerian] women" was a reminder of Algeria's place globally. A century into colonial occupation, Muslim women and Muslim society broadly in Algeria were largely uneducated and impoverished. Women's education, he argued, would turn the tide for Muslim society in Algeria, and even restore Algeria's status globally to the past glory it had shared with the Muslim Middle East. He wrote, "There is no reason for our delay in the caravan of life today, which we used to lead."[48] "Our" and "we" here refer not to an Algerian nation but the Muslim *umma*. For him, women's status was thus a marker of Algeria's loss of former shared Muslim glory, Algeria's weak global standing, and the potential for future renaissance.

For Muslims in Algeria, this regional renaissance was already underway in the Middle East. In *al-Bassair* Muhammad bin Ahmad al Mansur suggested that the articulate commentaries written by women in Middle Eastern newspapers signaled "the resurrection of Arab civilization in the East."[49] These women's eloquence was a marker of a broader social renewal underway. The titles alone from articles about the Middle East signaled these themes, such as "The Renaissance of the Iraqi Woman" and "The Modern Eastern Uprising in the Country of Afghanistan."[50]

Muslim women also took up the framework of educated mothers to argue that if educated, they could instill knowledge of this Islamic glory in the next generation. In 1934 a Muslim woman writing under the pseudonym "Séti BM" wrote to the editors of the reformist paper *La Défense* after reading "The Renaissance of the Iraqi Woman."[51] She explained that she was compelled to write to *La Défense* to ask why the Muslim women of Algeria were not given the same opportunities or resources, namely, schools, to advance like the women of Turkey or Egypt. She wrote that "because France does not understand the entire moral beauty of its task, our people stay in this state of ignorance and apathy." Like the schoolteachers, she underscored the state's failure to live up to the promises of "its task" of uplift for its colonial subjects.

Séti wrote that an educated mother could teach her children that "while others [Europeans] were in the most complete ignorance and barbarism, the Arab had his doctors, his poets, his writers, his astronomers, [and] his architects."[52] Her reference to a past of Arab glory functioned to decenter Europe's role as the sole imparter of civilization and modernity. Mothers could "make [their children] love their ancestors," which would enable the children to "revive such a glorious past" in the future. For Séti, an educated Muslim mother's capacity to instill within her children pride in a lineage of Arab glory was critical, because it offered Muslim children dignity in the face of colonialism. Her letter exemplifies how women's position as mothers could be leveraged to argue for the need for schools, in ways that referenced both past Muslim glory and contemporary news from the Middle East.

By the late 1930s the Muslim reform movement had established more of its own schools, which offered Muslim children a multidisciplinary education, including physical exercise, grammar and vocabulary, French literacy, history and geography of North Africa, math, and religion (Qur'an, Islamic principles, and the life of the Prophet Muhammad).[53] Like French colonial schools, they were in operation from October to June. Alongside the school, there were also reformist associations, theater troupes, and sports clubs. These schools were mixed-gender until "puberty," which made them the object of harsh critique from the Sufi sheikhs committed to strict gender segregation. Archival documents suggest there were plans to also open schools that taught girls artisanal training as well, but it is unclear whether they were ever realized.[54]

Muslim community members, including women, largely funded these schools.[55] Newspapers regularly published lists of donors to the schools whom they thanked for their contributions. Many women were on these lists for donating their wedding jewelry, dowry, or other money. Among women with limited financial means, dowry jewelry circulated as an alternate female financial system. It was passed down matrilineally and could be melted and sold piecemeal when needed. Dowry jewelry was a key means by which Muslim women contributed, whether in the form of money or the jewelry itself, to the establishment of reformist schools for Muslim boys and girls. The newspapers also joyously commemorated end-of-year celebrations in which community members gathered to watch female students debate certain topics, among them the woman's right to education in Islam.[56] These celebrations and their coverage in the press demonstrate that girls' education was a communal project—lobbied for, funded, and celebrated by community members. While the numbers of these schools remained limited because of funding difficulties, they indicate how multidisciplinary education for girls moved from a hope articulated by the *Voix des Humbles* schoolteachers in the early 1920s to a reality made possible through reformist community cooperation by the end of the interwar years.

Women's active participation in reformist education also came through associations affiliated with the reformists. Hundreds of Muslim women were active members of the El Kheira (or "Goodness") Association, for example. Surveillance documents noted that a third of the attendees at their events were usually women.[57] Notes from a 1938 meeting estimated that some four hundred Muslim women were in attendance. Speeches at these meetings focused on women's lives, and the organization had particular branches that worked toward a broad range of interests, including education and professional training for women. A newspaper reported that thanks to courses El Kheira offered, more than a hundred girls were now literate in French and Arabic. In 1941 the organization established its own artisanal training school for women.

The reporting on these schools continued the ongoing conversation about the compatibility between women's education and Islam, and educated girls took advantage of the press as a space to challenge concerns about their education. Girls and women stressed that these schools empowered Muslim women to fulfill their Islamic responsibilities. In 1938 *al-Bassair* published an article written by an educated girl in Constantine, "Bint Sayyida Asi Z. H. R.," who challenged this idea that education could lead to "leaky morals."[58] The descriptor "leaky" framed girls' morality as something fragile and easily susceptible to damage, as some Sufi communities contended. Like Houria Ameur and Seghir Hacène, who were published in *La Voix Indigène* in 1929 and 1932, respectively, Bint Sayyida Asi Z. H. R. critiqued Muslim men for their failure to support women's education for the women in their own lives. She wrote that these family members "believe if she is educated, she will rebel and behave inappropriately." She insisted that despite such fears, education would not lead to "copying Europeans blindly and wearing makeup." The fears were thus that women's education may not only enable licentious behavior but also facilitate assimilation to European gender norms. Like other commentators, she reframed women's education as rooted in Islamic ideals. She wrote that "true education will bring nothing but purity, goodness, Islamic behavior, and morality." Education would thus strengthen a girl's Islamic identity and "purity," an implicit reference to her sexual chastity.

The Educated Women of the Modern Middle East

Muslim reformist publications also praised how women in other Middle Eastern spaces had taken on greater social roles and called for similar transformation in Algeria. The Muslim reformist *al-Shihab* reported that in Afghanistan, "his majesty the King [Amanullah Khan] worked tirelessly by himself to make the *umma* understand the necessity of education."[59] Through the education of girls in particular, the article contended, Afghanistan had "reached the door to development in a stable and calm way." The phrase "stable and calm" worked to assuage fears that women's education would provoke too great a change to Algeria. Muslim reformist papers also published commentaries that called for Muslim women in Algeria to take on all the roles that Egyptian and Turkish women were playing in society, including "journalists, female doctors, lawyers, and even a pilot."[60] While the precise parameters of the feminist future they wanted varied, they agreed education was the critical first step toward this advancement. As another article stated, "Before we can have the liberation of women which we want [in the future], we need education [now]."[61]

Unlike other Middle Eastern spaces, discussions about women's education in Algeria were not framed predominantly in terms of the uplift of the future Algerian nation alone. Instead, these discussions proposed multiple modes of belonging that transcended geographical and temporal bounds and insisted on Muslims' right to see themselves as modern. Muslims in Algeria weaponized news from the Middle East to challenge colonial ideology about Muslim backwardness and to argue that Europe had no monopoly on modernity or civilization. Instead, they claimed ownership of their unique historical moment in which women's advancement and broader societal uplift were sweeping across the Middle East. References to concurrent developments in the Middle East or a shared Muslim past became a language that commentators across multiple communities adopted. This allowed them to engage in conversations about how Muslims in Algeria could participate in the "century of Progress" despite the considerable constraints on their daily lives as colonial subjects.

As the largest Muslim newspaper in Algeria, the Arabic-language *al-Najah* offered Muslim readers access to news from the Middle East. It had a wide readership that would have spanned multiple ideological communities. *Al-Najah* offered particularly consistent coverage of developments in Turkey to feed the Muslim public's fascination with Mustafa Kemal Atatürk. In 1922, after he emerged victorious in the Turkish War of Independence, the cult of personality around him was so strong that portraits of him were sold in Algerian marketplaces.[62] From the mid- to late 1920s *al-Najah* published news or commentaries about Turkey in almost every issue. They covered new reforms passed in Turkey, and they reprinted articles from Egyptian papers that were critical of how Mustafa Kemal Atatürk dismantled religious institutions and were interested in him and his private life. In 1925 publications in Algeria reported at length about his divorce, including coverage of his ex-wife's perspective.[63] In 1929 *al-Najah*'s editor, Smaïl Mami, even used the public thirst for material about Turkey to secure more subscriptions. He wrote that if more readers subscribed, the newspaper could appear daily (which it did briefly in 1930) and could offer readers even more news about Turkey.

Turkey mattered so much to secularists and Muslim reformists alike because of its political and economic independence from Europe, which they described as a victory for the *umma*. By this period, much of the region except Turkey, Iran, and the eventual Kingdom of Saudi Arabia were under some form of European colonial rule. In 1922 the newspaper *L'Ikdam* stated, "We salute with a deep respect and veneration . . . the savior of Turkey, the glory of Islam."[64] In 1923 the cofounder of *al-Najah*, El-Hachemi, wrote, "The [Turkish] coup d'état was a great event, and it pleased all the Muslims [of the world]."[65] An unsigned 1928 editorial in *al-Najah* stated, "Yesterday the Eastern states [Turkey and Iran] were enslaved. The Europeans had them by their necks, but today they only want to live free from this bondage and enjoy what modern states enjoy."[66] Interwar authors used the language of "bondage" to refer to the plight of the colonized, so the parallels to the colonized were clear to readers. These states had successfully "tak[en] back [their] freedom from" Europe and laid claim to their right to build their own modern states. Even in 1938, after Mustafa Kemal Atatürk's death, the nationalist newspaper *El Ouma* commemorated the fact that he upheld "the dignity of Islam."[67] His victory in Turkey, they wrote, ensured that "the crushing of the Crescent by the Cross" would not happen. Such commentaries used emotive language to evoke feelings of victory and shared pride among readers. Intellectual circles were abuzz over news about Turkey in the early twentieth century. Malek Bennabi described how even as a teenager who attended the Ecole Jules Ferry in Constantine, he closely following the news from Turkey by skimming newspapers in the local grocery store.[68] Later in a madrassa where he was training to become a magistrate, he and fellow students regularly discussed Mustafa Kemal Atatürk at the local café.

The way these Muslims in Algeria read Mustafa Kemal Atatürk illustrates the nuances to their international allegiances. Even though Mustafa Kemal Atatürk was known for his efforts to secularize Turkey, Muslims in Algeria still saw him as the strong Muslim leader who saved Turkey from the fate of the colonized states of North Africa and the Middle East. The language of "Crescent" and "Cross" referenced not religion but European dominance and Muslim resistance. This frame was not entirely new to Algerians. They equally celebrated the Ottoman Sultan Abdul-Hamid's victory over the Greeks in the 1897 Greco-Turkish War as a victory for the Muslim world.[69] Yet while Abdul-Hamid's official title was the caliph of all Muslims, Mustafa Kemal Atatürk dismantled Turkey's religious institutions, including the caliphate itself. While scholars and lay audiences alike have tended to overemphasize the explanatory power of religion in the Middle East, the framing of Mustafa Kemal Atatürk as a Muslim hero in spite of his secular reforms reflects the overlaps between religious language and discussions about political hegemony and resistance.

In their enthusiasm about how Mustafa Kemal Atatürk's reforms had transformed Turkish society, Muslim commentators in Algeria continually returned to the question of women's advancement.[70] Publications in Algeria also reported on the successes of the regimes of Reza Shah in Iran and Amanullah Khan in Afghanistan in terms of reforms for women, as well as women's rights movements in Egypt, Syria, Iraq, and India.[71] Many felt transformations in women's status were underway across the region, or "the order of the day," as one commentator described it.[72] The analysis that follows is thus shaped by the attention of commentators within Algeria, who most often referenced developments in Turkey and Egypt. Although Tunisia's feminist movement was also developing in the interwar years, it received almost no coverage in Algeria. While feminist movements in Syria and Lebanon were occasionally mentioned, they too received little coverage.

Commentators in Algeria identified the formula that seemed to govern developments across the Middle East: women's advancement had ripple effects and elevated the whole society. El-Hachemi wrote that women's uplift in Turkey enabled women to contribute their intellect and labor, which in turn uplifted the whole society.[73] In this formulation, women's advancement was not a by-product of Turkey's modernization but rather "one of the biggest causes." Benriba wrote in *La Voix des Humbles* that the "emancipation of the woman" that was underway "everywhere" had produced "evolution" and "prosperity" that benefited everyone.[74] *La Défense* reported that in Iraq the education of young girls granted them "a new mentality," which in turn worked to produce a "modern society" and a move away from "backward traditions."[75] The parallel to Algeria was clear. Algerian society suffered in stagnation because of its inability to capitalize on women's potential contributions. As an unsigned editorial in *al-Najah* in 1927 stated, unlike the rest of the Middle East, "no one [in Algeria] is taking care of the education of women . . . not the administration, not the Parliament . . . no one."[76] Calls for women's education in Algeria were similarly framed in terms of the potential uplift of Muslim society. Authors in *La Voix des Humbles* and *La Voix Indigène*, for example, claimed women's education would serve as a catalyst for "social reconstruction" and "social progress in Algeria."[77]

Commentators frequently contrasted the status of Algerian women with their Middle Eastern counterparts. On one hand, there was the "disastrous situation" of Muslim women in Algeria.[78] They were stagnant, "stuck in ignorance." The French's responsibility in this issue was obvious, but in his wedding speech, Abou-Ezzohra blamed Muslim society as well for this calamity. He reasoned that it was Muslims' "egoism," "lack of concern," and tolerance of the "corruption of customs" that had enabled this terrible state of affairs. Muslim women suffered as a result, but they were not alone. Women's education, he argued, was "the greatest factor of [their] evolution," and he concluded that Muslims were "punishing [them]selves" by not affording Muslim women an education. A range of social issues, including "the bad education of our children" and the high divorce rate, reflected this society in crisis. Yet Abou-Ezzohra was also filled with "hope for a better future" because the number of educated Muslim girls was increasing.

Other commentators also moved between the status of women in Algeria as compared to the Middle East. Muhammad bin Ahmad al Mansur compared the capabilities of women of the Middle East to Algerian women in *al-Bassair*.[79] He wrote that after he read "beautiful articles [written] by the Arab ladies of the East," he was "melting of sadness and misery when [he] consider[ed] the luck of Algerian women in Arabic education." An unsigned editorial in *al-Najah* stated, "Send your daughters to school to save them from poverty and to work toward the development of the region. This is why the liberated Eastern women do their work, just as men do their work, and that is perfection."[80] Education would simultaneously improve the immediate material circumstances of women and their families, as well as "develop . . . the region." Both women and men had their own particular role to play in this uplift project. The focus on "the region" here indicates how the idea of uplift was not limited to a national context. Instead, women's education was a vehicle for Muslims in Algeria to participate in the broader uplift of "the region." Commentators insisted that for Muslims in Algeria to evolve—in whatever limited way was possible under

French colonialism—they needed to take seriously the question of women's education.[81]

As commentators across communities envisioned women as equal participants in a vibrant, modern society, references to the Middle East assuaged concerns that perhaps women's advancement projects may have unpredictable results.[82] One author noted, for example, that Turkish women who were educated and were employed in office buildings, banks, and businesses occupied their new posts "honorably."[83] Their intact "honor" signaled to readers that their morality and modesty was not compromised by their new labor or increased public presence. Abou-Ezzohra described how since women's education became a priority in Egypt, Syria, and Iraq, women were now in leadership roles in "literary, scientific, athletic, and political movements."[84] As women took on these public and important roles in society, he noted, they "continued to wear their hijab." His juxtaposition of women's leadership with their hijab demonstrated for his readers that education would not necessarily lead women to lose their religiosity or Muslim identity.

Women's Rights and the Progress of Civilization

These discussions about women's education were multidirectional. While Muslims were invested in a discourse about Islam's capacity to be modern and in developments from Middle Eastern countries, they mobilized such discourse to critique France. While their definitions of progress differed, there was consensus among almost all interwar commentators that "progress" was something good to aspire to. Moreover, and crucially, for them, progress was universal. Algerian Muslim commentators did not simply lay claim to progress as something the French had and that they as Muslims were entitled to as a universal good. On the contrary, they argued that the very universality of progress meant that in some cases, the French could learn from Muslims. Women's inheritance and voting rights, for example, were two such key instances. The picture that emerges, then, is one of progress as a collective process in which Muslims in Algeria take it as foundational that they and the French are equal participants. This was a fundamental restructuring of power relations. Algerian Muslims and French settlers may be temporarily placed in unequal positions due to the power structures of colonialism, and Muslims may therefore need to make claims on France, but such claim-making was not a concession to French superiority.

Discussions about women were a forum to assert not only the compatibility between Islam and women's rights but also their ability to access progress as Muslims. Benriba wrote in *La Voix des Humbles*, "While the Turkish women can vote and enjoy full participation in politics as equals, her French and Algerian sisters are still unable to vote.... The progress of civilization is not Christian, not Oriental or Occidental, but universal."[85] On the question of women's suffrage, Turkey was more advanced than not only Algeria but France as well. Just as Muslims in Algeria framed Mustafa Kemal Atatürk's initial victory as a shared success, the progress of his reforms offered them the opportunity to claim their ownership of "the progress of civilization." To them, developments in Turkey proved that Muslim spaces could advance alongside (and even surpass, as on the question of suffrage) Europe. That Muslim countries have "advanced" beyond Europe in terms of women's inheritance rights and suffrage was a discursive challenge to the French colonial narrative of Muslim backwardness and misogyny. Such claims appeared in other Middle Eastern publications as well. One "Echoes from the Orient" column of *L'Égyptienne* quoted another publication that wrote, "What revenge of the weaker sex who, in Turkey, have gone beyond Europe!"[86] Such claims carried particular weight in Algeria's settler-colonial context because they challenged the colonial logics that used supposed Muslim misogyny to justify colonial policies and practices.

Through their attention to the rights Islam granted women, commentators reclaimed Islam as a modern force more feminist than other legal regimes. Algerian commentators were not alone in these claims about the importance of women's rights within Islam. The language of Amanallah Khan's constitutional reforms in Afghanistan, for example, similarly asserted that women's rights were such a crucial part of the sharia that to violate one necessarily meant violating the other.[87] In Algeria the reformist leader and editor of *La Défense* Lamine Lamoudi asserted in *Al Islah*, "No women in the world have rights like women in Islam."[88] He wrote that Muslim women had "moral rights and civil rights," most notably the right to maintain their own wealth and property, independent of their husbands or families.

Many commentators contrasted the rights Islam granted women with those enjoyed throughout history by European women. Muslim commentators in Algeria took great pleasure in noting that Muslim women had enjoyed the right to maintain their own wealth and property independent of their husbands or families and the right to divorce since Islam's inception, while these were relatively recent rights for European women. Writing in the communist *La Lutte Sociale*, Ahmed Smaili wrote that "Islam accords women rights that even 'civilized' Europe is far from knowing, except in the U.S.S.R."[89] Like the comparisons between women's suffrage in Turkey and France, such claims offered Muslim commentators the ability to push back against French colonial claims about Islam's inherent misogyny and inferiority.

From Students to Teachers: A Conclusion

Discussions about women's education exploded in the interwar Muslim press. They responded to the material reality that there were few educational options available for Muslim girls in Algeria. Commentators also looked abroad to the educated, modern women of the Middle East, whom they saw as an emblem of what was possible in Algeria. References to both Islam's feminist potential and news from the Middle East fueled arguments that if Muslim women could be educated, there would be uplift for all of Muslim society, despite the ways it was constrained by settler colonialism. Such claims in turn enabled commentators to reclaim Islam's emancipatory potential from women in the face of French colonial claims which equated Islam with misogyny. McDougall has explained that there was a broad "gradualist, reformist politics that fez-wearing, French-education professionals and turbaned or *chechia*-capped Islamic scholars draped in the burnus could comfortably share," which predominantly involved "education—in French and Arabic, for boys and girls, at all levels—and opposed administrative inequity, popular ignorance and 'superstition', and" the corruption of Muslim elites working within the colonial bureaucracy.[90] McDougall uses pieces of dress—the fez, chechia, burnous—to describe how multiple communities, each with their own particular set of allegiances and sartorial norms, were able to embrace the reformist position around particular issues, among them education at all levels for Muslim boys and girls.

By the end of the interwar period, there was still no consistent, formalized curriculum for Muslim girls in French colonial schools. Most continued to offer only artisanal training. In 1949 there was finally a fusion of Muslim and settler education tracks, so Muslim children were no longer segregated into their own classes and were taught with the same curriculum as European children. The numbers of Muslim boys and girls enrolled in secondary education and higher education increased from 1,358 in 1940 to 6,260 in 1954, as well as from eighty-nine Muslims enrolled in higher education in 1940 to 589 in 1954. Meanwhile, the numbers of Muslim reformist schools across Algeria continued to rise after the interwar period from seventy in 1935 to 144 in 1949 and 181 by 1954.[91] In 1951 there were 16,286 students enrolled in reformist schools across Algeria, 6,696 or 41 percent of whom were girls.[92] The influence of the Muslim reform movement continued to grow as well, alongside this expansion in schools. The AOMA's educational apparatus continued to formalize, with earlier generations of students becoming teachers, including women.

Reformist education for women expanded in the decades following the interwar years, beyond what Ben Badis envisioned. Reformist schools had an enormous impact for the girls who attended, the fruits of which Charlotte Courreye has argued were most visible in the 1950s. While Ben Badis was initially committed to educating women so that mothers would transmit Islamic values to their children, the reformist education system for girls multiplied and expanded in subsequent decades. Courreye has written that the generation of girls educated within these schools in the 1950s were so committed to their education, they resisted any attempts by their families to prematurely marry them off. Some of the girls educated in such schools in the 1930s and 1940s were also serving as teachers themselves by the 1950s. In a photograph of students at the reformist Ecole al-Tahdib in Algiers, open from 1954 to 1962, the female students are unveiled.[93] Their unveiling illustrates their willingness to break from strict Islamic doctrine, a departure from the informed mothers Ben Badis envisioned when he first began educating women in the 1910s.

These dynamics were also at play in the education and career of author and politician Zuhur Wunisi. Born in 1936 in Constantine, Wunisi was among the early generations of students to be educated in reformist

Table 3.7 Numbers of Muslim reformist schools and classes in 1949 by department

DEPARTMENT	SCHOOLS	CLASSES	CLASSES IN FOUNDATION	GIRLS' CLASSES
Algiers	34	51	7	2
Constantine	78	157	16	4
Oran	26	53	5	5

Source: *al-Bassair*, October 31, 1949

schools. There was such demand for Arabic-language education in the reformist schools that Wunisi began teaching even after only having completed her primary education. In her autobiography she describes a tense encounter she once had with an AOMA inspector of education, who wanted to ensure her teaching met AOMA standards.[94] She continued teaching concurrent with her education, which eventually included two degrees from the University of Algiers. She published across a variety of forums, including *al-Bassair*, the journal of the Muslim Boy Scouts, *al-Hayat*, and the official organ of the FLN, *al-Moudjahid*.[95] In 1955 in *al-Hayat*, she published an article in which she used the historical example of the seventh-century companion of the Prophet Muhammad, Asma bint Abi Bakr, to encourage women to engage in revolutionary warfare alongside men.[96] As part of the first generation of Muslim girls to receive an education in Muslim reformist schools, her education imbued her with both the historical knowledge and the ideological vision to articulate this call to arms for Muslim women.

In the post-independence period, Wunisi served in the Algerian parliament and held cabinet positions across multiple presidencies in the 1970s and 1980s. In the interwar years Ben Badis had written that he was against the participation of women in high political positions, yet Wunisi's expansive career, which began in reformist schools, illustrates how they served as a launching pad for women, beyond what Ben Badis originally envisioned.[97] Her story illustrates how the interwar years sparked feminist possibilities that expanded later. While there was disagreement among Muslims about women's education—what subjects it should include, whether it should be in French or Arabic, what its goals were—women took advantage of the openings available to them to write in to the press and demand better, as well as to gain an education and play a larger societal role, in the case of women like Wunisi. Of course, interwar debates also included authors like those in *al-Balagh al-Jazairi* who suggested women's education could corrupt Muslim society. Yet the gradual expansion of women's educational possibilities and growing support for women's education as a project in subsequent decades suggests that such voices were limited in their impact.

The next chapter turns to the debates over women's and men's headwear. Like those over education, these discussions saw Muslim dress for what it said about Muslim society. As with education, international references were key to how commentators in Algeria understood themselves, framed their sartorial choices, and envisioned more prosperous, feminist futures.

CHAPTER 4

The Haik, the Hat, and the Gendered Politics of the New Public

"If Turkey became equal to Europe by wearing hats," a commentator in *al-Najah* quipped in 1927, "one can become more elevated than Europe and Turkey by wearing something completely new, like a triangle-shaped hat."[1] The author was teasing Muslim men who wore the European-style brimmed hat by suggesting they believed Turkish modernization and advancement were due only to the Turkish adoption of the hat over older forms of headwear, like the tarbush (fez) or ʿamama (turban).[2] This commentator reminded readers that while the hat may have gained popularity during Turkey's modernization project, modernization itself should be the focus, not the hat. Newspapers in the interwar years saw a flood of discussions about headwear for both Muslim men and women. As they read news from the Middle East, Muslims saw themselves in a moment of enormous transition and possibility. It was within this context that dress came to signify one path—among many—toward the future. Commentators described possible futures as modern, traditional, Islamic, or Algerian in overlapping and uneven ways. Analyzing debates about both women's hijabs and men's hats together, against the backdrop of an interwar Algeria in transition, reveals how these forms of dress became a language for Muslims to redefine what was modern or traditional and articulate visions of Algeria's future.

Hijabs and hats became particularly contentious because Muslim gender relations were in a moment of crisis as analyzed in other chapters of this book. Working women were mobile in unprecedented ways, crossing the boundaries of their home spaces, leaving Muslim neighborhoods, and working in European homes. Their income granted them new decision-making powers within the home. Working- and middle-class women alike frequented cinemas, theaters, and association meetings. Muslim men's power was further threatened by women's limited access to education, employment, and financial stability under French colonial rule. Worried commentators warned of a potential crisis of virility if women's power and mobility went unchecked.

Desperate to make sense of these changes to interwar Algerian life and gender relations, commentators looked abroad, referencing news from and a shared history with the Middle East, and to Islamic tradition, citing the corpus of Islamic knowledge, which they arranged in a process akin to the writing of fatwas. Fatwas, or legal opinions issued by Muslim scholars, typically sought to answer particular questions. As scholars ruled on these questions, they cited and interpreted pieces of Islamic knowledge, including the Qur'an, Sunna, and Hadith literature, as well as the rulings of other scholars. They laid out these citations and interpretations to justify their final ruling on the subject at hand. In the interwar period, commentators in the press similarly brought together various pieces of Islamic knowledge to level arguments. This process was enabled by the Muslim reform movement, which encouraged lay Muslims to read Islamic texts themselves, but even nonreformist commentators engaged in this fatwa-like mode of argumentation. While Muslim thinkers cited fragments from the same corpus of Islamic knowledge—composed of the Qur'an, the Hadith literature, and Islamic history—to level their arguments for or against particular forms of dress, the meaning of these fragments was never fixed.[3] Sartorial practices thus became a key site for discussions about tradition's role in surviving colonialism both culturally and psychologically. While these debates over dress were shaped by concerns about assimilation and internationalism in the interwar years, in the following decades articles of dress became more closely influenced by nationalism and anti-colonial struggle.

The historiography of the veil in Algeria has been most preoccupied with its symbolism during the Algerian War of Independence. In *Burning the Veil* Neil MacMaster examined the French army's campaigns to unveil Muslim women during the war as an attempt to extend state power into Muslim homes. He argued that the French colonial state's insistence on the veil as a symbol of Muslim backwardness forced the FLN to in turn defend the veil and the patriarchal family as an essential part of the Algerian nation. This suggests that the post-independence Algerian state's attitudes toward women's veiling and family life were simply a response to older colonial pressure. This oversimplification does not account for the complex ways other social anxieties and international developments influence discussions about women and veiling.

Recent scholarship from scholars of the Middle East has demystified the veil by examining it as lived practice that involved the performance of particular ideologies, whether piety, colonial modernity, or a nationalist statement of defiance.[4] In this way it was not dissimilar from other forms of dress or style globally that came to symbolize allegiance to larger ideologies. While this analysis of interwar Algeria is rooted in press discourses and less attentive to the lived practices of these forms of dress, these discourses also illustrate how hijabs and hats came to represent the embodied performance of multiple overlapping social, religious, and political stances.

But why focus on men's hats as well in a book primarily about women? I argue that the inclusion of discussions about men's hats illustrates the ways debates about women's hijabs conformed to other discussions around gendered practices, as well as the ways they were distinct. Both sets of discussions addressed similar broad anxieties: Islamic principles being misunderstood or placed in jeopardy, dignity in the face of colonialism, negotiations of European and Muslim models of modernity, the emergence of national identity, and the value of tradition.[5] Discussions around men's and women's headwear both responded to French colonial gaze and pressure to assimilate, and revealed other social anxieties about custom, modernity, Islam, and the future nation. Whereas existing histories of veiling in North Africa and the Middle East situate the discussion of the hijab as a women's issue, I propose a gendered history of headwear, which places debates on Muslim masculinity and the tarbush alongside those on womanhood and hijab. This analysis demonstrates how ideas about self-representation, custom, Islam, and modernity were in flux in the interwar period for both men and women because of local as well as regional developments. The scholarship on hijab has been very attentive to the social, political, and cultural implications of veiling and unveiling.[6] Yet this historiography has often failed to engage with male sartorial choices or the broader historiography on shifting forms of gendered dress in the twentieth century.[7]

This analysis works to undo some of the scholarly insistence on framing the veil as something distinct to Muslims. By not situating veiling practices among other forms of gendered dress or other clothing items with political implications, historians have risked reproducing the colonial obsession with the veil and promoting the colonial idea that veiling was always an essential marker of Muslim identity, ignoring the flexibility and diversity in Muslim women's veiling practices.[8] This chapter moves beyond the obsession with the hijab as wholly unique or stagnant to consider its relationship to men's headwear. Analysis of both sets of discussions alongside one another illustrates how dress functioned not simply as a political or religious statement but as a dense marker of societal shifts, notably in terms of custom.

Al-Najah's joke about the "triangle-shaped hat" inserted a comedic bent to the ongoing news coverage of developments in Turkey and Egypt. It poked fun at the simplification of Turkish modernization to simply the changes in men's headwear, by suggesting Turkey "became equal to Europe by wearing hats." It also mocked the obsession with progress among some Muslims in Algeria and the idea that one could become more modern simply by mimicking the dress of others deemed modern. The joke instead suggests that if all that is needed to be modern is a hat, Muslims in Algeria could simply invent their own hat, the "triangle-shaped hat," to achieve a modernity even beyond Turkey or Egypt, and it reflects the ongoing interest in this larger regional moment of rupture. Commentators in Algeria used developments in Turkey to play with French colonial discourse, both challenging stereotypes that continually linked Islam to backwardness and claiming their right to universalist ideas of progress. Developments in Turkey proved that Muslim countries could advance alongside Europe—an argument also explored by Muslim reformists in the debates on dress.

Contentious Headwear across the Middle East

The Algerian debates over men's and women's headwear were part of larger ongoing debates about dress and imitation that had taken place across the Middle East since the late nineteenth century. In terms of the veil, male and female commentators across the Middle East questioned the necessity of both the face veil and the veil itself. Prominent women like Queen Suraya Tarzi of Afghanistan and feminist Huda

Sharawi generated controversy when they unveiled.⁹ Texts like the 1928 Lebanese book *Unveiling and Veiling* by Nazira Zein al-Din also sparked controversy and conservative backlash. Women's magazines in Palestine and Lebanon celebrated not only that women were unveiled but that they were well versed in the latest fashions from Europe, including wearing hats. For them, fluency in global fashion culture signified their participation in the modern world order. When an Egyptian official visited Constantine, one article in *al-Najah* noted with shock that both he and his wife were wearing hats, making them look like "American tourists."¹⁰

Debates about European hats were concurrently sweeping the Muslim world. Since the late nineteenth century, as Muslim societies across North Africa and the Middle East changed because of European intervention and colonization, religious authorities debated and discussed which appropriations from European culture were permissible. An 1897 cartoon in the Egyptian publication *al-Ajyal* titled "Blind Imitation" mocked young Egyptians for thinking that clothing alone could make them modern.¹¹ Scholars from Al-Azhar in Cairo argued that "the adoption of European attire by Muslims [was] a strong signifier of Europeanization and by implication . . . a weakening of an Islamic way of life," as Samira Haj has written. By contrast, the modernist Egyptian mufti Muhammad Abduh issued the famous Transvaal fatwa in which he argued instead that as long as "the person wearing a European headdress had no intention of forsaking Islam and taking up another religion, his action is not un-Islamic." Other contemporary Muslim scholars, like the Indian Muslim reformer Sayyid Ahmad Khan, argued that such issues "belonged to mundane affairs since Islamic did not prescribe a social dress for Muslims to begin with."¹²

In the late 1920s these ongoing discussions in the Egyptian press about imitation focused in on the hat. One cartoon mocked the dispute generated among religious scholars when the Afghan king prayed with his hat on while visiting Cairo, an episode also discussed in the Algerian press. The press also heavily covered "the tarbush incident," in which it was rumored that Mustafa Kemal Atatürk had yanked a tarbush off the head of an Egyptian diplomat. Despite this coverage that occasionally cropped up throughout the 1920s and 1930s, these discussions eventually became less contentious, with more or less consensus that while the tarbush was a symbol of Egyptian national identity, wearing a Western-style hat did not constitute a renouncement of Egyptian identity.¹³

These issues were equally contentious in Albania and Morocco. Etty Terem has written about an Albanian religious scholar who requested a fatwa from a Moroccan ulema, Muhammad al-Hajwi, about whether it was permissible for Albanians to wear the European-style hat. Terem maps out the various issues that al-Hajwi saw as interrelated to headwear, most centrally whether it was permissible for Muslims to imitate the style and dress of non-Muslims. On one hand, he argued that while the European brimmed hat did not undermine faith, it should be avoided because "it erases distinguishing markers of the nation." On the other hand, al-Hajwi noted that Muslim civil servants should comply with the Albanian edict to wear the hat, so as to not risk their dismissal and replacement with non-Muslim civil servants, which would eventually lead to the loss of Muslim representation within the government. In other words, the issue of the hat had to be contextualized within the broader social context of power relations in Albania. There were also questions about modernity and Islam's flexibility at stake. Terem summarized al-Hajwi's argument as follows: "Islam is a pragmatic, rational religion, compatible with minor inventions, and promoting the integration of the *umma* as a partner in a modern global order. Modern Muslims need to distinguish between harmful and beneficial appropriation of goods and technologies that originated in Europe."[14]

In French Mandate Lebanon the tarbush came to symbolize Lebanese identity and opposition to French colonialism. Yasmine Nachabe has analyzed, for example, how the tarbush symbolized authority in interwar Lebanese portrait photography. Wearing the tarbush in their portraits enabled men to project social standing and authority. Yet women were also a part of the tarbush's contested meaning in Lebanon, as women would sometimes don the tarbush in their portraits to challenge patriarchal authority.[15]

These regional discussions illustrate that Algeria was not alone in its concern over headwear and what it came to represent. The Algerian discussions illustrate multiple sets of concerns at once. While by the 1930s in Egypt the tarbush was largely a nationalist symbol, in the 1920s its meaning was still contested. Wilson Chacko Jacob stated, "In the 1920s the tarbush could simultaneously be a sign of the modern and the traditional, the civilized and the savage, the national and the foreign, the masculine and the effeminate."[16] The Algerian discourses about both the hijab and hats similarly demonstrate not neat correlations to particular categories but rather how commentators played with each of these categories. Interwar discussions in Algeria responded to Muslims' positions as colonial subjects after a century under colonial occupation, as well as developments elsewhere in the Muslim world. These dialogues demonstrate clearly the triangulated intellectual relationship between Muslim subjects, their pushback against their French colonizers, and their layered views on different regimes in the Middle East, most frequently the Turkish Republic. Women and men's bodies—and how they chose to dress them in public—were at the intersection of these transregional concerns and local anxieties about changing Algerian cities.

"A Hijab Convenient to Her Time and Place"

Veiling styles were variable across Algeria. Within the debates in the press about hijab, commentators used the term "hijab" to refer to the haik. In Algiers women's haik was a white cloth draped over the head that extended to calf- or ankle-length, often with a separate face veil that covered the lower half of the face while letting the forehead and eyes show.[17] Women in other cities wore different forms of the haik, with some extending only to the waist, for example. The haik itself could be constituted from a simple white cloth, or it could be embroidered at the edges as adornment. Dahbia Lounas, a woman from the rural town of Mirabeau near Tizi Ouzou, explained that women there did not wear the haik, which was more "for women of central Algeria, in the capital and its surroundings."[18] Instead women wore simple, long, loose dresses, which she described as the typical "Amazigh style." In the 1930s and later, women of her region did not cover their faces.

In terms of hijab styles, the haik is similar to the Iranian chador or the Mauritian malahfa, in that it is a simple cloth worn as an outer cloak over other clothes. While the haik is typically worn with a rectangular piece of fabric, the chador is a semicircle. Like the chador, the haik is typically held together by the wearer's hands. While the chador is typically held closed or could be tucked under the arms, the haik and malahfa both offer women a subtle flexibility in terms of how much of the body is exposed depending on the wearer's posture and movement.

Muslim and non-Muslim women across Algeria veiled in various ways before Algeria's conquest, but colonial contact also shaped veiling practices. From the beginning of the French colonial occupation of Algeria in 1830 and in the following decades, colonialism facilitated sexual violence and a new demand for prostitution.[19] French colonial attempts to regulate prostitution turned it from a casual occupation one could move in and out of to a permanently marginalized status.[20] About how this impacted veiling, Marnia Lazreg has written: "Colonial intervention meant a loss of status for . . . women, from decent (that is, Muslim) to immoral (used as prostitutes for Frenchmen's gain). The veil became women's refuge from the French denuding gaze. However, its form changed, became longer, and it acquired a new significance as a symbol of not only cultural difference but also protection from and resistance to the colonial-qua-Christian domination."[21] Her analysis suggests that urban women's haik became longer as a form of protection against both the physical occupation of French people and the violating French gaze.

While the haik is less commonly worn in Algeria today, it remains celebrated, sometimes in marches, as a symbol of Algerian cultural heritage. Many continue to associate the haik with women's involvement in the Algerian War of Independence, since some veiled women used their haik to smuggle weapons for the FLN, as discussed in Franz Fanon's 1959 essay "Algeria Unveiled" and depicted in Gillo Pontecorvo's 1966 film *The Battle of Algiers*. Today some Algerians distinguish between the haik and other forms of hijab or Islamic dress imported from the Middle East. Popular anti-Islamist sentiment in Algiers, for example, distinguishes between the "elegance" of the haik as compared to the so-called dirty Middle Eastern abaya, which drags on the street.[22] For some Algerians today, the term "hijab" evokes any kind of veil covering hair as a religious choice, while the haik recalls a cultural patrimony.

In interwar Algeria commentators referred to the haik with the term "hijab" in the Arabic-language press and simply the term "veil" in the French-language press. One major topic of discussion was whether the face veil component of the haik was Islamically mandated or could be removed. For supporters of the face veil, it was an important tradition that connected Muslim women in Algeria to their past. For those who called for its removal, the face veil was an outdated custom that inhibited women from participating in public life. For both its supporters and its detractors, then, the veil was a marker of custom—either one to be celebrated or one to be abandoned. Here the interwar discussions about the veil cohere to other contemporary discourses about what to do with customary clothing in modern times.[23] Globally consumption of clothing and makeup became a language for girls from a wide array of spaces to present themselves as modern, unlike women of earlier generations.[24]

In interwar Algeria one of the most prolific figures in the discussions about the hijab was Sheikh Abu Ya'la al-Zawawi, the imam of the Sidi Ramadan mosque, the second oldest mosque in Algiers, located in the casbah. His links to multiple communities reflect how interwar urbanization facilitated interconnection between multiple ideological communities. Born to a Kabyle-speaking family in the rural Azazga region of Tizi Ouzou around 1870, al-Zawawi only learned Arabic after his arrival in Algiers around 1890.[25] In his youth he was imprisoned for attacking a man who had assaulted his father, who was also an imam. While in prison he learned to speak French from the prison director, and he was ultimately released for good behavior after serving only three years of his seven-year sentence.

al-Zawawi's allegiances were complicated. While he became increasingly committed to the Muslim reformist movement in the 1930s, he never entirely disavowed Sufism or the zawiya system, which was responsible for the education of Sufi scholars. Although he critiqued the French administration at times, he was among the imams paid monthly by the administration—a practice disavowed by reformists.[26] Still, he was well received by reformists. An article in *al-Bassair* called him an "'*alim* [Islamic legal scholar] of two generations," reflecting both his age and his ability to move between both Sufi and reformist worlds.[27] Al-Zawawi also maintained a complicated relationship to European settler society. Within the press, for example, he defended his preference for French cafés and hotels over the Muslim *café maure*. As the imam of the Sidi Ramadan mosque in the casbah, al-Zawawi occupied an important intellectual role within Algiers.

His sermons were widely attended by large crowds, including women. In his *Livre de l'Algérie* reformist and nationalist leader Tawfiq El Madani described the powerful impact of al-Zawawi's sermons: "He has revolutionized and transformed the traditional and ancient function of the preacher to make it a useful and national role. He preaches for everyone on local and specific subjects. His discourse is a real lesson, and he does not stop until he is certain that everyone present, men and women, have fully learned it. I bear witness that his preaching has had an active impact on souls."[28] Al-Zawawi's impactful sermons were sometimes reprinted in the press in publications such as *al-Najah* and *al-Bassair*, as well as compiled into books. His influence also spread through his regularly published commentaries in various interwar publications.

Al-Zawawi wrote extensively on the subject of the hijab in a series of articles published between December 1925 and February 1926 in *al-Najah*. These articles discussed the relationship between unveiling and the reform taking place in Turkey, evaluating current events through Islamic sources and history. After offering quotations from the Qur'an and Muslim scholars, he wrote, "Everyone agrees the hijab should not cover the face, so if [Muslim women] go to work like this . . . it will be great reform. But if it is going to lead to her being like her Western neighbors in wearing less clothes," then that would be unacceptable.[29] He presented the style of hijab that allowed the face to be uncovered as a more moderate response to the unveiling becoming increasingly prevalent across the region.

In 1937 the Muslim reformist paper *al-Bassair* published a multi-issue debate on hijab within which the participants distinguished between the haik as Algerian "custom" and the parameters of hijab required by Islamic sources, which allowed for the face to be exposed. Articles contributing to the debate were featured in seven different issues of the weekly publication, between January and April 1937.[30] As commentators argued whether the haik was custom or Islamic requirement, they also debated its impact on women's participation in society. The 1937 debate began with a long article by Mustafa Ibn Hallush, who argued that covering the face, hands, and feet was an outdated custom that had no basis in Islam and needed to be abandoned. He described the form of hijab in which the face and hands were exposed as the "middle" ground "between the two extremes" of strict hijab and complete unveiling.[31] Ibn Hallush argued that an excessively strict form of hijab like the haik stood between present-day Algeria and a future, modern Algeria. He wrote, "The [customary] hijab inhibits the Muslim woman from participating in religious matters and society equally and from participating in the *umma* like a human being with rights and responsibilities."[32]

Two months later, Hamza Bukusha responded to Ibn Hallush in *al-Bassair*; he wrote that even if the ulema agree it was not Islamically mandated for women to cover their hands and face, it was "a beautiful custom" that should not be abandoned.[33] Then only thirty years old, Bukusha had studied closely under Ben Badis in Constantine. He would later become a leader of the Muslim reform movement in Algeria, imprisoned by the French during the Algerian War of Independence. For Bukusha, more important than whether it was Islamically mandated was the fact that it was "honorable" and had a long history.

Bukusha noted that the stricter form of hijab was practiced in the Middle Ages, as well as by Arabs and Greeks throughout history. The title of his article even referred to covering the face as an "honorable custom in Islam and before."

While many interwar commentators supported women uncovering their faces, Bukusha was by no means alone in his insistence that women's faces should remain covered. In fact, *al-Balagh al-Jazairi* repeatedly published articles that called for women to adopt several strategies alongside the face veil to anonymize themselves and ensure they not be seen.[34] One author urged women to maintain anonymity even at home in the presence of nonfamily men. If a woman was home alone and her husband's friend came to the door, for example, she should only answer if it was absolutely necessary. If answering the door was necessary, the author wrote, women needed to disguise their voices, as the sound of a woman's voice alone could be enough to attract men and compromise her modesty. For Ibn Hallush, however, the stricter form of hijab's association with the past was precisely the reason it should be abandoned in their modern moment. He noted that the stricter forms of hijab disappeared as nations "were civilized by science."[35] "Science" here implicitly referred to the Muslim reformist opposition between local, superstitious religious practice, on one hand, and the spirit of science and civilization, which they described as fundamental to Islam, on the other.

One month after Ibn Hallush's initial article, Djamila Debèche joined the debate with her own article on the topic published in the French-language reformist paper *La Justice*. Debèche would later found the first women's journal, *L'Action*, for Muslim women in 1947. Citing the Qur'an, the Sunna, and the writings of Rashid Rida and Ibn Arabi, Debèche argued the haik was not a religious requirement but merely a custom. She wrote that Muslim "young girls or women, as long as they are decent, can go out in the city, in makeup, with their faces uncovered, and without the haik."[36] Alongside her article, *La Justice* published a picture of Debèche unveiled.

Many referenced Islamic history to describe both more flexible styles of hijab as well as women's greater public presence. Reformists across the region, including in Egypt, also drew on Islamic history as a model of Muslim feminine emancipation.[37] Debèche too stressed that there was historical precedent for both a more minimal covering style of hijab and women's greater participation. She reminded readers that in the time of the Prophet and the imams who followed, most Muslim women left their faces and hands exposed and also maintained important public roles as teachers. An author writing under the pseudonym "Taciturne" wrote in *La Voix des Humbles* that Muslim women in early Islamic history had a public presence, especially tied to poetry, and many did not veil since it was only intended for the wives of the Prophet Muhammad.[38] Muslim reformism preached its own logics of historical time, which these commentators echoed. Omnia El Shakry has described how Muslim reformists in Egypt framed social issues within "a nonsecular concept of historical time—framing reform (*islah*) as a project of renewal (*tajdid*) in the face of the decline and digression of the Muslim world from the true path of Islam."[39] Reformists in Algeria similarly evoked the Islamic past in their calls for a more modern future Algeria, which would require reform of Sufi traditions that had supposedly deviated from Islam.

Muslim commentators in Algeria of multiple religious and political allegiances articulated a vision of a future in which Muslim women would enjoy greater participation in Algerian society, although they were often unspecific about what this future participation might entail. Debèche's article was introduced by Mohammed Benhoura, editor of *La Justice*, qadi, and leading figure in Algiers's reformist circles close to the reformist leader Sheikh Tayyib al-Oqbi. Decidedly not a nationalist, Benhoura would later be assassinated by the FLN during the Battle of Algiers. In his introduction to Debèche's article, Benhoura highlighted the similarity between her position and those recently expressed in *al-Bassair* by Ibn Hallush. He praised Muslim reformist leaders for their support for "the moral and social emancipation of the Muslim woman."[40] Their shared vision of an Algerian future in which women would enjoy "moral and social emancipation" reflects how thinkers from quite different intellectual communities came together around women's advancement. While Benhoura was a qadi and a leader within the reformist movement, Debèche would later be heralded by the French colonial administration as a model colonial subject for her openness to a European model of women's emancipation. What emerged in these discussions was thus a vision of a future Muslim woman—one who could participate in society "equally," according to Ibn Hallush.

As authors identified the parameters of the hijab Islam required for women, they consistently portrayed Islam as modern, flexible, and adaptable. In so doing they challenged the Orientalist and French colonial view of Islamic practice as something static from the past by positing that Islamic customs were well suited for the present and future.

Many noted that since Islamic law does not mandate the covering of the hands and face, women in different regions could wear hijab in different ways. It left room, for example, for the diverse styles of hijab worn by more rural Algerian women, who often worked alongside men in planting and harvesting crops. After the back-and-forth between Ibn Hallush and Bukusha, *al-Bassair* invited Al-Zawawi to contribute and marry the two perspectives. Al-Zawawi echoed his 1926 articles from *al-Najah* and commended Ibn Hallush for favoring the sharia form of hijab that would be "convenient to her time and place," or adaptable to their modern moment.[41] Al-Zawawi wrote that historically "Islam was not as strict with differences in hijab across different nations as people are now."[42]

Yet despite this potential flexibility of the so-called sharia form of hijab, commentators were largely in agreement that unveiling entirely was unacceptable. An unsigned editorial in the Muslim reformist *al-Shihab* lamented that increasing numbers of Muslim women, including "the wives of the Muslim princes and ministers," were unveiling completely.[43] They feared Muslim practice was in danger of being overrun by so-called Western practices. Al-Darraji wrote that his commentary about women's hijab was relevant to all Muslim women, "whether . . . Turkish or Arab or anyone else because the sharia applies to everyone in the same way."[44] Al-Zawawi reminded readers that Muslims "cannot decide ourselves what is right" and were bound by the dictates set by the sharia.[45] Others implied that unveiling would happen on its own with time. Ibn Hallush wrote that while the haik form of hijab was "burdensome" to women, he did not advocate for unveiling but rather to "leave it to time" and allow it to happen "step by step." Even Debèche, who herself was unveiled, wrote in her provocative explanation about how hijab was not a religious requirement that "we do not want to change everything in one day. Today we're content just to put these facts out there."[46]

Many commentators underscored that while they may complain about the so-called traditional haik, Islam itself was emancipatory for women. As in debates about education, they drew on both Islamic texts and early Islamic history. Through regional references—coupled with those about Islamic knowledge—Muslim thinkers reclaimed women's advancement as an Islamic project, as opposed to one imported from Europe. In her article about hijab, Debèche noted that Islamic law empowered Muslim women to enter into contracts independently, "a right French women do not possess."[47] Here Islam—far from being an unwaveringly misogynistic force—was rather one that grants Muslim women greater rights than some of her European counterparts. Debèche's comparison to "French women" makes explicit a key feature of these discussions in the French colonial context: the triangulated comparisons between French women, Muslim women, and the modernizing women of the Middle East, often Turkey. While Algerian discussions around dress were rooted in a comparative south-south gaze toward other Middle Eastern spaces, Europe remained an important counterpoint. By asserting that Islam was not inherently misogynistic but potentially emancipatory, these authors reordered colonial ideology and challenged the ideological basis of their inferior status vis-à-vis European settlers within French colonial society.

Aspects of these debates were not unique to Algeria. Women authors and activists in Egypt, Baron has shown, demanded their right to greater participation in Egyptian society in the late nineteenth and early twentieth centuries with reference to early Islamic history and women's rights in Islam.[48] What set Algeria apart, however, from other interwar Middle Eastern contexts where debates about hijab also raged was the settler-colonial context. This context continually reinforced claims that a Muslim women's hijab was a marker of not only her subjugation but also Muslim society's backwardness and incompatibility with modernity. In response to such claims, the Muslim discussions about hijab in Algeria sought to reframe hijab and Islam broadly as flexible and modern. Djamila Debèche's article, which went as far as to claim that hijab broadly was a custom not required by Islam, even received endorsement from Muslim reformists. This support suggests that the desire to represent Islam and hijab as flexible and modern was a point of convergence across multiple intellectual communities.

Hats and the Panic of the Present

Choices in clothing and headwear had long offered men a means of expressing their politics, class, local culture, and even profession. For Muslim men, as Omar Carlier argued, even facial hair had particular connotations. Nationalist leader Messali Hadj's combination of a "strong nose" and a full mustache, for example, connoted "social standing, virility, and honor." During the interwar period, however, multiple sartorial norms shifted. In early 1920s Algiers most Muslim men continued to wear *sirwal*, the traditional loose cropped pants. The term *sirwal* even remains the Algérois word for pants today. By 1935, however, most Muslim men in Algiers wore European-style trousers. Carlier has noted that this fact was made even more remarkable because the Great Depression forced many Muslims to buy used clothing exclusively.[49] This shift toward European-style clothing may have been a consequence of men's shifting taste in attire after having served in the French army in Europe during World War I.[50] By the late interwar period, only elite older men, administrators of Qur'anic schools, and functionaries in Muslim courts continued to wear *sirwal* and other traditional clothes "with different degrees of elegance and ornamentation" in order to assert their status as protectors of tradition. Of course, this varied across Algeria. In Constantine, for example, middle- and upper-class Muslim men would continue to wear the traditional robes throughout the interwar period.[51]

Despite the multiple items of clothing that were in flux in the interwar years, the press fixated on styles of men's headwear. Debates about men's self-fashioning focused exclusively on their choice between three different forms, each with its own connotations and meanings. The tarbush, or red fez, had a shorter history in Algeria, as it was adopted across the Ottoman Empire in the nineteenth century as an equalizing form of dress worn by Muslims, Christians, and Jews alike. In turn-of-the-century Algeria, the choice to wear a tarbush signaled allegiance to a new modernity, in contrast to the 'amama or turban, which was seen as dated. By the interwar period, with the exception of religious centers like Constantine, the tarbush was overwhelmingly the most dominant style, particularly for middle- and upper-class men. The tarbush could be purchased in various shades of red (which could signify religious affiliation), in different fabrics, and with different forms of tassels and adornments—all of which signified fashion trends as well as various forms of social distinction. The head covering that started the controversy, however, was the Western-style brimmed top hat, which the Arabic-language press simply called *qubba'a*, or hat.

Although it had the longest history in Algeria, the turban-style head covering or 'amama was rarely mentioned in the debates about headwear. By the interwar period, it was typically worn only by men such as Muslim reformist leaders or men affiliated with Qur'anic schools, mosques, and occasionally the Muslim courts. This limited use made it less politically contentious than the tarbush and the hat. Notably missing from these discussions was the chechia-style hat that Muslim men, particularly rural and lower-class, wore, similar to a tarbush in color and shape but softer in material, wider in diameter, and sitting lower on the head. The absence of the chechia in the debates in the press indicates that these commentators were particularly interested in the sartorial habits of the small but growing Muslim middle class.⁵²

While interwar Algerian discussions about dress were rooted in particular local tensions, they also reflected dynamics at play both globally and historically. In multiple contexts particular forms of clothing became symbols in the wake of political upheaval. Historians have explored, for example, how men wore liberty caps after the French Revolution, all-black ensembles during World War I, Mao suits after the Cultural Revolution, and brown jackets after the rise of fascism in Italy.⁵³ Historians have traced the spread of these clothing items and analyzed the multiple meanings they came to symbolize as they became adopted in increasing numbers. Historians have also considered how certain sartorial decisions reflected consumption of international taste patterns.⁵⁴ Kathy Piess has described dress as "a particularly potent way to display and play with notions of respectability, allure, independence, and status to assert a distinctive identity."⁵⁵ Clothing could be a language for men to distance themselves from local traditions and instead self-fashion as cosmopolitan or modern. Colonialism too produced a particular set of dynamics around clothing, with often a sharp divide in the dress of the colonized and the colonizers. Within this context, clothing could be a way for male colonial subjects to play with their relationship to colonial power. The Gabonese elites analyzed by Jeremy Rich or the Sapeurs in Brazzaville, for example, negotiated French colonial sartorial norms to produce their own hybrid forms of respectability.⁵⁶

While interwar discussions around men's hats reflected local discussions about Islam, colonialism, and modernity, they also speak to how some of these broader global dynamics played out in Algeria. Atatürk's 1925 hat law was the catalyst for these discussions, and commentators in Algeria described those who wore the hat as loyal to the emerging world order embodied by the rise of secular authoritarian regimes in Turkey and Iran. Others described the hat as a careless attempt by young people to be stylish—a marker of the widening generational gap. The hat also represented a particular tension with colonial power, with some arguing that the hat signified a shame in one's identity and an attempt to pass as a European settler. Finally, for many commentators the hat represented a rejection of local custom. The debates over the hat were, like the debates about hijab, about the place of customs in a modern society. Some saw the ʿamama and the tarbush as part of a long historical tradition that Muslims needed to maintain to ensure future prosperity. Supporters of the hat, in contrast, offered examples of Islamic history to demonstrate that many important leaders instituted their own forms of dress, and they situated Atatürk within this line of important leaders. For them, Atatürk and the hat signaled a new era of transnational Muslim greatness.

Globally, many sartorial norms shifted after World War I.[57] As colonial soldiers returned home from Europe, many of them brought European clothes and tastes with them. Ideologically too, World War I forced global populations to reckon with the large-scale violence that Europe, the supposed hub of modernity, had wrought. Yet the discussions in Algeria over clothing were predominantly influenced by Middle Eastern developments, as their timing reflects. The first commentaries on the hat began to appear in the press in September 1925 in response to new Turkish legislation. While the new Turkish laws initially only mandated particular types of hat for certain state employees, the Hat Law, passed in November 1925, officially banned Turkish men from wearing the 'amama or the tarbush, punishable by death. Some commentators described those who wore the hat as loyal to the emerging world order embodied by Atatürk's rise in Turkey.

Yet Islamic history was equally important for those who supported wearing the hat and who described Atatürk as part of a long lineage of important Muslim leaders whose reigns all involved new forms of headwear. They situated Atatürk within a longer history of Muslim advancement, which came in stages, each with distinct leaders and costumes. One *al-Najah* author, for example, described Atatürk as among the great reformers (*muslihun*) of Muslim history.[58] This author moved systematically through Muslim history and described how the 'amama that was common during the Umayyad caliphate was replaced by the Persian-style *qalansuwah*, or tall triangular turban, under the Abbasid caliphate. He cited the work of a sixteenth-century historian from Tlemcen, Ahmad Ibn Muhammad al-Maqqari, about how the Muslims of Andalusia abandoned the turban for another form of headwear. In defense of Atatürk's legal mandating of the hat, the author noted that Umayyad leaders were "extremely strict" about the 'amama, while "in the year 153 [hijri], al-Mansur [legally] required" men to wear the Persian style *qalansuwah*. By situating Atatürk within a lineage of powerful Muslim leaders, intellectuals in Algeria who supported the hat argued that Atatürk was ushering in a new era of Muslim leadership. They understood Atatürk's ban as part of a larger step forward toward modernity and civilization. Unlike those who presented Westernization as a threat to Muslim identity, these authors saw no contradiction in Atatürk's "large step toward Western civilization" and his status as a powerful Muslim leader. This author's commentary demonstrates how for some intellectuals in Algeria, Atatürk's embrace of the hat was not an affront to centuries of Muslim tradition but an important moment within it.

Perhaps because of the extent to which they were oriented toward Turkey, Muslim authors did not describe Muslims who donned the hats as making a playful or subversive move that asserted "independence and an insistence on equal treatment," as Marie Grace Brown has described Sudanese men's choice to wear trousers. Notably, it is Brown's analysis of tensions over the dress of Sudanese women that more neatly maps onto the Algerian debates about men's hats: in both cases, there was "concern that overindulgence in foreign trends led to weakness and cultural instability," which in turn led to an insistence that dress for both men and women remain "local and authentic" in order to maintain social cohesion and a strong future.[59]

As the number of men from Algeria educated in French schools and entering the French colonial bureaucracy grew, some Muslim thinkers feared their culture was at risk of disappearing. This situation provided an important context for concerns about headwear. The hat sparked a panic about the present, which was rooted in fears about how to survive colonialism both culturally and psychologically. Troubled commentators lamented the pressure to assimilate and the self-hatred that colonial ideology evoked within Muslims. For them, choosing to wear a hat signified a shame in one's Arabness and an attempt to pass as a European settler—a symptom of their powerlessness under colonialism. For many commentators, the hat represented a rejection of Arab and Algerian tradition. These commentators were less optimistic than those who described a future in which Muslim women would be "emancipated" in the dialogues about hijab. One author complained that the city of Bône (Annaba) was in decline and "the situation of the women . . . is really bad."[60] The market was full of prostitutes. "Young men" were wearing hats. The author wrote disapprovingly that "they say it is just to protect them from the sun," but they wore their hats "even at night!" Articles lamented that young boys were attending French schools and learning not about the glory of Arab civilizations but about European history and geography.[61] One author quoted Rashid Rida that wearing the hat meant "forget[ting] one's dignity."[62] He wrote that he who would "hide himself behind a hat" was "ashamed of who we are."

In April 1937 the Lebanese reformist intellectual Shakib Arslan was invited to speak at the conference of the Association des étudiants musulmans d'Afrique du Nord (Association of Muslim Students of North Africa, or AEMAN) in Morocco. He commended how most North Africans continued to maintain their Arab identity, unlike the Arabs of the East who were "copying from [Europe] in a blind way," which was dangerous because of the self-hatred it engendered.[63] While in this particular address he focused on mimicry of Europeans broadly, he had commented on hats in particular in 1926 in the Egyptian newspaper *al-Fath*, where he insisted that Egypt would lose its essential identity if Egyptian men adopted the hat.[64] In his address to AEMAN, he stated that those mimicking European customs clearly saw themselves as comparatively "small and weak." Another anonymous editorial similarly stated, "It is cowardly to pick the look of a people that do not consider you one of them, and do not consider you equals even if you wear what they wear and talk how they talk."[65] Here the hat was symptomatic of not only assimilation as a strategy but also the self-hatred colonialism engendered. Arslan reminded his Muslim audience that because of European prejudice, assimilation would never lead to a freer future.

For one commentator in *al-Najah*, while the choice to wear the hat might be understandable as an attempt by powerless people to seek access to power, the gesture was clearly little more than "try[ing] to imitate the powerful."[66] He admonished those wearers of the hat (implicitly Muslims in Algeria and perhaps the Turkish) for believing that changing their appearance to look more like those with power—namely, Europeans—would bring power. Instead, he advised, Muslims should focus on attaining "the root of the West's power and dominance: knowledge, work, perseverance, and vitality." This was a recurring trope in these discussions of the hat. Commentators distinguished between sources of European power worth emulating, knowledge and technology, versus more superficial markers of Europeanness, like the hat.

Many of these tensions—between colonizer and colonized, between shame and pride, between assimilation and tradition—were framed in religious terms. Muslim authors connected the question of the hat in Turkey to the looming threat of atheism. The conservative Sufi newspaper *al-Balagh al-Jazairi*, which frequently challenged reformists, admonished the newspaper *al-Najah* for covering Turkish developments so heavily.[67] They complained that such exhaustive coverage was equal to support for "the Kemalist project," which involved "replacing sharia with Western law," as well as "forbidding the tarbush and hijab and requiring hats." They interpreted Atatürk's actions not as an alternative model of Muslim modernity but as a direct mimicry of "Western law." The editors urged their readers not to be fooled by the label of "reform" that Kemalists used to disguise their real project: atheism. Within this view, the hat symbolized the erasure of Islamic practice. Another author reprinted Rashid Rida's judgment that if the intent of "Westernizers" was to promote disbelief (*kufr*) by encouraging others to wear the hat, then wearing the hat itself was an act of disbelief.[68] Controversy erupted after the visit of the reform-minded king of Afghanistan, Amanullah Khan, to Cairo, where, it was rumored, the king asked the religious authorities of Al Azhar University whether it was permissible to wear a hat while praying. Many facts about this encounter, including whether the question was even posed and whether the response was given, were contested even in Algeria.[69]

Writers frequently evoked the Qur'anic concept of *taqlid*, which in this context refers to "following." While *taqlid* could connote following in a positive sense, Muslim authors used it to signify blind mimicry of Europeans. One article warned readers that the religious scholars at Al Azhar University decreed that Islam "forbids you to try and look like others [non-Muslims]."[70] These scholars ruled that sharia emphasized the importance of "conserving nationality and unity." Articles about civilization and modernity complained that some Muslims were "copying nothing but bad morals from Europe."[71] The article then declared, "We have shown the judgment of God" on the hat and "have shown how that hurts our unity and our nationality." The article encouraged its readers to act either out of fear of God or at least out of "patriotism" and reject the hat. Similarly, one author described "wearing the hat and dressing in a Western manner" as "preferring the characteristics of the *umma*'s adversaries over their own nation's characteristics."[72] The hat was then the site of a struggle between the *umma* and their "adversaries," Europeans. The nationalist discourse around the need to stand unified against the hat was so totalizing that it came to encompass not only one's culture and politics but also one's religious commitment.

Headwear for a Dignified Future Nation

Muslim reformists proposed pride in Algerian history and traditions to combat this shame and "loss of dignity." James McDougall has analyzed how histories produced by Muslim reformist leaders, which spanned from precolonial Algeria to the present, enabled Muslims to envision themselves as part of a continuous, persevering Algerian people who could thus have a nationalist future beyond French colonialism.[73] The discussions about headwear similarly illustrate—perhaps more so than discussions about women's labor or girls' schooling—budding nationalist discourse. Unlike the new hat, both the tarbush and 'amama represented history that predated French colonialism. Although before the interwar period the tarbush had reflected difference, since it was a relatively new Ottoman phenomenon slowly replacing the 'amama, the debates about the hat during the interwar years reframed the tarbush as an Algerian tradition in opposition to the hat. The insistence on the tarbush as "tradition," when it had been so recently introduced, signals how quickly sartorial norms were not only changing but also being redefined in the interwar years. Unlike the face veil, which was a tradition that could be modified, Muslim reformists and others saw the tarbush as integral to their identity and thus necessary to uphold for a strong future Algerian nation.

In a poem about the tarbush, 'amama, and hat published in al-Najah, the 'amama represented Algeria's Arab history. The poem described the 'amama as "the crown of the Arabs" and a reflection "of the old glory."[74] The reference to "old glory" reveals the connections many commentators envisioned between tradition as embodied in the 'amama and the tarbush and the potential greatness of a people. To adopt the hat, then, represented participation in the erasure of this tradition of "glory" in the face of colonization and Westernization. References to the lasting presence of the 'amama and tarbush since the era of Arab "glory" functioned as a way to connect the Algerian present to an empowering vision of the past. These references to periods of Arab "glory" were analogous to the aforementioned allusions to early Islamic history as a model of how women could be Muslim and maintain important public roles.

These discussions were also—like those about hijab—future-oriented. About the 'amama, tarbush, and hat in Egypt, Wilson Chacko Jacob has written: "The three sartorial symbols and their differentiated evocations of nationalism and masculinity were situated unevenly in the international order—conditioned by the epistemic and physical violence of colonialism—wherein the subject's formation was measured against what was commonly regarded as the inescapable flow of modern time, with which Egypt was still playing catch-up."[75] The Algerian discussions were similarly about Algeria's attempt to "catch up" to "modern time." Commentators in Algeria idealized the Islamic past and used references to Islamic knowledge to argue that a return to the true principles of the faith could bring about a future that was at once Muslim and modern. Some envisioned the tarbush as an emblem of a powerful potential future, while others suggested that it was change, in the form of the hat, that would bring about a greater future. In the poem about the tarbush and the 'amama, while the 'amama represented an Arab past, the poet connected the tarbush to the prosperity of nations. He wrote that the tarbush represented the "happiness of nations and countries."[76] With it, "we build . . . castles of hope for the future and service to the homeland." The author associates the tarbush with the dream of a successful national project in the future. The cohesion and strength of this future nation depended on the commitment of the Algerian people to their traditions, like the tarbush.

Cohesion was critical for a future Algerian nation, both in the sense of a people and an independent nation-state. One author, writing in the Muslim reformist *al-Shihab*, argued that the tarbush was part of a broader range of "attributes and characteristics" of the Muslim "religion, language, literature, and true traditions" of Algeria.[77] Here he alluded to the Muslim reformist and eventually nationalist, saying, "Islam is our religion, Arabic is our language, and Algeria is our homeland." He argued a nation was only as strong as these "attributes and characteristics." Reiterating the connections other authors drew between men's self-fashioning and the greatness of Muslims, he warned of "weakening and decay" if the hat became more prevalent. Here tradition was not the vestiges of anti-modern ignorance to be wiped away as it was in discussions about hijab. Rather, it was a prerequisite for a strong Algerian future.

In his address at the AEMAN conference, Arslan cited the example of Japan to argue that maintaining traditions would not impede modernization.[78] He admired the long-standing Japanese belief that the emperor was part of the sun. He reminded his audience that despite the Japanese allegiance to this "ridiculous" belief, Japan was "one of the most advanced nations" in the world. In other words, tradition strengthened nations through a shared national culture, even when the traditions themselves may be of no discernible value. With his reference to Japan, Arslan joined Muslim reformists and thinkers like Debèche who challenged Europe's supposed monopoly on advancement and civilization.

Some critiqued the idea that the strength of the nation depended on tradition. As in the discussions about hijab, history was a critical part of how commentators evaluated whether the tarbush had value in the present. While *al-Shihab* frequently attacked Muslims who adopted the hat, they also reprinted an article from the Egyptian newspaper *al-Fajr*, which criticized other Muslim intellectuals for insisting on the need to uphold traditions, irrespective of their utility. The author described the tarbush as "the most ridiculous thing a creature has [ever] worn on its head."[79] He reminded readers that despite these ubiquitous references to the tarbush as a Muslim tradition, the tarbush originated in Greece. He questioned the utility of the tarbush, arguing that its red color and silk tassel initially had military value but there was no longer any reason to continue to wear it. He wrote, "Now, nothing is left but the trace of the old ages which do not help anything." He thus encouraged Muslims to abandon the tarbush since it offered neither utility or authentic Muslim heritage.

One author from Morocco whose article was reprinted in *al-Bassair* complained that all Westernized Muslims "know of civilization is . . . fashion."[80] Real civilization, he wrote, was that which would "bring together individuals, unify groups, work toward goals, work for the country, construct the nation, and elevate the social state [of the people]." In this nationalist formulation, plurality would fall away as individuals and groups united in service of the nation. This language combines the reformist rejection of plurality and insistence that there was one, single authentic mode of Islamic practice with the utilitarian ideals of nationalism. Yet while reformists were largely unified against the hat and unveiling, they were open to the diverse styles of hijab adopted by rural women. The hat and unveiling were so objectionable and impermissible because they represented assimilation to European norms.

The Gendered Stakes of Algeria's Sartorial Future

The Algerian discussions of men's and women's headwear remained separate. An individual's dress revealed multiple sets of allegiances, many of which were not always firmly decided but rather negotiated. A Muslim man's or woman's choice to don headwear would have been influenced by a number of factors, including but not limited to their social class, their geographic location, and their association with specific religious communities or professions.

Yet at the level of press discourse, these individual negotiations and choices became collapsed into decisions about custom and national cohesion. Particular pieces of headwear came to connote a particular stance on questions of custom, modernity, and nationalism. Despite being an Ottoman-era import, the tarbush came to symbolize Algerian and Muslim custom, while the hat represented modernization and secularization, either in the path of Atatürk or the French. Similarly in the discussions around the haik, proponents of the face veil argued it was an invaluable Muslim custom, whereas others argued it could be removed as part of the broader project to modernize Algeria. Reformist commentators who supported men wearing the tarbush and women removing the face veil envisioned both as emblems of a future independent Algeria that was firmly rooted in its Arab and Muslim identity. Interestingly, while some of these reformists were inspired by the Turkish Republic's independence from Europe, they saw Atatürk's embrace of the hat and outlawing of the tarbush as an egregious move to assimilate to European norms. Their perspective here was shaped by their experience as colonial subjects. In the face of attempts to assimilate Muslims to French norms, the tarbush represented their rejection of that pressure and insistence on the validity of their own identity. The growing Muslim reformist movement also envisioned the nation as inextricably linked to the Middle East by its Muslim identity, as opposed to Africa or the Mediterranean.

Discussions of the haik were also related to concerns about the future. These discussions differentiated between the haik, which commentators labeled Muslim tradition, and the hijab, which was Islamically mandated and, unlike the haik, could come in various forms and allow the face to be uncovered. Some reformists advocated the removal of the face veil of the haik to keep Muslim women's dress aligned with their interpretation of sharia (that women needed to cover their hair and bodies) while potentially allowing her to play a greater role in society. While for many the haik represented how Algeria could remain stagnant, women remaining veiled but uncovering their faces was envisioned as facilitating greater participation in public life and a more modern society. The removal of the face veil thus was an important step in the creation of a future Algerian society in which women were active participants but remained dressed according to the mandates of Islamic law. Yet reformists were not unanimous. Bukusha, an important reformist leader, argued that even if it was not Islamically mandated for women to cover their faces, it was a good custom that protected women from unwelcome attention. For him, the face veil was necessary for a future Algeria in which women did not modernize too quickly and thereby disrupt social equilibrium between the sexes.

In both sets of discussions, Islam's flexibility was important. Many commentators agreed that Islam was flexible enough to allow Muslims to participate in modern life and not be stifled by the requirements of their religion. Women could uncover their faces, participate more in public life, and still cover their hair. For proponents of the hat, wearing the hat similarly could distinguish oneself as modern without posing as an affront to their Muslim identity. For others, however, the hat was unacceptable because it was a symbol of the slow erasure of Muslim identity under colonialism.

History was used in different ways within both sets of discussions. Both Djamila Debèche and a commentator from *La Voix des Humbles* described how in early Islamic history women's dress was less covering than the haik. For them and others like Ibn Hallush, a return to the veiling of authentic Islam meant unveiling the face and hands. In the discussions about men's headwear, a poet in *al-Najah* described the tarbush and *amama* as symbols of former Arab "glory." Others who wanted to replace the outdated tarbush with the hat argued that the tarbush did not even have Muslim origins but rather Greek. For Bukusha, the face veil's pre-Islamic origins among Greeks and other Mediterranean cultures reaffirmed its status as an honorable custom throughout time worth upholding.[81] Both sets of discussions mentioned Greece as a marker of ancient society—either in need of abandonment for modernity to flourish or as an important cultural legacy not to be abandoned.

While both sets of discussions had similar stakes related to custom, modernity, and a future Algerian nation, commentators typically did not discuss men's and women's dress together. Still, examining the discussions alongside one another illustrates that anxiety about the hijab or haik was not in isolation of a wider cultural anxiety about assimilation and custom, which applied to men's headwear as well. There were important parallels in the two sets of discussions. Both invoked Islamic knowledge alongside regional developments. The link that was drawn between men's dress and political strength, which was absent from discussions about hijab, suggests that at the precise moment when so many Muslim thinkers were agitating for women's increased involvement in Algerian society, there were clear delineations on this involvement—namely, it was not yet envisioned to have urgently political stakes. In multiple colonial contexts, from Morocco to Bengal, scholars have argued that women's role in society was as the bearers of tradition.[82] While men had the opportunity to participate in a range of new, modern behaviors and activities, including new forms of education, consumption, and travel, women's lives remained tied to the home. Far from trying to cement the imagined relationship between women and tradition, Muslim intellectuals in Algeria sought instead to rescue the hijab from being a symbol of outdated tradition by insisting it be reformed. By contrast, they urged men to wear the tarbush in order to preserve the custom in the face of European colonialism and a rapidly secularizing world order.

Past and Future Headwear: A Conclusion

In the following decades, while hijab continued to be contentious, the debates about men's headwear largely fizzled out. In 1946 Djamila Debèche held a conference in Algiers titled "The Muslim Woman in Society," at which she gave a speech that discussed men's and women's headwear together.[83] She argued that the veil was "secondary" to education for Muslim women's advancement. The evidence was in Muslim men's evolution. Young Muslim men, she declared were often indistinguishable in dress from their European counterparts. Their education, she argued, paved the way for their assimilation to European norms and abandonment of their "Arab clothing [and] the chechia." Their education and shift in clothing reflected their openness to "modern ideas and French institutions because a new era of understanding encourages them into the path of progress." Like earlier discussions about men's and women's clothing, clothing represented progress for Debèche. Yet while earlier commentators envisioned a future inspired by Atatürk in Turkey or consistent with long-standing Algerian tradition, for Debèche progress meant assimilation to French norms and openness to French culture.

Interestingly, history mattered for Debèche too, just as it had in interwar discussions. For her presumably mixed audience of settlers and Muslims, she offered a long history of the status of Muslim women before Islam, of famous Arab women, and of women figures in early Islamic history. She then moved to the early twentieth century and discussed Qasim Amin's writings, Atatürk's reforms, and Egyptian feminists' successes. For her, this longer history indicated what was possible in the future for Muslim women. Muslim society could take inspiration from this history and contemporary developments, she argued, and campaign for women's education as a means of achieving progress.

In later years the meaning around each of the articles of headwear examined here shifted. Muslim men continued to adopt European-style clothing in increasing numbers, including the hat and the beret. Nationalists like Ferhat Abbas continued to don the tarbush. More women, including those educated in Muslim reformist schools, unveiled completely. Many continued to wear the haik. During the Algerian War of Independence, the haik took on new meaning as both a mode of camouflage and a rejection of the pressure to assimilate. The debates over dress in the interwar years reflect the instability of the meanings ascribed to particular forms of dress and the particularities of the moment in question, with its own pressures and imperatives. While in the interwar years those pressures focused on questions of assimilation and internationalism, later decisions around dress were increasingly influenced by nationalism and anti-colonial struggle.

As with discussions about women's labor and education, discussions about headwear became another domain in which Muslims in Algeria sought to push back against French stereotypes and assert a particular vision of how Muslims could embrace their own Muslim modernity, in conversation with developments abroad and new reformist interpretations of Islam. The remaining two chapters move to two different contexts. Chapter 5 considers how these tensions over Muslim women's labor, education, and dress also concerned French feminists, who, like Muslim society, were equally swept up in interwar discussions about the Middle East. The final chapter then turns to the postwar context to consider how these issues around Muslim women shifted as nationalism grew in popularity.

Chapter 5

French Feminists and the New Imperial Feminism

In a December 1934 issue of the Muslim reformist newspaper *La Défense*, a Muslim man named al-Gharbi penned a harsh critique of the oppression Muslims faced at the hands of settlers. He argued that colonialism locked Muslims into perpetual poverty, with Muslim women its most vulnerable victims. Urban Muslim women faced humiliation as they worked as domestic workers in settler homes. Rural women too, he wrote, earned meager wages, "three or four francs for twelve to sixteen hours of work a day," working in the fields for settlers. He described having seen "crowds of beggar [women] with their babies in their arms, made skinny by hunger and the cold."[1] For him the question of Muslim women's education and status could not be raised without attention to this oppressive poverty, and its root cause, colonial oppression. He wrote, "The emancipation of the Muslim woman will not come by conferences or newspaper articles, but by the evolution of an entire people, by obtaining their rights, by education more broadly, well-being, etc." He used the term "rights" to underscore that proponents of women's advancement in Algeria needed to also take up the work of larger change, including even Muslim political enfranchisement.

In the next issue of *La Défense*, the famous amateur ethnographer Marie Bugéja, who penned multiple texts about Muslim women, including a book titled *Our Muslim Sisters*, responded to al-Gharbi. Like other French feminists, Bugéja positioned herself as an important link between the French colonial administration and the Muslim population. For Bugéja the "conferences" and "newspaper articles" al-Gharbi dismissed were key sites for transmitting her work. She reminded him of all the work that, for "over thirty years," she personally had undertaken on behalf of the Muslim woman.[2] She wrote that she diligently studied the Muslim woman to then transmit her findings "not only for the public but [also] for [French colonial] administrators." She reminded him that she herself had always insisted that the key to women's advancement was not "conferences" and "newspaper articles" but "education for girls and boys, as prescribed by the Prophet." She referenced the Prophet Muhammad to convey her fluency in Islam. She closed by reminding al-Gharbi that she depended on the support of Muslim elites like himself to be able to fight on behalf of Muslim women. Although she was not personally named by al-Gharbi, she responded to his commentary as though it were a personal attack on her. I begin with their exchange because it reflects some of the tensions of this chapter.

Throughout the interwar period, French women—including metropolitan feminists, settler feminists, and settler women married to Muslim men—wrote about Muslim women in the metropolitan and settler press, in ways that intersected with Muslim discussions. Existing scholarship has largely depicted French feminists as flag bearers for the colonial cause or agents of empire.[3] Within this analysis, Muslim men and women are often silent actors, passive recipients of feminist attention. Yet the ways their discussions intersected with the intracommunal Muslim discussions that took place in publications like *La Défense* analyzed throughout this book reveal a much more tenuous position.

I include analysis of these French women in a book otherwise focused on Muslim society because I argue that their feminism was critically shaped by their ability to claim the currency of local Muslim support and their engagement with Middle Eastern developments. As mapped out throughout this book, the interwar years were a period of intellectual fluidity and experimentation. While there was an unofficial segregation of public life in interwar Algeria, in conference halls, school buildings, medical offices, and association meetings, French feminists connected with Muslim men and women. Approval and support from local Muslims were critical to these feminists' tenuous ability to position themselves as the ideal interlocutors between European and Muslim society to the state that largely ignored them. Like Muslim discussions, French feminists' perspectives responded to the local while also being shaped by an attention to developments in the Middle East.

Interwar French feminists were set apart from earlier generations of imperial feminists because they were profoundly impacted by the internationalism of their moment. They were anxious that Turkish women had achieved suffrage before them. They were watchful of the achievements of Egyptian feminists. French feminists feared that Middle Eastern women might soon surpass them in rights, thus threatening French claims to global superiority as well as these feminists' maternalism toward Muslim women in Algeria. What emerged was a new imperial feminism. Like the discussions about women in the Muslim press, their brand of imperial feminism was shaped equally by settler colonialism and interwar internationalism. This interwar generation of imperial feminists argued that they deserved full citizenship rights because the success of the colonial project depended on their unique access to Muslim women, and France's ability to claim global superiority was threatened by their disenfranchisement.

This global crisis, personified by the Turkish or Egyptian woman with her growing rights, set the stage for feminists' work within Algeria. Settler and metropolitan French feminists described the colonial project in crisis. Over a hundred years into France's colonial project, most Muslim girls still did not attend school. When pregnant or sick, Muslim women had little to no access to medical clinics or dispensaries. The French colonial state, they argued, had failed to improve the lives of Muslim women. French feminists set up a dichotomy between the hypocritical French colonial state, which claimed to care about civilizing its subjects, and French women—doctors, educators, intermediaries—who could marshal their unique skills toward this cause and impact the future of Muslim women on the other. These women presented their hard work and warm reception from Muslim society as a kind of currency that proved they could earn what the state could not: the enthusiasm and trust of Muslims.

Instead of treating French feminists as a single group, I map out a network of French women in different realms, including local educators, amateur ethnographers, women in publishing, and international feminist organizers. These women were united by their aspiration for a future in which both French and Muslim women would advance without disrupting French women's maternalism toward Muslim women.[4] They included more well-known figures like Marie Bugéja or Cécile Brunschvicg, the Jewish president of the Union française pour le suffrage des femmes (French Union for Women's Suffrage, or UFSF) and eventual politician. They also included lesser-known women, like Rosalia Bentami, the Jewish wife of the leader of the Young Algerians, Belkacem Bentami. While they approached discussions about Muslim women from varying social positions, all of these women presented themselves (and often their fellow French women) as able to reach Muslim women in ways the state could not. Yet despite this access, their claim to superiority remained tenuous because of their disenfranchisement.

The Threat of Middle Eastern Women

Like the Muslim press in Algeria, *La Française* reported heavily on Middle Eastern women, particularly from Turkey and Egypt. While these developments inspired hope for Muslims, for French feminists they fueled anxiety about their tenuous global standing. From 1933 to 1934 *La Française* offered continuous reporting on women's rights in Mustafa Kemal Atatürk's Turkish Republic.[5] In this period *La Française* covered developments in Turkey as much as if not more than other European nations. French feminists were impressed that not only could Turkish women vote, they could hold important leadership positions, including being elected to local and national legislative bodies. Within this context, the Middle Eastern woman became a powerful foil against which both French and Muslim women in Algeria were measured. To many, including Bugéja, the successes of Middle Eastern Muslim women proved that the Muslim women of North Africa were also capable of advancement. Yet the Middle Eastern woman's successes, particularly in the realm of suffrage, illustrated how she was capable of surpassing French women and thereby disrupting French women's claims to civilizational superiority over the Muslim women in Algeria.

The achievements of feminism in spaces like Turkey and Egypt became a metric by which to measure French feminism. Elsa Mornay wrote in the French feminist publication *Minerva* that Turkish and Egyptian women enjoyed so many rights that they essentially lived like Western women.[6] The vice president of the UFSF, Germaine Malaterre-Sellier, wrote an article titled "The Liberation of Muslim Women," which was reprinted in the Muslim newspaper *La Voix des Humbles*. Malaterre-Sellier ranked the world's countries based on women's rights. She wrote that French women "feel ashamed" when they "compare France to England, Germany, Hungary, [and] the Scandinavian countries."[7] In Turkey, "women have achieved equality in every domain." Malaterre-Sellier described

France alongside Arab spaces where women were agitating for more rights, including "Egypt, Palestine, and Syria." She wrote that feminism was spreading rapidly in the "Islamic world," and if French women were "not on guard, it is not impossible that Egyptian women would have political rights before them."

Turkey also loomed large in interwar French feminist thought because Istanbul was the site of the Twelfth Meeting of the Congress of the International Alliance for the Suffrage and the Civil and Political Activities of Women. Contributors, who called the congress simply "the Congress of Istanbul," wrote about this conference from November 1934 to June 1935. This conference was a key moment of engagement between French and Middle Eastern feminists. While Arab feminists wanted many of the same rights as their American and European counterparts, they directed their calls to the family more than the state.[8] It was on the basis of these shared goals that feminists engaged with one another at such conferences. By the late 1930s onward, international cooperation between European and Middle Eastern feminists fizzled out because of European feminists' failure to support the Palestinian cause.[9]

For these feminists, women's advancement in Turkey and Egypt rendered further visible French women's limited political standing in France. The failure of the French state to accord them suffrage, feminists argued, limited French women's capacity to serve as leaders. A commenter noted that while Malaterre-Sellier held an important position of authority within the United Nations as the "Technical Counsel to the French Delegation," within France she could not even be a *conseiller général*, or local administrator. This discrepancy, they argued, weakened France's global standing. Malaterre-Sellier's leadership within metropolitan, colonial, and international circles demonstrated what women could offer as intermediaries between the French regime and Muslims, and how they could bring glory to France, the article suggested. The article celebrated Malaterre-Sellier as "a distinguished ambassador of France and of feminism." It quoted Malaterre-Sellier on her ability to forge connections with Muslim elites across North Africa. She had said, "I love traveling in Morocco, Algeria, and Tunisia, and interacting with French feminists and the Muslim elite, who like us, are preoccupied by moral and social problems."[10] *La Française* also offered extensive coverage of Malaterre-Sellier's travels in Morocco.[11] The author noted a lot of anticipation surrounding her visit, and her supporters "were not disappointed." In each of the cities she visited, Malaterre-Sellier met with the

French colonial authorities, European settlers, and Muslims—reflecting her status as someone uniquely suited to navigate multiple publics. Not only did she meet with these groups, according to *La Francaise*, but she enjoyed a warm reception because of her "good reputation."

Even as they were threatened by the successes of Middle Eastern women, French women still sought to position themselves as intermediaries between Muslim women in Algeria and Middle Eastern women. *La Française* reprinted Abou-Ezzohra's wedding speech about the Islamic feminist movement sweeping the Middle East (analyzed in this book's introduction). Brunschvicg introduced it as "one of the most beautiful homages to the Muslim feminist movement" and noted that the UFSF hoped "an evolved indigenous woman" would accompany their delegation to the upcoming Congress of Istanbul.[12] They envisioned the conference as being an opportunity for a Muslim woman from Algeria to meet "Muslim women from Oriental countries." This collaboration, Brunschvicg wrote, would surely inspire this woman to "lead the movement of the emancipation of the French Muslim woman." Brunschvicg's commentary suggests that some of these French feminists, like Brunschvicg herself, imagined themselves not as the leaders of the movement for Muslim women's rights but as facilitators.

At the conference Malaterre-Sellier gave a speech on how the Orient and Occident each had a lot to learn from one another.[13] This language of mutual admiration was a distinct departure from the condescending language she had used toward Muslim women at the 1932 Constantine congress.[14] Together, she wrote, Muslim and European women could create "a better humanity, more just and more fraternal."[15] Interestingly, with the exception of Iran, all of the speeches *La Française* published were from representatives from multiple English colonies or spheres of influence, including India, Ceylon (now Sri Lanka), Jamaica, and Egypt.[16] After the conference, Malaterre-Sellier wrote that she was proud of the relationships she and other women from the UFSF forged with Tunisian feminists. She described these connections as a potential model for Algeria.

Failures of Social Services

Feminists understood the tenuousness of their ability to claim global superiority as French women in the face of Turkish and Egyptian women's achievements. This anxiety was a crucial context that established the stakes for their claims that they were the only ones who could ameliorate the French colonial state's failures in the realm of social services. Feminist publications like *La Française* and *Femmes de Demain* amplified local women's efforts to show that French women were capable, resourceful, and able to reach those the French colonial regime could not, especially Muslim women. Feminist publications in both France and Algeria focused on the failure of the French colonial regime to address the material needs of its Muslim subjects in the domains of schooling and medical care. Jane Bagnault insisted it was shameful that a century into French rule, only 3.7 percent of Muslim children were enrolled in schools.[17] This figure is less forgiving than the official ones, which in 1934 put this figure at 8.7 percent, or 78,000 out of 900,000.[18] French women distinguished between the state's failures, on one hand, and, on the other, the tireless work of French women (doctors, educators, intermediaries) to remedy the state's inadequacies.

Feminists praised the efforts of schoolteachers in the few existing French schools for Muslim girls, which inculcated students with French cultural values.[19] One such school was on rue Marengo (now rue Ben Cheneb) on the edge of the casbah of Algiers. Every year, *Femmes de Demain* reported on the school's celebrations for the Muslim holiday Eid El-Kebir and heaped praise on the school's director, Madame Wienlocher. This yearly event was covered by "Vonnick," a regular columnist of *Femmes de Demain*. A blonde woman whose photograph was included in the publication's first issue, she was introduced only with the claim that she was "particularly familiar with the life of the Muslims of Algeria" and would offer "documented studies" as well as reporting on settler high society.[20]

Vonnick was particularly touched by the students' performances.[21] She described how little Muslim girls, dressed in costumes, sang French songs and performed French plays. To their attendees, these performances conveyed how these Muslim girls were absorbing French history, culture, and traditions. The school and the efforts of its director indicated how France could, on one hand, respect Muslim culture through its celebration of this important Muslim holiday and, on the other, remake the holiday as a forum to show off the extent to which these girls could perform Frenchness. Vonnick wrote, "*Femmes de Demain* sees with pleasure our female educators organize an indigenous celebration according to French tastes."[22] This reporting again conveyed the message that French women could create hybridity, ease friction, and impart Frenchness without resentment.

To remedy the state's failure to provide adequate numbers of schools, many settler women created their own schools and crafts workshops for girls, including the L'Aiguille Musulmane (The Muslim Needle) school in Philippeville (Skikda), workshops by the White Sisters, and a vocational school created by Aurélie Picard Tidjani, wife of the leader of the Tidjani zawiya in Ain-Mahdi.[23] She was celebrated by the Muslim publication *L'Echo Indigène* with a front-page feature. Her achievements, the publication suggested, illustrated what beauty could come from Europeans and Muslims becoming closer to one another.

French women not only sought to fill the gaps in the state's educational facilities for women; they also sometimes clashed with authorities, complicating the scholarly claim that feminists operated solely as agents of empire. Jeanne Bottini-Honot, a feminist and member of the UFSF, was initially an instructor in a French colonial school that taught Muslim girls how to weave. Over time she became increasingly critical of the limited education the school offered local Muslim girls. She claimed the girls learned very little.[24] The few skills they did learn would not serve them after graduating, since many struggled to afford the raw materials needed to weave at home. She wrote that local Muslims were beginning to see French colonial artisanal schools as "dupery." She insisted that these girls instead needed an education that was "practical, not artistic." Taking matters into her own hands, she began teaching the girls basic domestic tasks. This move was met with such profound disapproval by local authorities that she was fired.

Bottini-Honot then founded her own school in Sétif, called the Muslim Housewife, where she taught Muslim girls to sew, knit, iron, bathe themselves and children, and create their own clothing.[25] In 1935 Bottini-Honot held a conference called "Raising Up the Indigenous Woman through Work" in order to publicize the school and raise monetary support. Local French colonial officials, both Europeans and Muslims, as well as Muslim elites attended. The Muslim reformist newspaper *La Défense* reported on the conference and Bottini-Honot's efforts with approval. Her school, they wrote, served the unmet needs of impoverished girls who would otherwise "wander in the streets" without purpose.

Bottini-Honot's conference featured several of her students dressed in clothing and white aprons they made themselves. Like the Eid celebrations at the school on rue Marengo in Algiers, the students' bodies showed off how they had been transformed from potentially aimless little girls to tidy, well-groomed, neatly dressed model young women. In her speech to attendees, she outlined how she envisioned her position with respect to the state. She described how "the actions of French women" were ameliorating the "lamentable" situation of Muslim women. These French women's important contributions, she asserted, should be supported by the state, and yet the state should not rely on French women alone to fulfill the state's responsibilities to Muslim women.

In 1939 Bottini-Honot wrote to Joseph Brenier, the head of the French League for Education, an organization established in the mid-nineteenth century to promote secular education throughout France and its colonies.[26] Bottini-Honot complained to him that far from being grateful for her work on behalf of Muslim women, local officials had tried to sabotage her efforts. These tensions between Bottini-Honot and local authorities suggest that French feminists' projects such as the Muslim Housewife should not be oversimplified as entirely "an instrument in service of [French colonial] politics," as some historians Sakina Messaadi have argued of French feminist efforts.[27] Even as Bottini-Honot saw her work as carrying out the ideals of the colonial project, her willingness to break with the colonial regime's policy on schooling and local colonial officials reveals the extent to which feminists asserted their right to be the authors of what the colonial project should entail.

La Française described Bottini-Honot as the one "who leads our efforts in Sétif"—thereby connecting her school to the overall feminist project of the UFSF. The publication framed Bottini-Honot's efforts in terms of how she was received by the Muslim population. Bottini-Honot wrote that it was important that local people felt the French were working hard for their benefit.[28] She reported on the gratitude of her students' mothers to both the audience of her conference and to fellow feminists. *La Française* published a letter written from a Muslim woman in the town of Chellala, near Sétif. The letter thanked Bottini-Honot for teaching her daughter Zineb how to "manage a household," an important skill that would serve her the rest of her life.[29] These mothers' approval was evidence, the newspaper suggested, of Bottini-Honot's fruitful proximity to Muslims.

Bottini-Honot's efforts equally illustrated settler women's maternal feminism and how they envisioned its wide impact. For Bottini-Honot, the Muslim woman was the most vital recipient of European attention and activism. She wrote that the "material and moral elevation of the Muslim household" and the "elevation of the indigenous people" would all happen "through the woman." In her letter Zineb's mother expressed gratitude for not only the domestic training Bottini-Honot imparted to Zineb but also the relationship they developed. She wrote that Bottini-Honot was "like [a] mother" to Zineb. Alongside this classic maternal feminism, though, *La Française* also wrote that the letter proved there were "enlightened" Muslims who could collaborate with French feminists on the shared "task of feminine liberation."

Rosalia Bentami's 1936 novel *The Hell of the Casbah* caused an uproar among European settlers for its frank depiction of the impoverished lives of Muslims in the casbah and its critique of the colonial state's failures.[30] Rosalia Bentami was a Jewish artist and the wife of Doctor Belkacem Bentami, one of the leaders of the Young Algerians, a group of Muslims who demanded a reform of the *Indigénat* and more political representation. Early in the novel, Rosalia Bentami described the enormous crowd of Muslim children, parents, and even grandparents that gathered around the school building on the first day of school each year.[31] Bentami described an "electric wave" of disappointment that rippled through the crowd as most realized their children would not be admitted because there were so many students and so few classes open to them. This was an indictment of the failure of the French state to meet the needs of its Muslim subjects.

Bentami's novel was a space to illustrate not only the state's failures but also their impact. She described that for impoverished young Muslims, "there is no family, no assistance, no refuge, no school, but only the streets, mother of vice, theft, and crime."[32] Muslim boys would often try to find informal employment, at the train station helping with baggage, for example, but often there were so few opportunities, she claimed, that they resorted to theft and drug use. Bentami disentangled the imagery commonly associated with Muslims, delinquency, from Muslim culture and instead connected it to poverty.

While of course some feminists parroted colonial rhetoric that emphasized the veil as a marker of Muslim women's backwardness and social exclusion, others insisted that education had a greater impact. Lucienne Jean-Darrouy was not only the editor-in-chief of *Femmes de Demain* but also the author of a regular column for women in *L'Écho d'Alger* and a music critic there as well. In *Femmes de Demain* Jean-Darrouy wrote that people should be more troubled by Muslim women's ignorance than their veils.[33] More urgent than unveiling, she argued, was all Muslim girls attending schools with the same frequency as Muslim boys. Amateur ethnographer Marie Bugéja similarly reminded her readers that the real veil "that needs to disappear is the veil of ignorance that keeps the spirit in a stagnation that we should not find after over a century of occupation."[34] She wrote in *La Française* that Muslim women could not be blamed for their own ignorance and their failure to assimilate when "the schools have not been given to" them.[35]

Medical care was another domain within which, like education, urgent intervention was necessary, and French women claimed they were working to remedy the state's failures. There were some state-run medical services, for example, programs that offered free care to mothers and infants. In 1934 the mayor of Montgolfier (Rahuia) reported that one such program helped 139 families, most of them Muslim, in its first four months of operation.[36] But feminists pointed out how these barely skimmed the surface of Muslims' medical needs.[37] In her novel Bentami wrote, "In the casbah, human beings die in the street, when they don't have all the pieces [of documentation] necessary to be hospitalized [among Europeans]." Throughout the novel Bentami refers to Muslims as "Arabs" or the "indigenous," but her use of "human beings" here signals her attempt to humanize this population for potentially indifferent settler readers.

Feminist publications instead celebrated French women for meeting the needs of Muslims, thereby more effectively carrying out the state's interests than the state itself, indicative of how they deserved suffrage. One commenter wrote that these female doctors were able to "penetrate the private lives of indigenous, where in principle the white person is excluded."[38] These doctors' unique access to Muslim women allowed them to forge intimate connections. Their clinics addressed such a profound need that Muslim women "came in crowds." Access to this many Muslim women thus meant these female doctors "can make the indigenous love France" and were thus "indispensable to the success of the civilizing project."[39] These arguments were not limited to print culture. In Paris in June 1936, Maryse Demour held a conference called "French Women in the Colonies" where she lauded how Muslim women could more easily trust French women because of their shared "maternal" bond.[40] Like settler feminists, Demour argued the success of colonialism depended on these women. Without them, she contended, "all territorial conquest would remain vain and unproductive."

For some feminists, these failures on the part of the state to meet the basic needs of Muslim women in schooling and medical care mirrored the state's failure to grant French women suffrage. Together, these failures threatened France's ability to claim global superiority, they argued. This perspective was also informed by a growing anxiety about the new rights of Middle Eastern women. Malaterre-Sellier was unafraid to critique the regime and reminded other French feminists that they were not obligated to "justify our country."[41] She wrote that "the European nations" that maintained control over most of the "Arab world [via colony,] mandate, or protectorate" were not sufficiently invested in "the liberation of Muslim women."

Malaterre-Sellier drew attention to the hypocrisy of the language of the civilizing mission on one hand and the realities of French indifference toward Muslim women on the other. She wrote, "Our Europe, which pretends to carry to other continents the flame of a superior civilization, shouldn't it understand . . . that the mark of a real civilization is to give women, like men, a means of developing their personality in all of the domains and in all activities?" She simultaneously critiqued the French colonial regime for its failures vis-à-vis Muslim women, as well as metropolitan France for denying French women political rights. These failures challenged the degree to which Europe successfully "carried to other continents the flame of a superior civilization." While her critique mentioned "Europe," she was arguing that the failed situation of women's rights in Algeria thus threatened France's global reputation.[42]

A settler schoolteacher named Jane Bagnault similarly described the intertwined destinies of French women and the Muslim women of Algeria. In the feminist publication *Femmes de Demain* she wrote, "It is so my Muslim sister no longer gives birth in the slum . . . that it is necessary that French women vote. . . . It is so little indigenous children no longer die in their cribs, lacking hygiene and elementary care, that it is necessary that the French woman votes. . . . It is so one day we can see big schools where French and Muslim children play and learn together" that it is necessary that French women vote.[43] Bagnault echoed older French feminists, like Hubertine Auclert, who wrote in 1900 that "if French women had the right to vote, their African sisters would have long been delivered of the outrageous practice of polygamy, and the intolerable promiscuity they live under with their cospouses."[44]

Some feminist critiques were targeted toward men in lieu of the state. *Femmes de Demain*'s editor-in-chief, Lucienne Jean-Darrouy, wrote in the publication's first issue that while men had "led Society toward progress," they could not accomplish everything alone. She contended that it was women who would be better suited to "the work of peace" and "the work of brotherhood."[45] True success and progress would require affording women a seat at the table politically through suffrage. Cécile Brunschvicg, secretary-general of the UFSF, dismissed the state's claims that they did not build more schools for Muslim girls because of budgetary concerns or out of a respect for Muslim culture.[46] To her, it was rather that the French state "lacked the courage and the energy" to offer Muslim women the means (an education) of gaining some power over Muslim men. She wrote that the French state feared worsening their already tenuous relationship with Muslim men and thereby enabled Muslim men's patriarchal treatment of Muslim women.

French Amateur Ethnographers

Feminists capitalized on the colonial context of endless fascination with Muslim women, who appeared to many Europeans as unknowable because of the veil, Muslim men's protective jealousy, and their supposed sequestration. Within this context, certain French women claimed their life circumstances gave them unique access to Muslim women, which they used to write amateur ethnographies. Their work capitalized on the public thirst for insider information about Muslims as well as allowed them to position themselves as uniquely authoritative on the subject of Muslim private lives. Like teachers and doctors, these women's warm reception by Muslim society was part of the currency they flaunted. Exchanges between these amateur ethnographers and Muslims, however, suggest the tenuousness of this currency.

Ethnographies functioned as political weapons within colonial Algeria.[47] French colonial rule relied on the maintenance of narratives of inherent, unending difference between Muslims and Europeans. Many of these ethnographies centered Algerian women as important sites for the civilizing mission.[48] In his introduction to Amélie-Marie Goichon's *La View féminine au Mzab* (1927), historian William Marçais wrote, "It is the French women who must run to save us from our misery [from ignorance about Muslim women] and undertake the necessary inquiries in this unexplored domain. . . . The solidarity among members of the same sex, which is stronger than the antinomy between civilizations, will loosen the tongues and make veils fall."[49] Here the female ethnographer is imagined as an instrument of colonialism. She alone can "make veils fall."

As ethnographies became increasingly popular, the genre remained only semiprofessional. Europeans in Algeria with varying credentials, including not only academics but also military generals, offered ethnographic accounts of Muslim women. As European women contributed to this craze for an ethnographic look at Muslim women, they built on generations of existing travel literature, including the harem literature, written by European women who similarly asserted their authority by being able to access such spaces.[50] The long-standing popularity of such harem literature ensured that there was already a large audience with a voracious appetite for this sort of content.

The prolific work of Marie Bugéja exemplified the public's thirst for this insider look into Muslim women's lives.[51] Marie Bugéja was married to Manuel Bugéja, a retired colonial administrator and also an amateur ethnographer.[52] Marie Bugéja published editorials and newspaper and journal articles, as well as presented at different conferences.[53] While Bugéja's critiques of the failures of the French colonial state were more subtly worded than those of some of her feminist counterparts, she too focused on many of the same themes: the state's failure to adequately provide resources, her unique position as an interlocutor between the state and Muslim women, and her warm reception by Muslim elites. The Muslim press, including *La Voix Indigène*, *L'Écho Indigène*, and *La Défense*, advertised Bugéja's books, lauded her activism, and offered her space for commentaries.[54] Bugéja took pride in noting to Europeans that "the indigenous know well" how knowledgeable she was about Islam.[55] To Muslims she emphasized the wide range of influence she had with Europeans. She recounted that a bookseller had reported to her that many tourists purchased her books and then traveled to the regions of Algeria she described. This proved the real-life material impact of her work. That impact, she wrote, was to make these travelers "admire our beautiful Algeria." She presented herself as responsible for generating interest in, understanding about, and respect for Algeria.

Ethnographies also took the form of memoirs. In 1929 Bottini-Honot published a memoir, titled *Among the Unknown*, about growing up in proximity to Muslims in the town of Souk-Ahras. She adopted the observational style of Bugéja and other amateur ethnographers. She distinguished between educated Muslim elites, whom she described as virtually indistinguishable from Europeans, and the Muslim "masses [that have] stayed primitive," whom "she took pleasure in observing at length."[56] She wrote that it was only once Europeans understood this "primitive mass" thanks to guides such as herself that they could begin "to study the ways to elevate" Muslims. In other words, any attempts to assimilate Muslims or ameliorate their possibilities depended on women like Bottini-Honot. Like other forms of ethnography, the project Bottini-Honot undertook involved control and authority through observation and knowledge.

As Bottini-Honot described typical Muslim homes in Souk-Ahras, she wrote that indigenous families, which often included extended family as well, often shared a single room, where they all slept "in disorder."[57] Bottini-Honot made explicit for her readers that parents had no privacy for sex. She wrote, "One must not be surprised to hear children recount what they have seen or heard at night." She continued on to describe that it would not be unusual for students to arrive at school and explain that they were absent because their mother had given birth. She then wrote, "The indigenous, like all primitive peoples, live very close to nature." Bottini-Honot's description of Muslim familial cohabitation moved between the pseudo-ethnographic assessment of "primitive peoples" and the voyeuristic gaze toward the Muslim couple, having sex within sight and earshot of their children.[58] Such descriptions of Muslim homes and family lives corresponded neatly to existing Orientalist tropes within travel literature published about North Africa and the Middle East.

French Feminists and Muslim Elites

French feminists also claimed they were uniquely positioned to foster interpersonal relationships with members of the Muslim elite, which made them ideal intermediaries between settler and Muslim societies. For these feminists, Muslim elites were educated, Francophone, and literate, and thus naturally the ideal segment of the Muslim population with which to connect because they were already assimilated to French culture. Feminists saw these elites as their natural allies in the struggle for increased rights for Muslim women, and they critiqued the state's failure to engage these men. Cécile Brunschvicg wrote that the French colonial regime was so impotent with respect to reforms for the Muslim woman that it failed even to "have the sympathy of the indigenous masculine elite."[59]

Again, French feminists positioned themselves as the sole actors who were compelled because of their "duty as feminists and as French women" to work alongside their Muslim men allies toward the amelioration of the Muslim woman's status.[60] Bottini-Honot wrote that feminist "groups like the UFSF of North Africa have proved the special character that feminism can take here."[61] They explained why they were more suited than their male European counterparts to successfully enact change. These explanations weaponized French women's feminine traits of compassion and generosity in the struggle for the hearts and minds of Muslims. French feminists positioned themselves as the group most able to "ameliorate relations with the Muslim population, where settler men and the state had already failed."[62] It was French women who lobbied the colonial state to build more schools for Muslim women. It was French women who united to form charity associations to help Muslim women. It was French women who could succeed where French administrators and men broadly had failed in uniting the two civilizations, Arab and French.

Feminists were quick to note that they were being called on by Muslim men to aid in the cause of Muslim women's advancement. In 1929 members of the Algerian branches of the UFSF attended a conference in Algeria organized by M. Meziam Oussedik called "Feminism, Its History, Its Results."[63] Oussedik lamented women's inferior status in both France and Algeria. A feminist in attendance, Alice La Mazière, reported that Oussedik argued that French women had proven their intelligence and thus deserved full political rights. He closed his talk by noting that he hoped "all these efforts will lead to the rapid amelioration of the lamentable situation of Kabyle women." French women marshaled such Muslim evocations of their leadership and calls for help as evidence that they had earned full citizenship rights.

La Française argued that another conference, the 1932 Congress of Mediterranean Women in Constantine, proved their capacity to serve as interlocutors between Muslim men and Europeans. For both Malaterre-Sellier and Bottini-Honot, Muslim attendance signaled that the two parties shared common goals and gave the French feminists "hope" that they had allies in their efforts on behalf of Muslim women.[64] Malaterre-Sellier was pleased that Muslim men brought their daughters to the conference, a move she interpreted as their openness to a more liberated next generation of Muslim women.[65] French women connected easily with Muslim elites, whom they saw as already "liberated by us intellectually and morally."[66] An author in *La Française* wrote that it was French feminists who "have heard the elite call for help" from the French colonial regime on behalf of Muslim women.[67] Bottini-Honot reported that the Muslim men who attended the conference "demanded that we intercede on their behalf with the administration to build more schools for indigenous girls."[68] This demonstrated that not only were French feminists uniquely qualified to address the needs of Muslim women, but they were also being called on by the Muslim population to do this work. Here again Muslim public opinion was invoked to prove the necessity of French women's intervention.

This discussion of Muslim men's pleas to French feminists to get involved also became another opportunity for feminists to critique the disparity between the rhetoric of colonialism and its impotence. A correspondent of *La Française* in Constantine wrote, "It is a shame that a Muslim is obligated to underscore the state of servitude of the women of his country to a government that pretends to have come to Africa to civilize the still barbarous population."[69] To this correspondent, the fact that it was Muslim men who were lamenting Muslim women's status signaled the hypocrisy of the French colonial state's failure to intervene. Interestingly, multiple open letters to conference attendees appeared in the Muslim press, including the one from Muslim woman Seghir Hacène analyzed in chapter 3 of this book. Such calls insisted that French women needed to do more for Muslim women and that Muslim women would not evolve based on a "more or less sincere discourse or under the effect of a magic wand."[70] Like Bugéja's exchange with al-Gharbi, such moments reflect contention between French feminists and the Muslims they claimed to speak for, and publications like *La Française* never reprinted or responded to these critiques.

Unlike the average Europeans who trafficked in stereotypes, these women claimed their proximity to Muslims as women enabled them to see the real Muslim life. A shift in focus from poor Muslims to elite Muslims, for example, could undo some European prejudices. Bottini-Honot wrote that "this elite [who attended the 1932 Constantine conference] is victim of the ancestral customs of their parents" and of "religious fanaticism."[71] Elite Muslims were thus being held back by their less enlightened brethren. In a searing editorial titled "Them and Us" in *Femmes de Demain*, Metropolitan journalist Paule Husset challenged the contempt with which most settler women treated Muslim women. She wrote that French women were unable to see Muslim women as their counterparts.[72] Instead, they saw every Muslim woman as like "their own cleaning lady." This was partially an issue of class. Husset asserted that while settler women treat every Muslim woman like the "Fatma who does the housework," they should not forget the Muslim middle and upper classes. She reminded her readers that they were educated Muslim women who probably had to struggle to earn their degrees from French colonial institutions. She described the various evolved Muslim women she knew personally. She described being in someone's home and meeting other young Muslim girls who normally were veiled, but among women they dressed in French clothes. One elite Muslim girl drove herself around Algiers in her own car and was training to be a midwife.

The ignorance of the French population—both in the metropole and in Algeria—about Muslims and Islam was another problem French feminists claimed they were uniquely positioned to solve. Sometimes this involved reprinting articles from Muslim publications. *La Française* occasionally amplified the voices of Muslim elites who called attention to the plight of Muslim women. They republished articles such as an editorial by Mohammed Tatouti in the settler paper *La Dépêche Algérienne*, the wedding speech of Abou-Ezzohra from the Muslim paper *La Voix Indigène*, and a report from Tahar Ameur to the *conseil général* of Algeria.[73]

Their introductions to these reprinted articles suggest that French feminists envisioned these articles as a key part of a larger project to educate their audience about Islam's emancipatory possibilities. Malaterre-Sellier wrote that at the 1932 congress in Constantine, French feminists learned from the Muslim attendees that "there is a growing movement to interpret the Qur'an in favor of women's moral, social, and political education."[74] Another commentator, M. R., wrote that the article being reprinted proved the misogyny Muslim women faced was rooted in custom, not Islam itself. In fact, she insisted, misogyny was "contrary to the spirit of Islam."[75] In the preface to an article written by a woman, C. Senieh, who was married to a Turkish diplomat, the newspaper's correspondent wrote that the article disproved the settler stereotype that the Qur'an mandated women's sequestration. She wrote that the article instead "proves that the true spirit of the Prophet was betrayed by texts written many centuries after his death and that he himself never wanted women's enslavement."[76]

In the later interwar years, Lucienne Jean-Darrouy, editor-in-chief of *Femmes de Demain*, published extensively to challenge popular depictions of Muslims in response to the ongoing debates about the Blum-Violette Law, which proposed extending citizenship to more Muslim men in Algeria. Settlers against the law cited Muslim misogyny as one of the reasons Muslim men could not be French citizens. They claimed French men would be endorsing Muslim men's cruel treatment of Muslim women if they granted them citizenship rights. One author asked how "Muslim men could be admitted into the French family where there was a situation so odious and so barbarous."[77] Jean-Darrouy conceded that the Muslim woman faced a particular set of challenges because of her religion, culture, and male counterparts, but she insisted that suffering at the hands of Muslim men was greatly exaggerated. In a series of articles that she published in February and March 1937, Jean-Darrouy challenged French settlers for pretending to care about Muslim women. She wrote that while feminists had long worked to alert the broader public about Muslim women's suffering, people "indifferent yesterday" were now pretending to care because of their opposition to the Blum-Violette Law.[78] Interestingly, she mentioned the reforms of Mustafa Kemal Atatürk in Turkey as evidence that Muslim societies could embrace feminist reforms, echoing the arguments that appeared in the Muslim press. She closed her article that the feminists behind *Femmes de Demain* would continue to work on "liberating Muslims from abusive customs while at the same time the Muslim man from an inferior political situation."

At the same time, Jean-Darrouy did not mince words when she addressed Muslim men. In April 1937 she penned an editorial titled simply: "Muslim Men, Your Wives Are Also Human Beings."[79] In it she challenged Muslim men's continual demands for the French state to build schools for Muslim girls while doing little to improve circumstances for the women in their lives. Again, her interconnectedness to Muslim elites was important. She cited three conversations she had with a Muslim teacher, a Muslim cleric, and a politician who all raised the question of more schools for girls. When she pressed them for more details about the women in their lives, one admitted his wife was illiterate and he had not tried to teach her to read. Another admitted that while he sent his daughter to school, he would soon insist she would veil herself because of her age. While Jean-Darrouy elsewhere herself advocated for more schools, in this editorial she turned her attention back to Muslim men. How sincere were their demands for more schools, she asked, if they were not willing to grant more freedoms to the women in their own lives?

Feminists and the Fight against Settler Prejudice

Metropolitan and settler French women wrote that settler prejudice toward Muslims made them indifferent to the plight of the Muslim woman. C. Fel was a teacher in Paris and also the assistant secretary of the teacher's union of the Paris area. In April 1931 she had recently returned to Paris from a 6,000 km road trip around Algeria with her husband. She reported to the metropolitan audience of *La Française* that settlers were "too full of superiority" to care about improving life for the impoverished Muslim masses.[80] She wrote that they opposed Muslim "emancipation" in part because it would make Muslims their equals. Likewise, Bagnault explained that Europeans had a limited image of Muslims, based on stereotypes, which they did not bother trying to complicate or nuance.[81]

Bottini-Honot and Bagnault, both schoolteachers, tied the question of prejudice to early childhood years. Bagnault wrote, "European mothers systematically distance their children from the indigenous." As a schoolteacher she described the regularity with which she observed parents transmit their disdain for Muslims to their children. This in turn led "European children to think they come before Muslim children."[82] Bottini-Honot wrote that part of the difficulty in side-by-side Muslim and European education was that Europeans saw Muslims as "undesirables" because their of their questionable "health" and "propriety."[83] Bottini-Honot linked the question of how settler children learned prejudice to their proximity to Muslims in housing. In her memoir, *Among the Unknown*, she described growing up in Souk-Ahras, 100 km south of Bône (Annaba) and 170 km east of Constantine. She emphasized how different the town was from other Algerian cities. Unlike Constantine, Algiers, Ksar Boukhari, and Tiaret, she noted, where Arabs were limited to a particular neighborhood, the Arabs of Souk-Ahras lived among Europeans, "sometimes in the same house." While in larger Algerian cities European "children are very often afraid of Arabs," in Souk-Ahras they played together and shared a "warm sympathy" for one another.[84]

Instead of trying to undo their gender difference with their male counterparts, French feminists underscored that it was their femininity that enabled them to connect to the Muslim population better than men could. In *Femmes de Demain*'s opening issue, its editor-in-chief, Jean-Darrouy, wrote that she hoped the journal would bring together French and Muslim women and remind them of their connectedness through their "female bodies and of course female hearts."[85] Husset wrote that French women needed to approach Muslim women not with exoticization or condescension but with "friendship," because of the "insoluble links between all of the women of the world."[86]

The Franco-Muslim Feminine Union also took on this work of cooperation and collaboration. They held conferences and workshops and took on aid projects with Muslim collaboration. On March 3, 1937, they held a conference at the Muslim reformist Cercle du Progrès in

Algiers.[87] *Femmes de Demain* reported on the union's activities regularly, including this conference. The union was so important, the publication asserted, because it represented a new step forward in women's engagement with one another. European and Muslim women came together "no longer in one of these gestures of charity that have always humiliated [Muslim women] in rescuing them, but in a simple, fraternal gesture." This statement praised the women of the union while implicitly critiquing the charity efforts of so many other settler organizations as condescending.

Reporting on the union stressed its commitment to collaboration with Muslim women over the condescension so common among settlers. Another article asserted that the union was started by French women who wanted to connect other settler women to Muslim women so that they could see Muslim women as more than simply creatures who inspire "pity or revulsion." Unlike other women's organizations, the union did not seek to "dominate" Muslim women but instead come together on the basis of "profound sympathy and feminine fraternity," as Paule Husset wrote in an article that praised the union for the creation of their dispensary in Algiers, which offered Muslim women consultations from female doctors.[88] Like other reporting on French dispensaries, this article too reminded the readers of how Muslim women were typically distrustful of settlers. Yet these female doctors had managed to overcome that distrust and offer help to almost two hundred people in the three months since its opening. Husset wrote that she was thrilled to see "women task themselves with this public service and organize it so benevolently." Again French women had effectively taken up a responsibility of the regime (a "public service").

Bagnault suggested that while men emphasized race or religion, "for [settler] women, the Muslim problem is a human problem."[89] Bottini-Honot also compared settler women's attitudes to that of their husbands. While men were cynical about transforming Muslim lives, settler women remained patient and compassionate, she wrote.[90] While men blamed culture and religion for Muslim delinquency, women understood that the root cause was poverty. While men disparaged Muslims as "thieves," it was their wives who insisted that their hunger forced them to steal. Even though some husbands treated their wives as if "they are naïve," settler women continued in their "difficult and thankless" work because of their "spirit of justice." To Bottini-Honot, then, settler women proved their essential role in transforming Muslim lives through their tireless commitment to humanizing Muslims, but also working on their behalf even in the face of disapproval from their husbands. Gender difference here was not an impediment to citizenship but an asset to women's capacity for leadership.

Of course, feminists too reaffirmed stereotypes, including, for example, of Muslims as unwaveringly superstitious. Marie Bugéja, for example, urged the French colonial state to build schools for Muslim girls, which would "deliver them from superstitions."[91] *La Française* once published an interview about the Muslim woman between one of its correspondents, Yvonne de Bruillard, and a thirteen-year-old Algerian boy, Ali, living in France.[92] To explain he was returning to Algeria, de Bruillard wrote that he was returning to "Africa, [where] his little Arab soul will again dominate him with its beliefs and superstitions." For de Bruillard, Ali's belief in superstitiousness was racialized, an inescapable part of Ali's "Arab soul," which could be combated in France but would inevitably reign in "Africa." For Bugéja, however, belief in superstition, like ignorance, could be cured with a French education.

Others, however, used comparisons with France to challenge the idea of Muslim particularity. A reviewer in *La Française* responded to Lucienne Favre's book *Oriental*, which described the material and "moral" impoverishment of a Muslim domestic worker.[93] Favre's Muslim protagonist was intensely superstitious. Yet the review's author, Henriette Sauret, offered details of the unscientific superstitions to which the French domestic worker in Paris also adhered. Sauret's comparison thus underscored the relationship between poverty and superstition, irrespective of culture or religion. Bugéja similarly compared gendered forms of dress, comparing the hijab to the corset.[94] She wrote that such a comparison demonstrated that civilization and barbarism could be found among both Muslims and Europeans, and it was only through education that groups could transition to civilization.

Some sought to connect French and Algerian women's suffering, both as victims of patriarchy. Fel wrote that like Muslims, who were "slaves of tradition and ancestral beliefs," French women were "slaves of the *code français*."[95] Brunschvicg wrote that Muslim women were oppressed because of the misogyny French women also faced, particularly masculine "egoism" and "jealousy."[96] Similarly, in her articles about the Violette Project, Jean-Darrouy compared the restrictions imposed on Muslim women to those also suffered by French women. She wrote that while deputies claimed to be indignant about polygamy among Muslims (which she noted hardly existed anymore), they were indifferent to French men engaging in adultery with mistresses.[97] French officials complained that Muslim women were supposedly sequestered in their homes, but, she asked, would a French woman not be approached by police if she tried to flee her home without her husband's permission? These comparisons signaled the shared experience of patriarchy, as well as the hypocrisy of the deputies in question.

French women saw themselves as the force that would not only challenge prejudice but eradicate it in the future. Bagnault urged her readership that "it is time to stop ourselves and let go of all the reasons we separate ourselves from our Muslim brothers."[98] Paule Husset wrote, "Between the Muslim woman and us, we have sowed too much contempt, indifference, and mistrust. Rest assured, European or indigenous readers, that the Women of tomorrow will . . . [eliminate] these odious prejudices."[99] The capitalization of "Women of tomorrow," which referred to women broadly united by feminism, suggested that the power Husset envisioned lay within modern European women to dismantle prejudice.

"Women of Tomorrow": A Conclusion

This chapter has argued that like Muslims in Algeria, interwar feminists' activism was shaped both by the internationalism of the interwar moment and the particularities of the settler-colonial context. French feminists positioned themselves as educators and interlocutors who had earned the trust of Muslim women despite the failures of the state to provide adequate education and medical care. They argued that they were the sole actors who could cross the cultural and social chasm created by settler colonialism and its de facto segregation of Algerian space. Intellectually too, these women asserted that their unique access to Muslim women empowered them to educate the broader settler public about their inaccurate prejudices toward Muslims. Like earlier generations of imperial feminists, they sought to reproduce maternal dynamics between themselves and the Muslim women they supposedly wanted to save.

Yet unlike earlier generations of imperial feminists, they were increasingly willing to break with the state and openly critique its failures to educate Muslim women, to offer a better material reality to Muslims broadly, and to offer full citizenship to French women. In their accounts of French women's leadership, feminist publications like *La Française* and *Femmes de Demain* cited support from the Muslim public as a crucial marker of these women's success. They depended on the evocations of this support from Muslims as a currency they could marshal to their public as evidence of their capacity for leadership, which proved they deserved full political rights. They also broke from earlier generations of imperial feminists in their internationalism. They felt their sense of global superiority was threatened by the contrast between Turkish and Egyptian women, whose place in their own societies and globally seemed to be on the rise, and French women, who still could not secure suffrage. Like the Muslim press commentators, they too were locked in a multidirectional relationship to Europe, settler colonialism in Algeria, and the women's advancement projects of the Middle East.

By the 1950s the French army also turned its focus to Muslim women. As the movement for Algerian independence grew, the French colonial regime was desperate to tighten its reins on the Muslim population. Muslim women, they concluded, were the key to changing Muslim hostility toward the French regime. If women could be convinced of the merits of assimilation, they could influence their husbands and transform their families. Army officers in the Psychological Warfare Bureau targeted Muslim women through posters, newspaper articles, and public unveiling ceremonies, where Muslim women were pressured into tossing their haiks into a burning fire to symbolize their emancipation from Islam's misogyny. In the interwar years French feminists were ahead of this later turn by state elements toward Muslim women. The final chapter now returns to Muslim society as an extended conclusion on how these multifaceted debates about Muslim women shifted in the postwar years.

CHAPTER 6

Muslim Women Address the Nation

In the summer of 1947, Muslim women wrote to the women's page of the publication *as-Salam: Revue musulmane nord-africaine de culture et d'actualité* (Peace: A North African Muslim Review for Culture and News) to complain that debate about the veil tended to ignore the real root of women's oppression: colonialism. A woman in Constantine, who signed her letter Mademoiselle K. A., wrote that many of the commenters and "scientists" offering their opinion on Muslim women's advancement failed to properly account for the damage created by empire, including "the miserable social conditions under which we live."[1] She argued that debating veiling was "folly, even crime" while at the same time "imperialism plants its destructive seeds in our earth." The imagery of "destructive seeds" evoked a vision of colonialism as not only exploitative but also having continuous growth with multiplying consequences. Mademoiselle K. A. had written in to *as-Salam* to respond to the editor of the women's page, Mademoiselle Anissa, who had asked readers to weigh in on whether education or veiling was more important to women's advancement. In response to this question, Mademoiselle K. A. insisted that empire created the "miserable social conditions" that limited Muslim women's possibilities, so neither unveiling or education alone would suffice to remedy women's suffering. Other women, including one who signed her letter "Houria," similarly wrote passionately of "the misery created by ferocious and inhumane colonialism" and its impact on Muslim women.[2]

In the postwar period, the French- and Arabic-language Muslim press regularly featured more women's voices. Layla Dyab had a literary column in five issues of *al-Bassair* in 1951 called "I've Chosen for You," in which she published excerpts from literature and also wrote about the limits on women's freedoms. In the nationalist publication *al-Manar*, Fadila Ahmad wrote about the need to educate women and no longer treat them as servants. The reformist publication *al Shula* also featured articles about the importance of education for women written by female students of reformist schools who published with only their first names. Fatima Zohra Guechi has explained that these articles by women were clearly written within a "national and religious" frame.[3] *As-Salam*'s women's page merits particular analysis because of the volume and wide range of letters from women it published.

The postwar discussions about women, while heavily influenced by earlier interwar discourse, also marked a turning point. By the postwar period, Algeria's intellectual landscape was in flux. The reformist movement had become decidedly more nationalist, culminating in its eventual brief relocation to Cairo in the 1950s to escape persecution from the French colonial state. In the interwar years many groups like the Young Algerians, the schoolteachers' association, and the Fédération des élus believed in the possibility of reforming the French colonial system so that there could be a future French Algeria in which Muslims could enjoy more or equal rights. By the postwar period, however, the failure of projects like Blum-Violette left many disillusioned that such reform was possible. In the postwar years nationalism developed a centrifugal power in which a broad range of issues were debated through the lens of the nation, as opposed to the interwar frame of *umma* oriented toward the Middle East.[4] Nationalist parties like the Parti du peuple algérien (Algerian People's Party, or PPA) echoed women's claims that linked their suffering to colonialism but centered the anti-colonial struggle. When the nationalist victory would be achieved, they argued, any hindrances to women's emancipation would equally melt away.[5]

This chapter examines the woman question in postwar Algeria primarily through the women's page of *as-Salam*, which offers access to a broad range of voices illustrating how nationalism's possibilities for women were contested and renegotiated from below. This offers a bridge between the interwar discussions about women and the later more documented participation of women in the War of Independence. While nationalism produced new regimes of respectability to which women needed to adhere, it also produced a language that women could marshal to challenge not only colonialism but also Muslim men. In their letters to Anissa, Muslim women highlighted the hypocrisies of Muslim men's critical gaze on Muslim women. They critiqued Muslim men for claiming they wanted women to play a greater role in society but continuing to harass women on the street. They underscored the disparities between the language of marriage as a patriotic union and men's refusal to grant women respect or authority within the home. And while men and women alike criticized Muslim women for behavior seen as assimilationist—unveiling, attending balls and frequenting other European settler spaces, drinking alcohol—women noted in their letters to *as-Salam* that educated Muslim men barely spoke Arabic, wore European clothes, and married European women. In their letters to Anissa, Muslim women sought to shift the debate's focus from women's honor and propriety to men's role in perpetuating women's troubles, including through street harassment.

A Page of Her Own in *as-Salam*

In September 1946 *as-Salam* appeared on Algerian newsstands. It offered readers cultural commentaries about international news, Arab cinema, and North African theater. *As-Salam*'s readership was concentrated predominantly in Algeria but also spanned Africa, Europe, the Middle East, and the United States. Its most novel feature was *as-Salam*'s prolific women's page, run by Mademoiselle Anissa. While Muslim women occasionally published in the male-dominated interwar newspapers, the women's page of *as-Salam* was the first such page devoted entirely to Muslim women in Algeria—almost a half century later than other Middle Eastern spaces.[6]

As-Salam's women's page typically featured an editorial by Anissa, letters from readers, articles on topics like a woman's role within a marriage or powerful Muslim women throughout history, and a beauty column written by a Moroccan woman, Zineb Rachid. In the following years, Anissa's women's page continued to grow, expanding from a single page to three pages within the typically twelve-page review. In their letters to the editor, male and female readers alike underscored that they were most interested in the women's page. By early 1948 the women's pages were so popular they moved to the first pages of the review. The publication's covers sometimes featured photographs of women, including the Egyptian actress Tahia Carioca and the Moroccan princess Lalla Aicha. The March 1947 cover featured a photograph of three Muslim students (figure 6.1) who had recently performed

FIGURE 6.1. Muslim women on the cover of *as-Salam*, 1947.
Source: BNF

a theater piece at the Opera of Algiers as part of a celebration titled the "fête feminine" celebrating their reformist school, al-Tarbiya wa-l-taʿlim ("Upbringing and Education"). The caption of their photograph on the cover stated, "Algeria in the Middle of Renaissance: Our young girls participating in their grandiose project of generation with their entire souls, just like our boys." The article that corresponded to the image also featured an advertisement for L'Oréal henna, which featured a woman in a white haik with a few strands of beautiful wavy hair revealed (figure 6.2), one of the few advertisements featuring a veiled woman ever to appear in *as-Salam*.

The pages of *as-Salam* reflect multiple new realities of the postwar years: nationalism's increased currency, the rise of global beauty culture

FIGURE 6.2. Woman in haik in L'Oréal henna ad, from *as-Salam*, 1947.
Source: BNF

marketed to Muslim women, and concerns over a new generation of Muslim schoolgirls educated in French colonial schools. Mademoiselle Anissa, concerned with all three developments, outlined her own regime of conduct for young women. Her editorials and the letters of readers together indicate the shared feeling that the conduct of this generation of Muslim girls could either propel forward nationalist uplift or betray their people with frivolity and assimilation to European norms. Yet other women responded to such claims and sought to refocus the conversation away from women's comportment and toward colonialism and Muslim men.

The women's page of the first issue echoed the reform-minded ethos of the publication and featured an article on the "heroine of Turkish feminism," Sabiha Gokchen, the daughter of Atatürk who had become the world's first female fighter pilot in 1937.[7] In this inaugural issue, Anissa offered an overview of the problems Muslim women in Algeria faced. She wrote, "Under the tent, or in the house, for us Muslim women, it is the same life of erasure."[8] She recommended a comprehensive education project to remedy the "forgotten" status of both rural and urban women, which included "school for the young ones, conferences, newspapers, cinema, and radio for the adults." While Anissa envisioned herself as a guide for Muslim society, she presented the women's page as a space of "sisterhood" for communal exchange and collaboration. She urged her female readers, "Write to me, my sisters, so that we can establish between us an active correspondence and so the flowers of friendship grow within our large feminine community . . . a platform . . . to hear your voices, I hope to receive your critiques, articles, etc."

While Anissa framed her initial call for letters in terms of "friendship" and "sisterhood," Anissa's posturing was equally like that of an amateur ethnographer. In November 1946 she announced she would begin a "study on the emancipation of the Muslim woman."[9] She asked readers: which was more important in Muslim women's advancement—education (which she defined as a basic religious education) or unveiling? In the following eight months, she printed a selection of the replies she received in each issue. Seven months later in June 1947, she published the results (both qualitative and quantitative) of her study (figure 6.3).[10] Based on the letters, she calculated that 60 percent of respondents were for a religious education first, and then unveiling, 17 percent for religious education and no unveiling, and 20 percent felt unveiling needed to happen first.

NOUREL

RESULTAT DE NOTRE ENQUETE
sur l'émancipation de la Musulmane en Afrique du Nord

par Mlle ANISSA

Je suis heureuse de donner à mes lectrices et lecteurs les résultats de l'enquête que je mène depuis des mois sur les raisons, les possibilités et les moyens de l'émancipation de mes sœurs en Afrique du Nord.

Au cours de cette enquête, plusieurs correspondants m'ont demandé ma propre opinion en la matière. *Je suis pour l'émancipation intégrale de la Musulmane en Afrique du Nord, dans le cadre des lois et des traditions de l'Islam.* Mais mon opinion n'a qu'une valeur relative. Je ne puis prétendre à refléter l'opinion unanime des Musulmans, tout au moins celle des hommes. Je vais donc, en toute objectivité, donner, d'une façon scientifique, les conclusions de ce long et grand débat. Je remercie M. le Directeur d'*AS SALAM* qui, en me permettant de « soulever » le voile sur cette question, dans sa jeune et prometteuse revue, m'a donné des conseils sur la manière de présenter les résultats de cette enquête.

Si ces conclusions ne représentent que les idées de celles et de ceux qui m'ont écrit, elles fournissent du moins la possibilité de préciser les données générales et les lignes maîtresses de l'orientation de cet important problème :

1°) *Durée de l'enquête :* novembre 1946- juin 1947 : 8 mois.

2°) *Pays touchés par la revue AS-SALAM et qui pouvaient participer à l'enquête :*

Algérie, Tunisie, Maroc, France, Angleterre, Suisse, Belgique, Hollande, Allemagne, Tchécoslovaquie, Turquie, Syrie, Irak, Inde, Egypte, Tripolitaine, Hoggar, Soudan, Sénégal, Guinée, Cameroun, Togo, Etats-Unis d'Amérique.

3°) *Nombre de lettres reçues:*

Algérie	12.033
Maroc	3.150
Tunisie	8.420
France	2.720
Angleterre	905
Etats-Unis	703
Egypte	250
Syrie	115
Tripolitaine	3
Turquie	121
Tchécoslovaquie	1
Les autres pays	0
Total	28.421

4°) *Etudes reçues sur l'émancipation de la Musulmane sous formes de thèses, pièces de théâtres, etc... :*

Tunisie	12
Algérie	11
Maroc	3
Total	26

5°) *Classement des correspondances reçues par ordre d'importance et d'origine* (pourcentage du total général) :

Tunis	14 %
Alger	13,1 %
Tlemcen	8 %
Rabat	7,8 %
Oran	5,5 %
Casablanca	5,4 %
Marrakech	4 %
Bône	3 %
Oujda	3 %
Fès	2.7 %
Constantine	2,4 %
Paris	2,1 %
Oxford	1,7 %
Mascara	1,2 %
Bel-Abbès	0,5 %
Marseille	0.3 %
Lyon.	0,2 %
Kenchela	0,2 %
Bougie	0,2 %
Djidjelli	0,1 %
Colomb-Béchar	0,1 %
Meknès	0,1 %

Le restant du pourcentage est représenté par les lettres reues de diverses localités.

Le pourcentage par région ou pays est le suivant :

Département d'Alger	19 %
Tunisie	18,1 %
Maroc	15 %
Département d'Oran	12 %
Départ. de Constantine	7,9 %
France	7 %
Autres pays	20,9 %

6°) *Classement des correspondances par confession, sexe, âge et rôle dans la famille :*

MUSULMANS : 24.240 lettres.	
Jeunes filles	7.001
Jeunes gens	10.711
Pères de famille	2.540
Mères de famille	1.703
Anonymes ou indéterminés	2.288
CHRETIENS : 3.257 lettres.	
Jeunes gens	0
Jeunes filles	17
Pères de famille	1.234
Mères de famille	2.002
ISRAELITES	
Jeunes filles	2
Divers ou indéterminés : 924 lettres.	

7°) *Pour l'émancipation :* 95 %.

Contre l'émancipation : 4 %.

La Musulmane doit-elle imiter l'Européenne :

80 % : non.
18 % : oui.
2 % : Indécis.

8°) *Le Voile :*

Les opinions, à ce sujet, ne sont pas toujours très nettes dans les lettres reçues. En général, ceux qui se prononcent contre le voile mettent comme condition l'éducation religieuse et l'instruction, au préalable.

Les réponses peuvent être classées ainsi :

a) Euducation religieuse et instruction d'abord, supression du voile ensuite : 60 %.

b) Suppression immédiate du voile. « Faites confiance à nos femmes qui doivent, elles-mêmes, participer à leur propre éducation et au relèvement de notre peuple » : 20 %.

c) Education religieuse, instruction et maintien du voile : 17 %.

d) Statu quo : 1 %.

e) Indécis : 2 %.

Conclusions générales qui se dégagent de la majorité de l'opinion de mes correspondantes et correspondants :

1. — La Musulmane doit être émancipée. Cette émancipation la mettrait en harmonie avec l'évolution de la société dont personne ne doit contester la profondeur et l'ampleur.

2. — Elle doit évoluer dans le cadre de l'Islam. Toute occidentalisation, en raison même du libertinage et de l'athéisme qu'elle suppose, entraînerait la perte de nos femmes et une désorganisation mortelle de notre société. L'Islam recommande le respect de la femme, son droit à la vie, sa participation aux luttes livrées par l'homme, mais exige la décence, l'équilibre familial, l'attachement de la femme à son époux et au bien de son foyer. L'Islam condamne le luxe tapageux des toilettes, le vin, les dancings, la débauche, l'impudence, les tenues inconvenantes, les attitudes étudiées dans un but de luxure, l'exhibitionnisme, le désir de vouloir briller par la beauté et les toilettes plutôt que par le savoir et la vertu.

L'Européenne cherche à plaire, cultive, sous couvert d'originalité l'excentrisme et manifeste une tendance de plus en plus marquée pour le nudisme. Elle voudrait être à la fois blonde et brune, spirituelle et naïve. Sa plus grande passion, c'est d'être admirée, « regardée ».

La Musulmane doit être pudique, renoncer au vain plaisir de plaire pour s'attacher à être avant tout *estimée* et *respectée*. Le physique importe peu. La vraie richesse d'une Musulmane est dans l'exemple de sa conduite, la richesse de sa vie morale, sa foi en Dieu.

L'Europe paie en ce moment l'imprudence qui l'a poussée à extirper du cœur de la plupart de ses femmes le sentiment religieux. La Musulmane doit joindre à sa ferveur religieuse un patriotisme exemplaire qui lui permette de lutter aux côtés de ses frères.

Bien que notre enquête épistolaire sur l'émancipation de la Musulmane en Afrique du Nord soit terminée, nous croyons devoir publier la lettre qui nous envoie M. Hamdadui dont les suggestions sont courageuses et simples. Cette rubrique est une tribune libre où toutes les opinions doivent trouver leur place.

...Voici la dernière lettre que nous vous offrons:

Alger le 30 mai 1947.

Mademoiselle :

Je viens de lire pour la première fois votre rubrique, « Nour el Mahall ». Sa lecture me suggère quelques reflexions que je vais vous exposer en toute franchise. Les voici :

Aux temps glorieux du Prophète et des Califes légitimes et justes, les Musulmanes remplissaient leur mission sociale avec la même ponctualité que leurs pères, leurs frères ou leurs maris. Le métier des armes et la « politique » ne les dispensaient pas de l'accomplissement de leurs obligations religieuses.

Ce sommet n'est pas toujours atteint actuellement par « celles qui sont devenues maîtresses dans l'art d'exhiber un visage violemment peint ».

La Musulmane est arriérée par manque d'instruction. Le monde Islamique tout entier a dû effectuer un mouvement de régression. Hommes et femmes, grands et petits, se rendent compte de notre état de décadence qui n'est que la conséquence logique d'un régime lamentable avec son million d'enfants illettres, son million de gourbis, ses affamés, sa mortalité infantile qui atteint la proportion désolante de 2/5, etc. etc...

Cette ignorance, cette affreuse misère, aurait pu vous inspirer, chère Mademoiselle l'évocation juste et loyale du grand mérite de la femme musulmane, car elle a préservé notre nation de l'extermination et de l'assimilation, toute ignorante et enterréé vivante qu'elle était.

Ce sujet nous conduirait très loin. Il s'agit tout simplement de mettre en valeur les vertus de nos sœurs, facteurs importants qui sont à la base de l'existence même de ce peuple algérien que nous voudrions tant voir émancipé. Considérez l'irresponsabilité, la triste situation de nos sœurs, considérez aussi leur immense mérite et vous ferez en sorte de ne pas les abaisser.

Tout d'abord les coutumes de la Musulmane sont simples et n'ont rien d'extraordinaire. La femme chrétienne elle-même semble mécontente de sont sort et de la loi qui régit sont existence. Il suffit pour prouver cela de voir le résultat des congrès féministes. Contrairement à cela la Musulmane est satisfaite de son sort. Emancipation ne veut pas dire occidentalisation. Pour nous, cette « émancipation » doit se borner à la stricte application de la loi Islamique.

Si la femme Européenne travaille comme un homme, la Musulmane s'occupe chez nous de son ménage et ses enfants. Si la nécessité l'oblige à aider son mari en apportant sa contribution au budjet de la famille, elle travaille chez elle en faisant de la couture, du tricot, etc.

D'aucuns prétendent, que la femme Musulmane est « achetée » par son mari qui la considère comme une esclave. C'est absolument faux. La Musulmane est plus libre que l'européenne. Elle peut disposer de sa fortune à son gré, vendre et acheter sans avoir besoin d'autorisation ni des tutelles. Quant à la question de l'achat de la femme... il n'y a qu'une dot apportee par le mari. En Europe c'est la femme qui « achete » son mari puisque c'est elle qui doit apporter la fameuse dot; Et ce fait n'est pas très raisonable. Ce qui se fait chez nous, est, après tout, plus noble. Si le « sadaq » atteint de nos jours la somme extraordinaire de cinquante, cent ou cent-cinquante, mille francs, cela se doit également au régime qui rend si chère et si difficile notre vie, car un trousseau ne coûte pas moins de cent-mille francs !...

Certains de nos sœurs ont l'air bien attristé de se voir privées de la société des hommes, de se voir exclues de toute distraction. Qu'elles passent de l'autre côté de la barricade. Les Européennes n'ont-elle pas leurs partisanes du nudisme ?... Il n'est pas étonnant que nous ayons aussi nos « pin-up girls ». Les Musulmanes vertueuses ne souffrent pas de devoir se conduire différemment. Tout d'abord, elles ne sont ni emprisonnées ni « enterrées vivantes ». Elles jouissent d'une grande liberté, assitent à des fêtes charmantes et sortent lorsqu'elles le désirent. Aucun plaisir honnête leur est interdit. Quant à les mêler aux hommes nous n'en voyons pas l'utilité. A part quelques têtes folles qui aiment se faire remarquer, nos dignes sœurs respectent la tradition. Notre religion nous oblige à la propreté.

NOTRE CONCOURS

Nous avons le plaisir d'annoncer à nos lecteurs que le jury chargé de décerner un prix de *DIX MILLE FRANCS* au meilleur travail littéraire concernant l'émancipation de la Musulmane en Afrique du Nord se réunira dans le courant du mois de juillet.

Les résultats seront rendus en temps voulu.

ان شئتم خير اللباس
فاقصدوا محل
رابح الساسي
نهج باب عزون رقم ١٨
– الجزائر
LES ELEGANTS et
LES ELEGANTES
savent où s'habiller
SASSI RABAH
Tailleur, Spécialiste
Civils et Militaires
Robes pour Magistrats
et Professeurs
Impasse de la Flèche
Rue Bab-Azoun
ALGER

FIGURE 6.3. Ethnographic Report from *as-Salam*, 1947.
Source: BNF

As-Salam's women's pages enjoyed active participation from a wide readership. According to her own statistics, in the first eight months of the woman's page alone, Anissa received 28,421 letters. She received letters from (in order of frequency) Algeria, Morocco, Tunisia, France, England, the United States, Egypt, Turkey, Syria, Libya, and Czechoslovakia. Of the 24,240 letters Anissa claimed to receive from Muslims, 8,701 were from Muslim women (80 percent, or 7,001, from "young women"). The letters published in *as-Salam* offer scholars access to a broad range of voices both from within and outside of Algeria—from Muslim schoolgirls to uneducated mechanics to European professors. While many wrote in from North African urban centers—Rabat, Oran, Algiers, Tunis—others wrote in from small villages and towns across Algeria.

That many of the individuals who wrote in to the women's page signed their letters with initials raises questions about anonymity and reliability. From 1958 to 1962 a journal was published in Algeria titled *Femmes nouvelles* (New women), supposedly directed by a Muslim woman, Djemila Tarahoui. Some historians have read this as a source that featured Muslim women's voices.[11] Yet Terrence Peterson has demonstrated, however, that the publication and its supposed letters to the editor were written by intelligence officers within the French Army's psychological warfare bureau.[12] This raises questions about whether Mademoiselle Anissa's columns and the supposed correspondence she received could have been fictions produced by to try to sway public opinion. Yet there are no indications that this was the case in the places where *as-Salam* appears in the archival record, including in colonial surveillance documents. Additionally, as Stephanie Newell has argued, the anonymity of sources does not diminish their usefulness in historical analysis.[13] Her work demonstrates how editors and contributors evaded colonial censorship through articles left unsigned or signed with pseudonyms. In Algeria women's use of initials or pseudonyms similarly enabled them to avoid potential backlash for themselves or family members.

The Educated Muslim Woman's Guide to Respectability

There were some clear continuities between the interwar and postwar discussions about women, particularly about education. Interwar calls for women's education in the press had materialized into intercommunal collaboration by the postwar period. In January 1947, for example, a group of Muslim elites and leaders, including Sheikh Bashir al-Ibrahimi, president of the reformist AOMA; Algeria's first female doctor, Aldjia Noureddine (later Benallègue); and nationalist leaders Ferhat Abbas and Mohamed Khider formed the Provisional Committee of Support for the Muslim Algerian Student, which came together to work toward a nationalist program of action for uplift through education.[14] One of the group's platforms outlined in this initial meeting was increased access to schools for Muslim girls. They were not alone in this mission. New associations, founded by and devoted to Muslim women, also lobbied for more and better education.[15] The numbers of French colonial schools had increased, but their curriculums remained limited. Beginning in 1947, public school classes were opened specifically for teaching literacy to anyone over the age of 14. In 1958 there were 392 classes for women, attended by 8,600 women ages fourteen to forty (mostly in their twenties) out of a total of 1,900 classes attended by 46,150 men and women. The classes for women taught French language alongside other skills including sewing and childcare. By 1954 the proportion of students enrolled in primary school with respect to total Muslim students was 33 percent in Oran, 26 percent in Algiers, and 22 percent in Constantine.[16]

While the numbers of Muslim children enrolled in schools remained relatively low compared to the total proportion of school-age children, they slowly increased after the interwar years. In 1930 only 5 percent (or 68,000) of Muslim school-age children were enrolled in French colonial primary schools. These numbers continued to steadily rise and reached 8.8 percent (or 111,000) in 1944 and 14 percent (or 302,000) by 1954. The numbers of Muslims enrolled in French colonial secondary education slowly rose from 1,358 students in 1940 to 6,260 in 1954. Finally, the numbers of Muslims enrolled in higher education also continued to rise from 89 in 1940 to 589 in 1954. The curriculum of Muslim girls' education shifted in the postwar years as well. On February 13, 1949, a new reform merged Muslim and settler tracks of education so that the two groups were now classmates with the same sets of textbooks.[17]

Muslim reformist schools that emerged in the interwar period also continued to proliferate; the ninety schools in 1947 had doubled to 181 by 1954. Reformist publications stressed the importance of the Islamic education these schools offered women. *Al-Bassair* published "A Call for the Elevation of Muslim Woman" by a woman's group, the Association for the Elevation of the Muslim Woman, in Tlemcen.[18] It argued that the women educated in French colonial schools "ignore the truth of our religion, but the guilt is not theirs," only a reflection of their limited possibilities. An Islamic education for Muslim women, on the other hand, was an urgent undertaking to repair "the crookedness found in our internal state." Like interwar calls, this postwar one also insisted that it was through women's education that Algeria could "elevate our nation," "take its place among the advanced nations," and "build the glory of North Africa."

Oral interviews can offer some more details about women's experience with schooling. Fatma Zohra Benaik, who was born in 1932, went to Qur'anic school as a child and then the Shabiba school in Algiers in the 1940s. The Shabiba school was a reformist school for boys and girls, funded by the reformist leader Tayyib al-Oqbi.[19] Some of her teachers were Muslims who had been educated in Europe. She explained that while French colonial schools reinforced ideas of Muslim "inferiority," the Shabiba school offered students a more political education, including about the French colonization of Algeria.[20] She described how girls' education was largely an urban phenomenon and still difficult to access in rural Algeria. While more women could receive an education in the 1940s as compared to previous decades, these numbers remained small. Dahbia Lounas, who was a school-age child throughout the 1940s in the town of Mirabeau near Tizi Ouzou, reported that she never attended any kind of schooling and was illiterate like most women around her.[21] Similarly, she did not know any women of her mother's generation, who were school-age children in the 1920s, who attended any schools. While she knew some men who had been educated in her father's generation, neither her father nor her uncles were ever educated. She reported that even in the 1940s, many around her felt that if one attended French schools, their mind would be "colonized by the French." By contrast, Benaik's entire family, situated in Algiers, was literate in both French and Arabic. Her father owned a small café in Algiers, and the family listened to the radio together every morning. Lounas, on the other hand, remained illiterate even into adulthood. This suggests that even as education for Muslims slowly expanded, it was geographically limited in its reach.

In the interwar years commentators described a movement for women's advancement located outside of Algeria from which they urged the broader public to take inspiration. By the postwar years Muslim women in Algeria described how this energy had taken root within their country. In another postwar publication *L'Action* Halima Benabed noted that while women still had very limited access to professional positions—"around twenty teachers, around twenty midwives, two or three professors, a doctress in medicine"—more important was "the spirit you find everywhere in the cities... the march toward knowledge and progress."[22] Three years later, in *as-Salam*, Madame H. S., a midwife from Algiers, wrote that the era in which "the Muslim woman was just an object of pleasure has passed!"[23]

The marker of this greater public interest in women's advancement, according to Benabed, was the overwhelming public support for women's education. Muslims in Algeria now understood, she wrote, that their evolution depended on women's education. Since places were still limited in French colonial schools, communities relied on Muslim reformist schools and were enthusiastic about their daughters learning Arabic. Benabed described how everyone participated in this push for women's education. Even though most women themselves remained uneducated, they took part in this movement for girls' education by contributing money to establish new schools, supporting poorer students, attending celebrations for girls' schools, and admiring the students' monologues, as they had in the interwar years.

By the late 1940s, though, there was public anxiety about this new class of educated Muslim young women and how best to channel their advancement in ways productive for the nation. In *as-Salam* Anissa outlined her own model, which readers echoed, in which Muslim women should be educated, contribute to the nation through their labor, and remain focused on familial and communal uplift despite the pressure to assimilate or take part in new forms of consumption more readily available. This correspondence, published within *as-Salam*, demonstrates how in the postwar period a wide range of voices echoed claims about the importance of women's education but often within a specifically nationalist framing. One letter to Anissa from a schoolteacher, Smain H., described ideal Muslim women simultaneously as "patriots, good mothers... educated, workers."[24] This emphasis on women as "educated" and "workers," though, did not exclude women engaged solely in the labor of childrearing and household management. The reader similarly framed domestic responsibilities as "a demanding social mission" that required "effort [and] sacrifice." In this nationalist vision, all women had a role to play in the uplift of the nation, the stakes of which multiple readers contended were high. Commentators echoed interwar claims that educated women who channeled their education in service of the nation would contribute to "the renaissance of our people."[25] Nationalist publications like *al-Manar*, journal of the nationalist party

Mouvement pour le triomphe des libertés démocratiques (Movement for the Triumph of Democratic Liberties, MTLD), praised the role of women in Pakistan and Indonesia, where they participated in nationalist military struggle.[26]

This important social mission assigned to Muslim women demanded strict adherence, according to Anissa and some of her readers, to particular codes of conduct. Anissa's guides and how-to columns delineated for Muslim women the most minute details of appropriate comportment and behavior.[27] These discussions about Muslim young women's comportment responded directly to long-standing fears articulated in the interwar years that women's education may lead to too much assimilation or distract women from their role as mothers.

As Anissa presented herself as a sort of guide for Muslim women from *as-Salam*'s inaugural issue, she was quick to assert that the model of advancement she proposed for Muslim women was not mimicry of European women. She wrote that Muslim women did not want the "agitation and masculine allures of Occidental people" for themselves.[28] In the interwar years too, some commentators disparaged European society as excessively masculine and thus imbalanced. Instead, Anissa presented herself as someone who wanted to reform women's position in society slowly and gently. In that same editorial in the inaugural issue, she wrote, "We cannot risk disrupting the social equilibrium and harmony of our households, which Europeans envy."[29] She asserted a pride in the "harmony" of Muslim households, in which both genders had their own distinct roles. Her invocation of European envy as a marker that this equilibrium needed to be protected allowed her to reinvert the long-standing assertion that Muslim inferiority was rooted in the deviancy of Muslim households. Like interwar commentators, Anissa reframed potential shame about Muslim patriarchy within the home as pride in "social equilibrium and harmony."

The code of conduct Anissa outlined included how to properly consume cinema culture. Anissa wrote that while it was acceptable to take interest in cinema, her readers should not "become those stupid girls obsessed with photos of actors . . . to the extent of neglecting their work."[30] Even as *as-Salam* devoted considerable space to coverage of developments in cinema and theater, Anissa urged young women to police themselves so that such frivolities did not disrupt schoolwork. Anissa warned that when girls were unfocused with respect to their schoolwork, "This tells our grandparents, often the enemies of Progress, that modern civilization entices [us] to more bad than good."

Schoolgirls needed to prove with self-discipline and focus that they could balance their access to new forms of leisure with their larger mission as educated mothers of the next generation. Any frivolity or extravagance risked provoking this older generation ("the enemies of Progress") and thus damaging the cause of women's advancement. The tension between concerns about frivolity and global beauty culture marketed toward Muslim women was on display within the pages of *as-Salam*. At the same time as *as-Salam* featured articles that advised women about makeup and how to dress stylishly on a budget, Anissa's column urged women not to prioritize "the latest fashions" or "pretty dresses" over the needs of the nation.[31] The beauty and style columns in *as-Salam* were one of the earliest instances of beauty marketing targeted to Muslim women, yet they were printed alongside commentaries that reminded women not to devote too much energy to such frivolities.

Both Anissa and her readers insisted that unveiled women practice modesty. A girl from Oran, "S. H. Bintou Chaab" (S. H. Daughter of the People), wrote that evolution was not simply throwing off the veil and parading around "decked out in a ridiculous manner in front of the world."[32] By "ridiculous" she meant with skin exposed. She continued, "We must not confuse 'emancipation' with 'exhibition.'" She thus urged Muslim women to maintain modesty in their clothing, whether veiled or unveiled. Like Anissa, she worried about judgments from fellow Muslims. She warned fellow young girls, "We must not give arguments to our enemies." Educated women thus saw themselves at the forefront of internal cultural conflict, where they were forced to carry the burden of modern women's propriety.

In an editorial that urged unveiled Muslim women to continue to practice modesty, Anissa urged them not to "do damage to the cause of all of the women of the Muslim world with your extravagance."[33] In this framing, Muslim girls in Algeria were part of a larger community of Muslim women globally who sought advancement but faced criticism from fellow Muslims wanting to limit this advancement. The broader region was also part of discussions about who should serve as role models for Muslim women. One young man from Hammam-Lif complained that while some valorized Egyptian women for being modern, "notice how they do not mind showing their cleavage."[34]

While interwar commenters worried that the new class of working women would enter spaces of Muslim male sociability like cafés, postwar commenters were concerned about schoolgirls who would have easy access to European heterosocial spaces like "balls."[35] One young man from Mostaganem chastised Muslim women who unveiled "to be happy" and dance with young European men.[36] His mocking tone about girls' desire "to be happy" echoed others' concerns about frivolity. The schoolteacher Smain H. similarly complained about Muslim women "who do not think of anything but pleasure and luxury [and] receptions."[37] Again, these anxieties were linked to the broader cause of women's advancement. One young woman from the Belcourt neighborhood of Algiers, Leila, wrote that the Muslim women who equated civilization with "drinking wine, smoking cigarettes, [and] keeping bad company" were "slowing down our evolution."[38] There was largely consensus between Anissa and other women who wrote into *as-Salam* that educated, modern girls needed to ensure they were representing Muslim women well so as to prevent conservative backlash from the older generation and others. Muslim women were thus urged to model with their comportment and conduct how advancement would not lead them to deviate from their commitment to Islamic values and service to the nation despite the pressure to assimilate.

Muslim Women Address the Nation

One major shift in the postwar discussions was how women made use of the rhetoric of nationalism and its emphasis on women's roles as shapers of the next generation to demand women's advancement. As in the interwar years, much of the public discourse around women's advancement was focused on women themselves—including on their schooling, their comportment, and their mobility. Yet in the postwar years women increasingly made use of the forums available to them, like *as-Salam*'s women's page, to turn attention to men. They shifted the terms of the debate from women's comportment to street harassment. They argued that for women to be able to advance, men needed to pay them more respect, both within the household and on the street. Looking back on the period, one woman stated, "After the Second World War, Algerian women decided to take their independence [from men] by force."[39]

In *as-Salam*'s first issue Anissa urged Muslim society to pay attention to the Muslim woman, whose plight they had "forgotten." She asked, "Are we not the framework of Muslim society, the guardians of the home and the traditions, the spouses, the mothers?"[40] Here Anissa set a tone that readers echoed in their letters. The emphasis on women's domestic roles should not suggest such women wanted only a limited expansion of women's power. As Afsaneh Najmabadi has argued for early twentieth-century Iran, women's roles as mothers and household managers became a powerful and effective rationale in their arguments for increased rights.[41] Muslim women made use of the symbolic labor women performed as guardians of the next generation and the nation as the basis on which they made demands from other members of the nation for a variety of ends, including better access to education. In July 1946 female students weaponized the rhetoric of patriotic motherhood when they petitioned *as-Salam* readers for 3 million francs to fund an all-female dormitory. They explained that girls from across Algeria who moved to Algiers for college struggled to find an affordable place to stay. Their appeal described women as "a brick in the social edifice we want to create with the glory of our country."[42] Their language presented women as the pillars critical to not only social well-being, "the social edifice," but also national "glory." They continued, "They carry the seed of our future, of our faith, the flame of our Renaissance and of our place in history." These quotes all demonstrate how older reformist arguments about women's education and its centrality to communal uplift, "glory," and "Renaissance" were remade with more decidedly nationalist rhetoric ("our country"). Moreover, nationalist rhetoric was not only a list of demands made of women but ideals that women too could use to make their own demands.

Some readers also made use of the language of nationalism to critique ongoing discussions about appropriate comportment and conduct for Muslim women. Letters from readers reveal that Muslim women's respectability was a contested terrain, not simply the articulation of a set of ideals. Awareness of these tensions helps tease out the political and social work that respectability performed in this postwar nationalist moment. As Brian Harrison has written, "Respectability was always a process, a dialogue with oneself and one's fellows, never a fixed position."[43] Men and women alike articulated a vision of the ideal, respectable Muslim woman—devoted to her family, focused on her labor in service of both her family and her nation, dressed modestly—and women consistently raised questions about these ideals.

Women challenged Muslim society's emphasis on the veil. A young girl named Khadidja wrote that men did not understand how burdensome the haik was. She described it like a "shackle," because wearing it was so inconvenient that it limited women's movement outside of the home.[44] Others questioned the symbolic value attributed to the veil. A midwife from Algiers, Madame H. S., questioned why "a piece of fabric" was the "symbol of [women's] virtue."[45] Some men also argued that a woman's character should not be reduced to her status as veiled or unveiled. A young man from Tazmalt, for example, wrote that he had seen "dishonorable veiled women and honorable unveiled women," and thus a woman's conduct was more important than her choice to veil.[46] One young woman from Bougie (Béjaïa) insisted on her right to determine her own codes of conduct. She wrote that even though she was unveiled, she was not "depraved."[47] She did not "go out without the permission of [her] father" and "never [went] to balls." She insisted her morality was not compromised by her lack of a veil and asserted her right to negotiate the bounds of appropriate behavior for Muslim women.

Women directed critiques at Muslim men for their obsessive gaze on Muslim women's comportment and conduct. They used discussions about Muslim women to deflect any concerns about their own conduct, particularly with respect to assimilation and closeness with European women. Women complained that they were judged by different standards than European woman. Mademoiselle H. Said from Oran wrote, "Our young people are full of indulgence for European women, but intransigent, intractable on the conduct of Muslim women."[48] This critique—leveled by multiple women who wrote in to *as-Salam*—pointed to the hypocrisy of Muslim society's treatment of Muslim women. These critiques were an opportunity for women to note that the promises of nationalist rhetoric—in which the nation was a single family—had fallen short for Muslim women. The language of family reappeared in women's critiques. H. Said wrote that Muslim women's modesty was "exploited egotistically by our brothers against us." Her use of "our brothers" here signaled both the nationalist frame of nation as family and the unfairness that women would be treated so exploitatively by members of this national family. Natalya Vince has argued this nationalist "familial" framing was a way nationalists deflected concerns about men and women working alongside each other in the struggle for independence.[49]

One regular, everyday marker of this unfair treatment of Muslim women by Muslim men was verbal harassment in the streets. Muslim girls who enrolled in French colonial schools, which were often in European neighborhoods, had to traverse much of the city daily en route to school. One young woman, "S. T.," described how men "mocked" and "bothered" her "along the whole route" to her high school.[50] The harassment was relentless, continuous, and debilitating. Despite being "one of the most dedicated girls in the whole class," exhausted by the harassment, she ended her schooling prematurely at the age of sixteen.

Many women wrote in to *as-Salam* to complain of street harassment, and they asserted that it was not limited to any particular type of woman or even comportment. While S. T. was veiled, another schoolgirl from Oran wrote that her little sister was teased on her way to school for not wearing a veil.[51] Another woman, Houria Illal, wrote that both veiled and unveiled women faced street harassment. She wrote that veiled young women walking alone in the street would be "followed by a band of young idlers, who are the plague of our society." One woman from Oran, Asnia H. M., wrote that "when [Muslim women] triumph over stupid objections from old women and go out unveiled, they are met with insults from young men." As they named the problem of harassment, Muslim women shifted the object of women's safety from potential sexual impropriety implicit in concerns about dances, for example, to verbal harassment from Muslim men. Illal described their harassment in terms of the constant assault of "ideas"—likely sexual in nature—women were forced to hear from their harassers. She wrote that unveiled women like herself were "the object of very impolite propositions." While commenters wrote that Muslim women were unsafe in European spaces, Illal responded that it was Muslim men, not Europeans, who harassed them in the streets. Illal wrote that, unlike Muslim men, "the Europeans leave us alone if we appear correct." She elaborated that while European men may make comments to Muslim women who appeared to be of "loose morals," they left most Muslim women alone.[52] Such critiques remapped concerns about Muslim women's safety from abstract threats of potential impropriety or licentious contact with European men at dances to the regular, everyday harassment they faced from Muslim men.

For Muslim women, street harassment was a symptom of a larger problem: despite the rhetoric of nationalism that valorized women as important pillars of the nation's glory, Muslim men regularly disrespected Muslim women. Asnia H. M. wrote that she was "offended by the attitude of the young men of our race." Street harassment was evidence, she argued, that men "do not respect the honor and freedom of the Muslim woman." She used the language of the national family to underscore the extent to which this treatment was a betrayal. "Our brothers humiliate us," she lamented.[53] Some male commenters also acknowledged the harassment women regularly faced. Selim Taleb from Sidi-bel-Abbes wrote that commenters could not encourage all Muslim women to unveil because they would have to deal with too much agitation from not only their parents but also from fellow Muslims.[54] A factory worker, Abdelkader Haddadi, lamented that unveiled women had to face "bands of *zazous*" who called out to them as they walked through the city, a reminder that openness to unveiling was not limited to elite Muslims.[55] Another young man from Tazmalt, who signed his letter simply "B. M. A.," wrote that while he himself was uneducated because of insufficient space at the "indigenous school," he urged Muslim women to persevere in their education and ignore "the words of their detractors."[56]

As had occurred in the interwar years, readers of *as-Salam* suggested that Muslim women could not serve as ideal companions to increasingly educated men because of their own lack of education and experience. This mirrored transformations taking place across the colonized world, as elite men—having received the benefits of a colonial education—looked for "new women" who would mirror their new cosmopolitan status and outlook.[57] A woman from Tablat, Nedjma Gamar, wrote that Muslim women were so devoid of cultivated intellect that they were nothing more than "cleaning ladies" for their husbands and nannies for their children.[58] Others reaffirmed the nationalist fantasy of a wife as a critical partner and source of support for her husband. A commenter from Mostaganem wrote that men faced so many stresses at work, they needed to be able to depend on their wives as their confidantes and partners.[59] Yet because Muslim women had so little access to education, men suffered.

Marriage as an issue raised questions of equity and authority. Some Muslim women contended that their marriages were another site of their humiliation by Muslim men. Nationalist rhetoric described marriage as a partnership in which each spouse played an important role, which produced "social equilibrium and harmony [in] our households," according to Anissa in *as-Salam*'s first issue. Yet despite this ideal, Muslim women contended that they were continually mistreated by Muslim men. An unsigned editorial stated that for Muslim women, marriage was simply a form of domestic service, since men demanded "obedience" from their wives.[60] S. H. Bintou Chaab went even further, claiming men treated the Muslim woman "like a slave." She wrote, "Her opinion is never listened to, [and] she is always under the constant domination of her husband, her master." The realities of married life, in other words, did not reflect Anissa's description of "equilibrium and harmony."[61] Such letters recentered Muslim men as figures who abused their position of power within marriages. One young person from the Collège de Blida wrote that the Muslim man left the house without his wife, not because Islam required women's sequestration or because his wife was insufficiently educated, but because he wanted to behave as if he was single even when he was married.[62]

Nationalism also provided the grounds for women to argue that attention should be turned from the miniscule details of women's comportment to how Muslim men had so thoroughly assimilated to European culture, thereby violating nationalism's commitment to cultural cohesion. While details of women's lives were scrutinized and women were warned not to behave too much like Europeans or even keep European company, men were assimilating in much more tangible ways, including their clothing. A young Muslim Algerian woman living in France, Mademoiselle Mina, noted that Muslim men no longer wore the burnous, the traditional Amazigh hooded long cloak.[63] She questioned why men were permitted to transition away from customary dress, but for women such transitions were equated with a turn away from Islam. This was about not only personal hypocrisy but also collective identity. Mohammed-Lamine Boutaleb lamented that since men stopped speaking Arabic from age five when they entered French colonial schools, Muslim men and women "did not even share a common language."[64] For Boutaleb and others who noted this, men's and women's different linguistic capabilities were not only a marker of different education levels but represented a fundamental violation of Muslim identity, since Muslim men so easily abandoned their native tongue. H. Said wrote that men's "hypocritical respect for our traditions" produced ignorance and isolation for Muslim women.[65] These letters framed Muslim men's assimilation as a slight against not only their Muslim counterparts but Muslim society writ large, since it would ultimately weaken social cohesion based on shared identity.

The most troubling reflection of men's duplicity lay in mixed marriages, which had become increasingly common, even among working-class and rural Muslims. For Muslim women, men's willingness to marry outside "of their own race" represented the ultimate hypocrisy. While Muslim women were held to the highest standards in terms of modesty and chastity under the guise of national cohesion, Muslim men were free to marry Europeans.[66] Chérifa B. wrote, "Don't talk about female vanity when . . . [there are so few] women who abandon their religion, or following the example of their parents, marry any European."[67] Muslim women interpreted marriage to European women as an act of betrayal. Mademoiselle H. Said called it "desertion."[68] A woman from Oran, Khouira B., wrote that Muslim men were "abandoning the women of their own race."[69] She pointed out that Muslim men who did not marry women "of their own race" had no business chastising Muslim women. These mixed marriages, women argued, would have a disastrous impact on Muslim society. Asnia H. M. wrote that a fusion of Muslim and European cultures was "grave and contrary to the divine will."[70] This same rationale was cited in concerns about the potential assimilation of Muslim schoolgirls to European norms. Yet in these discussions that centered Muslim men, women contended it was men who violated the nationalist call to maintain difference and strengthen one's own community.

Muslim women's attack on mixed marriages was also a critique of Muslim leadership, since many Muslim activists and politicians had European wives, including nationalist leaders Messali Hadj and Ferhat Abbas. Madame H. S. wrote that ordinary Muslim men were marrying European women in part because of the example set by Muslim politicians.[71] She asked, "Which one of them [Muslim politicians] dares to present himself in front of his people with a woman of his people as his wife by his side?" These commentaries about mixed marriage, like the discourses of respectability, reveal the political ethos of the moment. Questions of leadership, self-presentation, and performativity of race and culture were all lenses through which the questions of dignity in the face of empire were refracted. These all undergirded their critique of double standards for women's behavior.

Djamila Debèche, *L'Action*, and Women's Emancipation in a French Algeria

In September 1947, exactly one year after *as-Salam's* first issue was published, a new publication devoted to Muslim women appeared on newsstands: *L'Action: Revue sociale féminine artistique* (Action: Social artistic women's review). *L'Action* was founded and edited by thirty-two-year-old Djamila Debèche. Like the schoolteachers who initiated the debates about women's education in the interwar years, Debèche was a liminal figure who straddled the worlds of both Muslims and settlers. Although she was born in the small village of Bordj Okhriss and spent her early childhood in Ouled Si Ahmed, she eventually moved to Monaco with her grandmother where she lived throughout her teenage years before returning to Algeria.

Debèche had a long career in publishing and broadcasting in Algeria that spanned the interwar and postwar periods. In 1936, at the age of twenty-one, Debèche began writing for the Algerian newspaper *L'Écho de la presse musulmane*. In 1937 *La Justice* published a lengthy editorial by Debèche in which she argued hijab was not a religious requirement.[72] Between 1939 and 1944 she was a broadcaster on Radio Ptt d'Alger in the 8:30 p.m. Saturday evening spot. Her broadcasts included social and educational material intended for Muslim women. In 1947 she published a novel, *Leila: Young Girl of Algeria*, the same year she founded *L'Action*. In 1955 Debèche published another novel, *Aziza*.

In both the interwar and postwar years, Debèche was an exceptional figure. Alongside *La Voix des Humbles*'s Muslim women contributors, Debèche was one of the few women to be regularly published in the interwar press. Her article in the reformist newspaper *La Justice* took the provocative stance that Islam did not mandate veiling at all, and her article was published alongside a photograph of her unveiled (figure 6.4). Her article adopted the frames common among interwar writers, including references to Islamic knowledge, Islamic history, and contemporary developments in the Middle East. Her writing in the postwar period,

Mlle Djamila DEBECHE, *publiciste*
Cette jeune fille musulmane, qui habite Nice, effectue ainsi tous les jours ses sorties en ville sans que cela puisse constituer une atteinte aux préceptes islamiques.

FIGURE 6.4. Djamila Debèche, from *La Justice*, 1937.
Source: BNF

including her novels and her writings in *L'Action*, was more concerned with the place of Muslims like her, who moved between Muslim and European worlds comfortably, in an increasingly nationalist Algeria.

While *as-Salam* was in print from 1946 to 1950, *L'Action* only lasted ten issues and was out of print by the summer of 1948. Muslim newspapers in colonial Algeria struggled to maintain both a readership and the necessary financial backing, so many were short-lived. While *as-Salam* offered coverage of regional politics and cinema, *L'Action* was more highbrow and published short stories as well as ethnographic accounts of different Muslim tribes, holidays, and even neighborhoods. Debèche's ambiguity over her audience may have contributed to the review's inability to succeed. While *L'Action* presented itself as a publication for both Muslim and settler audiences, such ethnographic accounts functioned to educate a settler audience about Muslims.

Alongside an analysis of *as-Salam*, *L'Action* illustrates that although the rhetoric of anti-colonial nationalism was on the rise, Muslim society was by no means unanimous in its aims. Indeed, as James McDougall has written, the terms and goals of nationalism remained contested even throughout the War of Independence.[73] *L'Action* was decidedly more ambivalent about nationalism and even politics writ large than *as-Salam*. Like the schoolteachers, Debèche was among the last generation who believed in the emancipatory potential of a French Algeria for Muslims before it was no longer possible. At the same time as Anissa offered her own vision of the ideal Muslim woman and her readers responded with their own (often nationalist) visions of women's possibilities, older ideals of Franco-Muslim collaboration remained in circulation in forums like *L'Action* and persisted well into the Algerian War of Independence.

Unlike the women who wrote in to *as-Salam* who saw Muslim women's status as a consequence of the brutality of colonialism, Debèche still remained optimistic that collaboration with the French could ameliorate the problems Muslim women faced. While she did not say so outright, it was implied throughout *as-Salam*, which sought to bring Muslim elites and European settlers closer together through mutual understanding. Even as late as 1959, she continued to write articles petitioning the French state to do more for Muslim women.[74] In those articles she echoed interwar discussions using brief histories of Islam and Atatürk's reforms to argue that Islam was emancipatory for women and that Muslim countries could be modern. Like interwar discussions about women, *L'Action* also reported on developments in Turkey and

Egypt, and it offered histories of women's powerful position in the Islamic past, including profiles on particular women such as Khadija and the women of the court of the Abbasid caliph Harun al-Rashid.[75] In an article about the holiday Mawlid, Debèche offered an explanation of Islam's feminist history.[76] She wrote that Islam transformed society through its regulation of family life in which "the woman became the equal of the man to a certain extent." She praised Muhammad in particular for "the considerable project of women's emancipation [that he] realized." Such articles demonstrate the longevity of these interwar claims even beyond reformist communities. *L'Action* was also oriented toward international feminist organizing for women. Its second issue, for example, offered extensive coverage of the October 1947 International Feminine Congress in Paris. Subsequent issues also reported on the successes of women's rights projects in spaces like Argentina.

In her novels Debèche critiqued the societal focus on Muslim women's comportment in ways that echoed *as-Salam*'s readers. The protagonists of Debèche's novels, *Leila* (1947) and *Aziza* (1955), were, like her, trapped between two worlds. Although their social circles were primarily European elites, they resented the racism they faced from settler society as well as their alienation from Muslim society for being too Western. A passage from *Aziza* offers a commentary on Muslim men's hypocrisy similar to that presented in *as-Salam*. At a party in Algiers, Aziza unexpectedly reconnects with a childhood playmate, Ali Kemal. Aziza (like Debèche) left her village as a young child after being orphaned, and by the time she meets Ali she is very assimilated to European norms and most of her friends are settler elites. Although they have much in common, Ali's brother Allel tells Aziza she is not a good match for Ali and she would be better off marrying a European. Aziza says, "The elegant Western outfit he was wearing made me doubt the sincerity of his words. He wasn't even wearing a fez [tarbush]."[77] While Allel deems Aziza too European, she notes he too was assimilated enough to wear "Western" clothes without even the traditional tarbush, which some Muslim nationalists, including Messali Hadj, for example, wore alongside suits. Like the letters from *as-Salam* readers, Debèche challenged the unfair scrutiny directed toward Muslim women, while Muslim men's assimilation was accepted.

Unlike *as-Salam*, which published letters from readers, in *L'Action* Debèche instead chose to respond to letters on a single page, "From You to Us." Without the context of the readers' letters, the page functioned more as a space for Debèche to thank her readers than a space

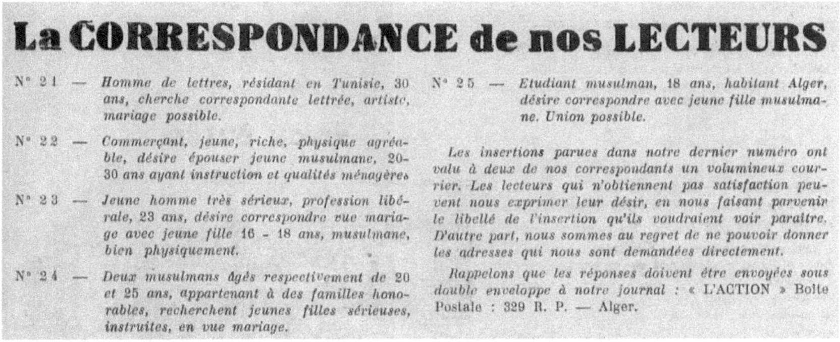

La CORRESPONDANCE de nos LECTEURS

N° 21 — Homme de lettres, résidant en Tunisie, 30 ans, cherche correspondante lettrée, artiste, mariage possible.

N° 22 — Commerçant, jeune, riche, physique agréable, désire épouser jeune musulmane, 20-30 ans ayant instruction et qualités ménagères.

N° 23 — Jeune homme très sérieux, profession libérale, 23 ans, désire correspondre vue mariage avec jeune fille 16 - 18 ans, musulmane, bien physiquement.

N° 24 — Deux musulmans âgés respectivement de 20 et 25 ans, appartenant à des familles honorables, recherchent jeunes filles sérieuses, instruites, en vue mariage.

N° 25 — Etudiant musulman, 18 ans, habitant Alger, désire correspondre avec jeune fille musulmane. Union possible.

Les insertions parues dans notre dernier numéro ont valu à deux de nos correspondants un volumineux courrier. Les lecteurs qui n'obtiennent pas satisfaction peuvent nous exprimer leur désir, en nous faisant parvenir le libellé de l'insertion qu'ils voudraient voir paraître. D'autre part, nous sommes au regret de ne pouvoir donner les adresses qui nous sont demandées directement.

Rappelons que les réponses doivent être envoyées sous double enveloppe à notre journal : « L'ACTION » Boîte Postale : 329 R. P. — Alger.

FIGURE 6.5. Personal advertisements from *L'Action*, March 1948.
Source: BNF

of community dialogue. One glimpse into *L'Action*'s Muslim readership was the personal advertisements it started posting in its third issue in November 1947 (figure 6.5). Although some were posted by Muslim women, most were posted by Muslim men, interested in marriage to a younger Muslim woman. Many specified that she should be educated or *"évoluée."* Some even requested women of specific professions—"preference for a midwife or teacher." Many noted that they had a comfortable financial situation, an indication of the elite status of *L'Action*'s Muslim readers. While most clearly indicated they were looking for marriage and to start a family, others, like an eighteen-year-old student in Algiers, wrote that he desired correspondence with a Muslim young woman and that marriage was "possible."[78]

Although *as-Salam* and *L'Action* were in print at the same time, neither explicitly mentioned the other. In *L'Action*'s final issue in April 1948, which featured a photograph of Debèche (figure 6.6), she wrote in response to an unposted letter from a reader: "I have nothing in common with the *collaboratrice* of the Algerian review about which you've talked to me. That person who is so charming is, in effect, of European origin."

As-Salam was a review, and Mademoiselle Anissa never revealed her full name, so she could have been the subject of Debèche's dismissive tone.[79] In the May 1950 issue of *as-Salam*, Anissa described the outpouring of responses she had to her inquiry about whether mixed marriages were acceptable. She wrote that she was visited by someone who may have been Debèche. She wrote: "Mlle B. B. who calls herself Muslim and praises wine, who calls herself Arab and can't say a word in Arabic (she was raised in Nice) paid me a visit. She came to tell me her ideas

Figure 6.6. Djamila Debèche, from the final issue of *L'Action* in April 1948.
Source: BNF

about the subject [of mixed marriage]. For an entire hour she exposed me to incoherent theories inspired by naiveté and stupid pretension."[80] Anissa likely used B. B. in lieu of D. D. to slightly anonymize her attack. Debèche was raised in southern France and wrote for the publication *Le Petit Niçois* as a teenager. The vitriol directed at Debèche here—"naiveté and stupid pretension"—speaks to the extent to which they had different aspirations for Muslim society.

Anticolonial Feminist Futures: A Conclusion

Thirteen years before Franz Fanon would publish "Algeria Unveiled," which detailed the long history of the entanglement between colonialism and Muslim women's veiling, Muslim women wrote into the women's page of *as-Salam* to argue that women's veiling practices were inextricable from empire. Scholarship on the veil in Algeria has paid particular attention to its important role within the Algerian War of Independence as a marker of Algerian defiance in the face of pressure to unveil and assimilate. During the Algerian War of Independence, the veil took on political meaning in response to the intensification of French efforts to push unveiling, including public unveilings and veil-burning ceremonies. As famously depicted in *The Battle of Algiers*, the veil also became a means of camouflage for women fighters. For others, it simply meant insisting on their right to be Muslim and resist the pressure to assimilate.

In the second half of the 1940s, the women's page of *as-Salam* offered Muslim women and men a forum to critique the discussions about women that had unfolded and intensified in the preceding decades. While a small number of elite women wrote in to interwar newspapers, in the postwar period a wider segment of Muslim society wrote in to *as-Salam*. As they entered the ongoing discussions about Muslim women in large numbers, they articulated a counter critique of both colonialism and Muslim men. They wrote that it was colonialism's exploitation of Muslims that limited Muslim women's possibilities, and so questions of education and veiling were futile without consideration of colonialism's impact. Muslim women also critiqued the obsession with women's veiling, initiated by the French but also upheld within Muslim society. This obsession with veiling was part, they argued, of an unfair focus on Muslim women, while it was Muslim men who rejected their people by adopting European dress, speaking French, and marrying European women.

The contributions of the women and men who wrote into *as-Salam*'s women's page should neither be minimized nor overstated. On one hand, they illustrate the ways women and their allies took advantage of new spaces like the women's page to publish critiques of colonialism and the disrespect they faced from Muslim men. Such commentaries illustrate how the codes of conduct outlined for women within nationalist discourse were being disputed and negotiated. And yet, while the growing nationalist movement benefited from women's participation, it largely minimized their concerns. As Vince and others have charted, women were told their concerns did not need to be foregrounded because they would naturally be resolved once Algerian independence was won.

Conclusion

On the evening of February 24, 1954, Muslim men and women gathered at the Opéra of Algiers. The building, which bordered the casbah, had been constructed between 1850 and 1853, only two decades into the French occupation of Algeria. Its principal architect, Charles Frédéric Chassériau, was also responsible for the design of a number of important structures in Egypt, Algeria, and France, including the consulate of France in Alexandria, the Marché des Capucins in Marseille, and the boulevard de l'Impératrice Eugénie in Algiers with its arcades that were meant to recall Paris. That evening in February 1954, the Opéra hosted the annual gala of the Association des femmes musulmanes algériennes (Association of Muslim Algerian Women, AFMA). The night was an opportunity for members and supporters to gather, enjoy performances of dance and Andalusian music, and raise funds for the organization's operations. AFMA's efforts included agitation for increased access to education for Muslims, as well as material support to poor families and to women whose husbands had been arrested or detained as political prisoners.

Amid the festivities that night were speeches by the organization's president and founder, Mamia Chentouf, and its secretary-general, Nefissa Hamoud. Chentouf addressed the audience in Arabic. She contended that women's limited participation in social and intellectual

CONCLUSION

life was one of causes of the "decline of the nation."[1] She lamented that some Muslim men were so ignorant that they "oppose[d] the liberation of the Muslim woman in the name of Islam." Chentouf insisted that instead, it was the rights Islam accorded women that "liberated her." Chentouf described the contradiction between Islam's feminist possibilities, the former glory of Islamic history, the current state of "decline" Muslims in Algeria suffered, and the enduring misogyny Muslim women in Algeria continued to face. Two days later, the PPA's nationalist newspaper *L'Algérie Libre* reported on the gala with a quotation from Chentouf as the article's title: "Women's emancipation is a religious obligation and a social necessity."

Chentouf's speech that evening drew on many of the same themes that had preoccupied interwar Algerian commentators, including Islam's support for women's advancement and the need to reform Muslim women's status for society to progress. She echoed the interwar commentators who insisted that women's advancement reflected a commitment to Islamic principles, not a project of French assimilation. Her choice to address the audience in Arabic also indicates the orientation of the association broadly, which, like the other nationalist organizations in its milieu, insisted on Muslims' identity as both Arabs and Muslims. While she drew on Islamic evidence, she was unveiled. Her ability to deliver such a speech in front of a crowd within the Opéra of Algiers—one of the monuments of the French colonial project—reflects how these interwar ideas gained a new legitimacy within a nationalist frame on the eve of the Algerian War of Independence.

Chentouf's life was formed by many of the interwar dynamics this book has analyzed. Her childhood involved multiple migrations. She was born in 1922 in a small village, but her father's support for the reformist Association of Oulémas was so contentious among the village's Sufis that the family eventually migrated to the nearby seaside town of Nemours. Nemours was coincidentally also the town where the domestic worker and communist activist Rahma ben Drahou lived and worked. In Nemours Chentouf's parents were able to secure her a position within a French colonial primary school and eventually in 1935 an upper-level French colonial school in Mascara, a town 250 kilometers east of Nemours. Later, as a midwifery student at the University of Algiers, she would join the AEMAN, as well as Messali Hadj's nationalist party, the PPA-MTLD.

In 1947 Chentouf founded the AFMA, an auxiliary to the PPA-MTLD, with Hamoud. While sources point to the presence of women (and their *youyous*, which signaled affirmation and support) during Hadj's public speeches in the 1930s, the party lacked any formal organ specifically for its women adherents until the creation of the association. Indeed, this blind spot with respect to women until 1947 reflected nationalism's ambivalence about the problems Muslim women faced. The PPA-MTLD, for example, had never had a coherent policy with respect to women since the foundation of its newspaper, *Étoile nord-africaine*, in 1926.[2] Its position broadly was that women suffered because of the conditions created by empire. When the nationalist struggle would succeed in the creation of an independent Algeria, the problems Muslim women faced would inevitably fade away. Yet the PPA-MTLD was able to mobilize women into participation in the nationalist struggle through a range of networks, including Muslim reformist schools and eventually the AFMA.

Despite Muslim women's growing activism since the interwar years, French colonial administrators continued to claim that Muslim women's religion and customs prohibited their advancement. In a 1952 letter to the minister of the interior, Governor-General Roger Léonard wrote that Muslim women's limited opportunity "results from customs and Quranic principles [and thus] escapes the direct action of the legislator."[3] He opened his letter with this claim and then called for greater access to education for Muslim girls in Algeria as an important first step toward greater participation in public life. He closed his letter with the assertion that Muslim women's rights depended on "the reactions of a society, attached to its religious customs, and infinitely sensitive to any measure that appears to be a violation of its consciences." He called for more education for Muslim women, an empty platitude in between the opening and closing of his letter, where he echoed long-standing claims by administrators that Muslim patriarchy was too intransigent and Muslim society too sensitive for the state to be able to intervene in any regard on behalf of Muslim women. This stance both absolved the state from its failure to educate Muslim women or improve the material conditions of their lives, while also shifting the blame to nebulous Muslim customs.

Less than eight months after the Association of Muslim Algerian Women's gala, on November 1, 1954, the FLN attacked a series of targets across Algeria—an event that launched the start of the Algerian War of Independence. This book concludes with Chentouf's story not to suggest there was a neat, linear progression from Muslim women's limited participation in public life at the start of the twentieth century to their prominent position on the eve of the Algerian War. Rather, this book has mapped how interwar discussions about women were seeds that bloomed—with the support of other factors—into later developments.

In the later decades of the twentieth century Algerian feminism became more organized and vocal. In the 1980s in particular there was a proliferation of women's publications, academic texts, associations, and marches.[4] Algerian feminists like Chérifa Benabdessadok, Chafika Dib-Marouf, and Souad Khodja published academic texts on feminism that took up many of the questions first posed by interwar commentators. They asked: How could categories of tradition and modernity be questioned and remade? What would it mean to consider such questions without the colonial gaze? Could Islam be an emancipatory force for women? Decades later, in 2019, a group was founded in Algeria called Les Archives des luttes des femmes en Algérie (The archive of women's struggle in Algeria). With a Facebook group of thousands of members, the group has photographed and disseminated several Algerian feminist publications, including some pages from Djamila Debèche's 1947 *L'Action*.

While much of the historiography on Muslim women in twentieth-century Algeria has focused on their participation in the War of Independence, this book has turned our attention instead to the interwar years.[5] The interwar discussions about women reflect a moment of colonial internationalism.[6] Interwar commentators were critical of empire, and yet many remained ambivalent about nationalism. They were invested in news from abroad, most frequently from the Middle East, and they used this news as material to help them work rhetorically through the crisis of their present moment. At the center of this temporal anxiety were concerns about women. The future—full of possibility—became the space onto which commentators could project their aspirations for both Muslim women and Muslim society in Algeria writ large. These tensions of course persisted into the rest of the twentieth century, but both nationalism and the eventual FLN government attempted to subsume them under the singular identity of Muslim, Arab, Algerian.

Attention to this period with a turn away from the teleology of the War of Independence reveals a whole host of actors and discussions that the focus of nationalism has rendered insignificant. In 1962 writer Kateb Yacine stated, "To write in French is almost, on a much more elevated level, to snatch a gun from the hands of a paratrooper."[7] As early as May 1922, the schoolteachers who were part of the Association of Schoolteachers of Indigenous Origin used their platform, *La Voix des Humbles*, to raise critiques and to agitate, in French, for change. Like the Young Algerians of that same generation, they were culturally and politically assimilationist and yet also raised critiques of the French colonial project. Like other publications, they too suffered from surveillance and censorship from the state. Central to the transformation they envisioned for Muslim society was the position of Muslim women and their limited access to education. My intention here is not to posit a new origin story of Algerian anti-colonial nationalism with these schoolteachers at the center. Rather, I propose an expansion of our notion of what constitutes radical imaginings. The fluid possibility of the interwar years enabled transnational imaginings of how women's advancement could transform Algeria.

Thinking with feminism as a possibility rather than a fixed identity allows us to analyze the ideas, commitments, and negotiations of multiple social, political, and religious groups together. This offers a path forward from the scholarly interest in the "agency" and "resistance" of Middle Eastern women, both of which have been complicated in recent decades by scholars Saba Mahmood and Judith Tucker. In the case of colonial Algeria, Sarah Ghabrial has explored how as women navigated the bifurcated legal system, they may have pushed back against the pressures of patriarchy in their own lives while reinforcing colonial assumptions about Muslim misogyny.[8] Augustin Jomier has explored the case of Mzabi washers of the dead who used their powerful position to enforce patriarchal norms.[9] Ghabrial and Jomier have further complicated the older categories of "agency" and "resistance" by showing how even as women resisted one form of power, they may have upheld another.

Attention to interwar discussions about women, this work argues, reveals the contours of multiple sets of power relations—between women and men, rural and urban, poor and elite, Sufi and reformist. As commentators envisioned new futures for women and for Algeria broadly, they had to contend with these social divisions and work through (or sometimes conveniently avoid) how such divisions would be resolved in the future. While their versions of advancement varied and were envisioned toward varying ends, most saw women's advancement as a critical means toward a better future. Even some reformists who envisioned women's social role as predominantly within the home still sought to create more equitable power relations within the family and more (albeit limited) opportunities for women's advancement. In Algeria discussions about women and feminist imaginings matter, I argue, because they constitute a realm of emancipatory action that was able to operate under the constraints of colonialism. The enduring scholarly interest in nationalism has obfuscated attention to such imaginings as historically significant. While they sometimes intersected and upheld nationalist thought, these discussions about women also connected Algeria to the broader Middle East and reflected a geographic and intellectual gaze that was multidirectional.

My analysis's focus on labor, education, and dress in chapters 2, 3, and 4 echoes ongoing processes of modern subject formation underway across the Middle East and much of the world. Of effendi status in Egypt, for example, Lucie Ryzova has written, "At the center [of effendi status] was a claim on modernity, institutionally codified through (modern) education and (modern) employment, and expressed by (modern) dress."[10] These three domains, labor, education, and dress, in other words were contested sites of debates about modernity and social change elsewhere too. In Algeria, this work demonstrates, these discussions were shaped by how colonialism constrained Muslim colonial subjects. Instead of the kind of white-collar labor that made effendis in Egypt, Muslim women in Algeria were limited to domestic service. Instead of discussions about the importance of education to train men to work for an "inwardly expansive modern state" as in Egypt, discussions about education analyzed here focused on the limited access and curriculum available to Muslims in Algeria. In discussions about dress too, while the Egyptian effendi could codeswitch between traditional and modern modes of dress, in Algeria the connotations of different forms of dress were shaped by the settler-colonial context.

In the end, interwar discussions about women reflect fluidity. Social divisions were at once rigid categories that divided Muslim society, but simultaneously fluid enough to be navigated and moved between by multiple actors and communities. Algeria's place in the emergent international world order was also fluid. In some ways it belonged to the Middle East or the Muslim world, and in others it was on the cusp of its own national project. The status of women too was fluid. Some doors, like those of Muslim reformist schools, were opening to women, while others, such as access to most professions, remained firmly shut. While more elite urban women maintained a limited public presence, other working-class women moved between homes, neighborhoods, and even cities as part of their work. In later decades some of this fluidity would narrow as nationalism's centrifugal power strengthened. Yet the interwar moment remains important because of the possibilities for women's advancement that arose as feminism, internationalism, and Muslim reform intersected.

Notes

Introduction

1. Abou-Ezzohra, "En instruisant nos filles nous deviendrons meilleurs, extrait d'un discours prononcé à l'occasion d'un mariage," *La Voix Indigène*, July 12, 1934, 2.

2. Though it is admittedly Eurocentric, I use the term "interwar" throughout this book because of its usefulness as a shorthand for the period in question and because, as Marc Matera and Susan Kingsley Kent have shown, it was truly a global historical moment, as populations across the world enjoyed new access to global news and formed various international solidarities.

3. Laure Blévis, "La citoyenneté française au miroir de la colonisation: étude des demandes de naturalisation des 'sujets français' en Algérie coloniale," *Genèses* 53 (2003): 25–47.

4. Marya Hannun, "States of Change: Women, Islamic Reform, and Transregional Mobility in the Making of 'Modern' Afghanistan" (PhD diss., Georgetown University, 2021), 204.

5. For the sake of clarity to nonspecialist audiences, I am using the term "settler" to refer to the European population of Algeria, legally classified as "Algerians" in some periods of the colonial era. My intent is not to assert that there was always an Algerian nation this population was outside of. To the contrary, at the time these people were citizens of the legal and geographic space called "Algeria." For clarity's sake, though, I find "settler" allows for the clearest and most immediate distinction between Europeans living in Europe and Europeans living in Algeria, as well as those legally classified as "Algerians" in the colonial era and those classified as "Algerians" post-1962.

6. Martin Evans, *Algeria: France's Undeclared War* (New York: Oxford University Press, 2012), 38.

7. Mahfoud Bennoune, *The Making of Contemporary Algeria, 1830–1987* (Cambridge: Cambridge University Press, 2002), 77.

8. Gilbert Meynier, *L'Algérie révélée: La guerre de 1914–1918* (Paris: Editions Bouchene, 2015), 405.

9. Donal Hassett, *Mobilizing Memory: The Great War and the Language of Politics in Colonial Algeria, 1918–39* (Oxford: Oxford University Press, 2019).

10. Judith Surkis, *Sex, Law, and Sovereignty in French Algeria, 1830–1930* (Ithaca, NY: Cornell University Press, 2019).

11. Charlotte Courreye's *L'Algérie des Oulémas* is one recent text that begins to pull out some of Algeria's connections to the Middle East (mostly Egypt).

Charlotte Courreye, *L'Algérie des Oulémas: Une histoire de l'Algérie contemporaine (1931–1991)* (Paris: Éditions de la Sorbonne, 2020).

12. Samira Haj, *Reconfiguring Islamic Tradition: Reform, Rationality, and Modernity* (Stanford, CA: Stanford University Press, 2009), 4–5.

13. Judith Butler, "Contingent Foundations: Feminism and the Question of 'Postmodernism,'" in *Feminists Theorize the Political*, ed. Judith Butler and Joan Wallach Scott (New York: Routledge, 1992), 16.

14. Margot Badran, *Feminists, Islam, and Nation: Gender and the Making of Modern Egypt* (Princeton, NJ: Princeton University Press, 1996), 19–20.

15. Margot Badran, *Feminism in Islam: Secular and Religious Convergences* (London: Oneworld, 2009).

16. Badran, *Feminism in Islam*, 4.

17. While recent texts have brought in a range of new perspectives on the topic, feminism in the colonial North African context remains underexamined. See Jean Said Makdisi, Noha Bayoumi, and Rafif Rida Sidawi, *Arab Feminisms: Gender and Equality in the Middle East* (New York: IB Tauris, 2014).

18. Amy Aisen Kallander, *Tunisia's Modern Woman: Nation-Building and State Feminism in the Global 1960s* (New York: Cambridge University Press, 2021); Valentine Moghadam, "Feminism, Legal Reform, and Women's Empowerment in the Middle East and North Africa," *International Social Science Journal* 59, no. 191 (2008): 9–16; Margot Badran, "Between Secular and Islamic Feminism/s: Reflections on the Middle East and Beyond," *Journal of Middle East Women's Studies* 1, no. 1 (2005): 6–28; Fleischmann, "Other 'Awakening'"; Lila Abu-Lughod, ed., *Remaking Women: Feminism and Modernity in the Middle East* (Princeton, NJ: Princeton University Press, 1998); Kumari Jayawardena, *Feminism and Nationalism in the Third World* (London: Zed, 1986).

19. The *youyou* or *zagharid* in Arabic is a North African ululation sung by women independently or in unison to show excitement, celebration, or praise, often at particular rituals, like weddings.

20. Natalya Vince, *Our Fighting Sisters: Nation, Memory, and Gender in Algeria, 1954–2012* (Manchester: Manchester University Press, 2015).

21. Roxanne Panchasi, *Future Tense: The Culture of Anticipation in France between the Wars* (Ithaca, NY: Cornell University Press, 2009), 4.

22. Sara Pursley, *Familiar Futures: Time, Selfhood and Sovereignty in Iraq* (Stanford, CA: Stanford University Press, 2019).

23. Manu Goswami, "AHR Forum: Imaginary Futures and Colonial Internationalisms," *American Historical Review* 117, no. 5 (December 2012): 1462, 1464, 1467.

24. Benoy Kumar Sarkar, "The Futurism of Young Asia," *International Journal of Ethics* 28, no. 4 (July 1918): 540.

25. James McDougall, *History and the Culture of Nationalism in Algeria* (New York: Cambridge University Press, 2006).

26. Manijeh Moradian, *This Flame Within: Iranian Revolutionaries in the United States* (Durham, NC: Duke University Press, 2022), 25.

27. Roger LeTourneau, "Social Change in the Muslim Cities of North Africa," *American Journal of Sociology* 60, no. 6 (May 1955): 534.

28. Vince, *Our Fighting Sisters*.

29. Augustin Jomier, "Muslim Notables, French Colonial Officials, and the Washers of the Dead: Women and Gender Politics in Colonial Algeria," *French Politics, Culture and Society* 39, no. 1 (2021): 18.

30. Arthur Asseraf, *Electric News in Colonial Algeria* (New York: Oxford University Press, 2019).

31. Aaron Spevack, *The Archetypal Sunni Scholar: Law, Theology, and Mysticism in the Synthesis of al-Bajuri* (Albany: State University of New York Press, 2014).

1. The Rise of the Woman Question in Interwar Algeria

1. Mohamed Hamed Filajl, "La Femme Musulmane," *La Défense*, November 2, 1934.

2. Mustafa bin Hallush, "Hijab al-Mar'a 'Ada la Din" [Women's hijab is a custom and is not religious], *al-Bassair*, January 29, 1937; Hamza Bukusha, "Hijab al-Mar'a Dīn wa-l-Mubalagha fihi 'Ada Sharifa fi al-Islam wa-qablahu" [Women's hijab is religious and the exaggeration of it is an honorable custom in Islam and before it], *al-Bassair*, March 5, 1937; Sheikh Abu Ya'la al-Zawawi, "Hawla Hijab al-Mar'a" [About the veil of women], *al-Bassair*, March 19, 1937; Mustafa bin Hallush, "Hawla 'Adat al-Hijab" [About the custom of the hijab], *al-Bassair*, March 26, 1937.

3. Allison Drew, *We Are No Longer in France: Communists in Colonial Algeria* (Manchester: Manchester University Press, 2017), 22.

4. James McDougall, *A History of Algeria* (Cambridge: Cambridge University Press, 2017), 131.

5. Drew, *We Are No Longer in France*, 22.

6. McDougall, *History of Algeria*, 133–34.

7. Marie Baroy, "Rôle du travail de la femme dans l'évolution sociale de la Casbah" (master's thesis, Université de Alger, 1943), 122.

8. Marguerite A. Bel, *Les arts indigènes féminins en Algérie* (Algiers: Ouvrage publié sous les auspices du Gouvernement Général de l'Algérie, 1939).

9. Julia Clancy-Smith, "A Woman without Her Distaff: Gender, Work, and Handicraft Production in Colonial North Africa," in *Social History of Women and Gender in the Modern Middle East*, ed. Margaret L. Meriwether and Judith E. Tucker (Boulder, CO: Westview, 1999), 33.

10. Dahbia Lounas, interviewed virtually by Sara Rahnama, October 31, 2021.

11. Kamel Kateb, *Européens, "Indigènes" et Juifs en Algérie (1830–1962)* (Paris: Editions de l'Institut national d'études démographiques, 2001), 276.

12. Zeynep Çelik, "A Lingering Obsession: The Houses of Algiers in French Colonial Discourse," in *The Walls of Algiers*, ed. Zeynep Çelik, Julia Clancy-Smith, and Frances Terpak (Seattle: University of Washington Press, 2009), 134–60; David Prochaska, *Making Algeria French: Colonialism in Bône, 1870–1920* (New York: Cambridge University Press, 1990); Allan Christelow, *Muslim Law Courts and the French Colonial State in Algeria* (Princeton, NJ: Princeton University Press, 1985); Sarah Ghabrial, "Le 'fiqh francisé'?: Muslim Personal Status Law

Reform and Women's Litigation in Colonial Algeria (1870-1930)" (PhD diss., McGill University, 2014); Surkis, *Sex, Law, and Sovereignty*; Joshua Cole, *Lethal Provocation: The Constantine Murders and the Politics of French Algeria* (Ithaca, NY: Cornell University Press, 2019).

13. There were exceptions to this rule, in the form of smaller political newspapers that reflected new political developments, such as communist or fascist newspapers.

14. Peter Dunwoodie, *Francophone Writing in Transition: Algeria, 1900-1945* (Bern: Peter Lang, 2005).

15. Stephanie Newell, *The Power to Name: A History of Anonymity in Colonial West Africa* (Athens: Ohio University Press, 2013), 47.

16. Fanny Colonna, "Training the National Elites in Colonial Algeria, 1920-1954," *Historical Social Research* 33 (2008): 291.

17. Colonna, 189, 289.

18. Dunwoodie, *Francophone Writing in Transition*, 15.

19. This figure is for 1936. See Colonna, "Training the National Elites," 16. There are no statistics on female literacy in French, but almost all of the articles published by Muslim women in the interwar period appeared in French-language newspapers. The government likewise did not collect literacy rates for Arabic. Most Algerian men and some women would have attended Quranic schools (*kuttab*) as small children. As Arthur Asseraf has noted, "Rote learning from the Quran did not necessarily allow adult men to read a newspaper in the renewed Modern Standard Arabic" (*Electric News in Colonial Algeria*, 88).

20. Saïd Faci, *Mémoire d'un instituteur algérien d'origine indigène* (Constantine: Attali, 1931) and *L'Algérie sous l'égide de la France contre la féodalité algérienne* (Toulouse, 1936); Mohand Lechani, *Le malaise algérien* (Algiers: Pfeifer et Assant, 1939); Rabah Zenati, *Bou-el-Nou* (Algiers: La Maison des Livres, 1945).

21. Abderrahmane Bouchène, Jean-Pierre Peyroulou, Ouanassa Siari Tengour, and Sylvie Thénault, eds., *Histoire de l'Algérie à la période coloniale (1930-1962)* (Paris: La Découverte, 2012), 547-52.

22. Claire Marynower, *L'Algérie à gauche (1900-1962): Socialistes à l'époque coloniale* (Paris: Presses Universitaires de France, 2018).

23. Claire Marynower, "Réformer l'Algérie? Des militants socialistes en 'situation coloniale' dans l'entre-deux-guerres," *Histoire/Politique* 1, no. 13 (2011): 112-24.

24. Claire Marynower, "'À nos sœurs indigènes... le meilleur de notre affection': Militantes socialistes dans l'Oranie des années 1930," *Genre and Colonization* 1 (Spring 2013): 192-231.

25. Fonds Associations, Archive of the Wilaya of Algiers.

26. The numbers of such individuals were also on the rise in the interwar years because of a series of laws that marginally increased the numbers of Muslim elected officials. The Fédération des élus had over one thousand members at its inception in 1927.

27. Dunwoodie, *Francophone Writing in Transition*, 65.

28. Patrick Weil, *Qu'est-ce qu'un Français? Histoire de la nationalité française depuis la Révolution* (Paris: Éditions Grasset & Fasquelle, 2002).
29. Kamel Kateb, *Européens, "Indigènes" et Juifs en Algérie*, 194.
30. Raymond Betts, *Assimilation and Association in French Colonial Theory, 1890–1914* (Lincoln: University of Nebraska Press, 2004).
31. McDougall, *History of Algeria*, 103.
32. McDougall, 122.
33. Surkis, *Sex, Law, and Sovereignty*, 80.
34. McDougall, *History of Algeria*, 123.
35. McDougall, 130.
36. Alice Conklin, *A Mission to Civilize: The Republican Idea of Empire in France and West Africa, 1895–1930* (Stanford, CA: Stanford University Press, 1997), 159.
37. Within the écoles normales, Muslims were a small minority in the overwhelmingly European student body. Most of the contributors to *La Voix des Humbles* would have graduated from one of these schools.
38. Colonna, "Training the National Elites."
39. Memo by Governor-General William Merlaud-Ponty, Fonds École Normale de Bouzareah, Archives Nationales d'Algérie, Algiers.
40. Jonathan Gosnell, *The Politics of Frenchness in Colonial Algeria, 1930–1954* (Rochester, NY: University of Rochester Press, 2002), 48.
41. "L'Enseignement des indigènes: un interview avec M. le Recteur Hardy," *L'Echo Indigène*, July 4, 1934.
42. "Le Bolchévisme et les instituteurs indigènes," *L'Ikdam*, November 29, 1920.
43. Prochaska, *Making Algeria French*, 10.
44. Vince, *Our Fighting Sisters*.
45. Julien Fromage, "Innovation politique et mobilisation de masse en 'situation coloniale': un 'printemps algérien' des années 1930" (PhD diss., École des hautes études en sciences sociales, 2012).
46. McDougall, *History of Algeria*, 161; Courreye, *L'Algérie des Oulémas*.
47. Courreye, *L'Algérie des Oulémas*, 35, 38, 50.
48. Courreye, 67.
49. McDougall, *History of Algeria*, 43.
50. Zahir Ihaddaden, *Histoire de la presse indigène en Algérie: des origines jusqu'en 1930* (Algiers: ENAL, 2003).
51. Asseraf, *Electric News in Colonial Algeria*, 49.
52. McDougall, *History of Algeria*, 161.
53. McDougall, 161.
54. Letter from Commissaire central de la police de Constantine au préfet de Constantine, July 30, 1923, ANOM ALG GGA 15H 22, Dossiers de presse, Gouvernement général d'Algérie, Archives nationales d'outre-mer, Aix-en-Provence, France (hereafter ANOM).
55. Letter from the Prefect of Constantine to the Governor-General, September 1, 1931, ANOM ALG GGA 15H 22, Dossiers du Presse, Gouvernement général de L'Algérie, ANOM.

56. Letter from the Resident General of France in Tunisia to the Governor-General of Algeria, April 11, 1921, MN 19 2, Notes et rapports sur les relations entre les indigènes algériens et les jeunes tunisiens, Archives nationales de Tunisie, Tunis.

57. Other texts that offer more comprehensive overviews of the Muslim press are Zahir Ihaddaden, *Histoire de la presse indigène en Algérie des origines jusqu'en 1930* (Algiers: ENAL, 2003), and Dunwoodie, *Francophone Writing in Transition*.

58. Drew, *We Are No Longer in France*, 94 (quotation), 5.

59. Newell, *Power to Name*.

60. Derek Peterson, Steph Newell, and Emma Hunter, *African Print Cultures: Newspapers and Their Publics in the Twentieth Century* (Ann Arbor: University of Michigan Press, 2016).

61. Asseraf, *Electric News in Colonial Algeria*, 42.

62. Ami Ayalon, *Reading Palestine: Printing and Literacy, 1900–1948* (Austin: University of Texas Press, 2004), 103.

63. Malek Bennabi, *Mémoires d'un témoin du siècle: l'enfant, l'étudiant, l'écrivain* (Algiers: Samar, 1965), 128.

64. Asseraf, *Electric News in Colonial Algeria*, 191.

65. Ami Ayalon, *The Press in the Arab Middle East: A History* (New York: Oxford University Press, 1995), 61.

66. *al-Najah*, October 22, 1926.

67. "Déclaration," *L'Égyptienne*, February 1, 1925.

68. *Filastin*, October 1929, quoted in Ellen Fleischmann, *The Nation and Its "New" Women: The Palestinian Women's Movement, 1920–1948* (Berkeley: University of California Press, 2003), 165.

69. Fleischmann, *The Nation and Its "New" Women*, 154.

70. Muriam Haleh Davis, *Markets of Civilization: Islam and Racial Capitalism in Algeria* (Durham, NC: Duke University Press, 2022), 3.

71. Colonna, "Training the National Elites," 189.

72. Drew, *We Are No Longer in France*, 21.

73. Ethan Katz, *The Burdens of Brotherhood: Jews and Muslims from North Africa to France* (Cambridge, MA: Harvard University Press, 2015); Sophie B. Roberts, *Citizenship and Antisemitism in French Colonial Algeria, 1870–1962* (New York: Cambridge University Press, 2017).

74. McDougall, *History of Algeria*, 110.

75. Joshua Cole, *Lethal Provocation: The Constantine Murders and the Politics of French Algeria* (Ithaca, NY: Cornell University Press, 2019).

76. Ali Merad, *Le réformisme musulman en Algérie de 1925 à 1940* (Paris: Mouton, 1967), 67, 62.

77. Dahbia Lounas, interview conducted digitally by Sara Rahnama, October 31, 2021.

78. Courreye, *L'Algérie des Oulémas*, 35.

79. Hannun, "States of Change," 27.

80. Marnia Lazreg, *The Eloquence of Silence: Algerian Women in Question* (New York: Routledge, 1994), 83.

81. Julia Clancy-Smith, "The House of Zainab: Female Authority and Saintly Succession in Colonial Algeria," in *Women in Middle Eastern History: Shifting Boundaries in Sex and Gender*, ed. Nikki R. Keddie and Beth Baron (New Haven, CT: Yale University Press, 1991), 256.

82. Jomier, "Muslim Notables," 18.

83. Joshua Cole, "À chacun son public: Politique et culture dans l'Algérie des années 1930," *Sociétés et Représentations* 38 (February 2014): 21–51.

84. Mahieddine surveillance report, ANOM ALG ALGER 9H/37, Surveillance Politique, Gouvernement général de L'Algérie, ANOM.

85. Théatre populaire algerien, ANOM ALG ALGER 4I/190, Service des liaisons nord-africaines, Administration des indigènes, Préfecture d'Alger, ANOM.

86. Hadj Miliani and Samuel Sami Everett, "Marie Soussan: A Singular Trajectory," in *Jewish-Muslim Interactions: Performing Cultures between North Africa and France*, ed. Samuel Sami Everett and Rebekah Vince (Liverpool: Liverpool University Press, 2020), 82.

87. "Nouveau moyen-âge et renaissance arabe," *L'Afrique du Nord illustrée*, January 28, 1933.

88. Chris Silver, *Recording History Jews, Muslims, and Music across Twentieth-Century North Africa* (Stanford, CA: Stanford University Press, 2022), 47, 56, 59, 60 (quotation).

89. Unsigned document, February 1940, Archive of the Archdiocese of Algiers (henceforth AAA), Algiers.

90. Omar Carlier, "Messali et son look. Du 'jeune Turc' citadin au zaim rural, un corps physique et politique construit à rebours?" in *Le corps du leader: Construction et représentation dans les pays du Sud*, ed. Omar Carlier and Raphaëlle Nollez-Goldbach (Paris: Harmattan, 2008), 263-299.

91. J. L. L., "La Situation en Afrique du Nord," *L'Afrique française*, July 1936, 395.

92. "Rapport de Police Spéciale d'Alger," No. 3226, April 14, 1939, ANOM ALG ALGER 4I/67, Service des liaisons nord-africaines, Administration des indigènes, Préfecture d'Alger, ANOM.

2. Domestic Workers in a Changing City

1. Yvonne Mussot, "Enquête sur la femme musulmane," *Oran républicain*, June 12, 1937. Throughout the book I use this formulation to offer both colonial and Arabic names for cities.

2. This brief feature in *Oran républicain* is the only archival trace of Ben Drahou I was able to locate.

3. Letter from the Mayor of the Commune of Arba to the Prefect of Indigenous Affairs, July 8, 1929, ANOM ALG ALGER 2I 50, Administration des indigènes du territoire civil, communes mixtes, Administration des indigènes, Préfecture d'Alger, ANOM.

4. "Artisanat, travail de la laine, main d'œuvre féminine . . ." 1927-39, ANOM ALG ALGER 2I/50, Administration des indigènes du territoire civil, communes mixtes, Administration des indigènes, Préfecture d'Alger, ANOM.

5. *Oran républicain* featured a Muslim page on Fridays and a women's page on Saturdays. Yvonne Mussot, "Enquête sur la femme musulmane," *Oran républicain*, June 5 and 12, 1937.

6. Scholarship has paid an exciting new attention to domestic workers in the twenty-first century, including Caroline Kahlenberg, "New Arab Maids: Female Domestic Work, 'New Arab Women,' and National Memory in British Mandate Palestine," *International Journal of Middle East Studies* 52 (2020): 449-67; Attiya Ahmad, *Everyday Conversions: Islam, Domestic Work, and South Asian Migrant Women in Kuwait* (Durham, NC: Duke University Press, 2017); Sumayya Kassamali, "Migrant Worker Lifeworlds of Beirut" (PhD diss., Columbia University, 2017); Ray Jureidini, "Sexuality and the Servant: An Exploration of Arab Images of the Sexuality of Domestic Maids Living in the Household," in *Sexuality in the Arab World*, ed. S. Khalaf and J. Gagnon (London: Saqi, 2006).

7. Abdelhafidh ben El-Hachemi, "Religion Doesn't Demand That of Us," *al-Najah*, May 27, 1927.

8. Hanan Hammad, *Industrial Sexuality: Gender, Urbanization, and Social Transformation in Egypt* (Austin: University of Texas Press, 2016), 14.

9. Evans, *Algeria*, 35.

10. G. Laloë, *Enquête sur le travail des femmes indigènes à Alger* (Algiers: Typographie Adolphe Jourdan, 1910).

11. Sarah Ghabrial, "'Muslims Have No Borders, Only Horizons': A Genealogy of Border Criminality in Algeria and France, 1848-Present," in *Decolonising the Criminal Question: Colonial Legacies, Contemporary Problems*, ed. A. Aliverti, H. Carvalho, A. Chamberlen, and M. Sozzo (Oxford: Oxford University Press, 2023).

12. Kamel Kateb, *Européens, "Indigènes," et Juifs en Algérie*, 166.

13. Alternatively, these statistics can also be represented as 12.4 percent in 1926 (of a total Muslim population of 4.5 million) to 14.9 percent (of a total Muslim population of 5.5 million) in 1936. John Ruedy, *Modern Algeria* (Bloomington: Indiana University Press, 1992), 121.

14. McDougall, *History of Algeria*, 134. McDougall also maps out the effects of the overpopulation of Algerian cities in this moment, notably in makeshift shantytowns that developed on the outskirts of urban centers.

15. Kateb, *Européens, "Indigènes," et Juifs en Algérie*, 271.

16. Letourneau, "Social Change in the Muslim Cities of North Africa," 529.

17. Father Letellier, Report on the Casbah by White Fathers, December 3, 1941, 1, Archives of the Archdioses of Algiers in Algiers, Algeria.

18. Omar Carlier, "Medina and Modernity: The Emergence of Muslim Civil Society in Algiers between the Two World Wars," in Çelik et al., *Walls of Algiers*, 63.

19. Father Letellier, Report on the Casbah.

20. Mlle B, "Le travail de la femme dans l'évolution sociale de la casbah d'Alger" [Women's labor in the social evolution of the casbah of Algiers] (1946), 34, available at BNF. These were predominantly from Kabylia.

21. Laure Lefèvre, "Recherches sur la condition de la femme Kabyle" (PhD diss., Université d'Alger, 1939), 153, available at the Archives of the Wilaya of Algiers.

22. Zeynep Çelik, "A Lingering Obsession: The Houses of Algiers in French Colonial Discourse," in Çelik et al., *Walls of Algiers*, 135.

23. Rosalia Bentami, *L'Enfer de la Casbah* (Algiers: Impr. du Lycée, 1936), 69.

24. Nadia Hijab, "Women and Work in the Arab World," in *Women and Power in the Middle East*, ed. Suad Joseph and Susan Slyomovics (Philadelphia: University of Pennsylvania Press, 2001), 41-51.

25. "Artisanat, travail de la laine, main d'œuvre féminine..."

26. Clancy-Smith, "A Woman without Her Distaff," 34.

27. "Artisanat, travail de la laine, main d'œuvre féminine..."

28. Charles-Robert Ageron, *Les Algériens musulmans et la France (1871–1919)*, vol. 2 (Paris: Presses Universitaires de France, 1968), 849.

29. Marie Baroy, "Rôle du travail de la femme."

30. Lazreg, *Eloquence of Silence*, 29-35.

31. Clancy-Smith, "A Woman without Her Distaff," 27.

32. Judith E. Tucker, "The Arab Family in History: 'Otherness' and the Study of the Family," in *Arab Women: Old Boundaries, New Frontiers*, ed. Judith E. Tucker (Bloomington: Indiana University Press, 1993), 195-207.

33. My attention to these shifting constellations has benefited from the historiography on the danger associated with Black women's movement in the United States, including Hazel Carby, "Policing the Black Woman's Body in an Urban Context," *Critical Inquiry* 18, no. 4 (Summer 1992): 738-755; Tera Hunter, "The 'Color Line' Gives Way to the 'Color Wall,'" in *To 'Joy My Freedom: Southern Black Women's Lives and Labors after the Civil War* (Cambridge, MA: Harvard University Press, 1998): 98-129; and Marcia Chatelain, "'Modesty on Her Cheek': Black Girls and Great Migration Marketplaces," in *South Side Girls: Growing Up in the Great Migration* (Durham, NC: Duke University Press, 2015), 59-95, as well as the historiography of women's mobility in the Middle East, including Farzaneh Milani, *Words, not Swords: Iranian Women Writers and the Freedom of Movement* (Syracuse, NY: Syracuse University Press, 2011).

34. Maurice Borrmans, "La femme de ménage musulmane en service dans les familles européennes" (master's thesis, University of Algiers, 1955), 4.

35. "The Danger of Women," *al-Najah*, November 19, 1926.

36. Carl Nightingale, *Segregation: A Global History of Divided Cities* (Chicago: University of Chicago Press, 2012), 13, 78.

37. Baroy, "Rôle du travail de la femme."

38. "Artisanat, travail de la laine, main d'œuvre féminine..."

39. Mussot, "Enquête sur la femme musulmane," June 12, 1937.

40. Troupe théâtrale "Alif-Ba," March 3, 1941, ANOM ALG ALGER 4I/183, Service des liaisons nord-africaines, Administration des indigènes, Préfecture d'Alger, ANOM.

41. Miliani and Everett, "Marie Soussan," 90.

42. "Artisanat, travail de la laine, main d'œuvre féminine..."

43. "Artisanat, travail de la laine, main d'œuvre féminine..."

44. al-Gharbi, "La femme musulmane," *La Défense*, December 7, 1934.

45. In 1939 Mussot married Joseph Charles Enkaoua, a member of the powerful Jewish Enkaoua family of Algeria. Here she may have also been talking to her own community of Algerian Jewish women, since many Jewish Algerian women donned the haik as well. By the interwar period, most urban Jewish

women had unveiled, but rural Jewish women continued to wear the haik. Yet Mussot's columns in *Oran républicain* either focus on Muslim women as objects of study or speak to women broadly without distinction, so she likely was not speaking to Jewish women here. Hadas Hirsch, "Veiling," in *Encyclopedia of Jews in the Islamic World* (Leiden: Brill, 2010).

46. Mussot, "Enquête sur la femme musulmane," June 12, 1937.

47. "La jeune fille musulmane [The young Muslim girl]," *La Voix Indigène*, August 11, 1932.

48. Sheikh Yahya bin Muhammad al-Darraji, "Al-Mar'a al-Muslima wa-l-Hijab fi al-Shari'a al-Islamiyya [The Muslim woman and hijab in Islamic Sharia]," *al-Najah*, January 25, 1926.

49. In Victorian Britain too, Lynda Nead has shown that men conflated women in public with prostitutes in order to limit women's movement. Lynda Nead, *Victorian Babylon: People, Streets and Images in Nineteenth-Century London* (New Haven, CT: Yale University Press, 2000), 65. In her study of mobility titled *Walking the Victorian Streets*, Deborah Nord wrote, "The figure of the fallen woman—the street prostitute and ultimately the bourgeois wife with a past—served as a means of representing first the novelty and buoyancy and then the danger and inevitability of urban experience." Deborah Epstein Nord, *Walking the Victorian Streets: Women, Representation, and the City* (Ithaca, NY: Cornell University Press, 1995), 13.

50. al-Darraji, "Al-Mar'a al-Muslima."

51. Fatima Mernissi, *Beyond the Veil: Male-Female Dynamics in a Modern Muslim Society* (Bloomington: Indiana University Press, 1987), 31.

52. Abdelhafidh ben El-Hachemi, "Religion Doesn't Demand That of Us."

53. "The Danger of Women," *al-Najah*, November 19, 1926.

54. Ali ben Ahmad ben Muhammad El-Namri, "The Education of Girls and Unveiling," *al-Balagh al-Jazairi*, November 28, 1930.

55. This appeared as part of Ramadan's calls for better access to education for Muslim women, further analyzed in chapter 3. Muhammad Salih Ramadan, "Ta'lim al-mar'a" [The education of the woman], *al-Bassair*, November 19, 1937.

56. al-Namri, "Education of Girls and Unveiling."

57. Mohamed ben Mabrouk, "La femme musulmane," *L'entente franco-musulmane*, June 1, 1939.

58. Surkis, *Sex, Law, and Sovereignty*.

59. Many pamphlets were circulated by Catholic groups among settlers in Algeria that compared, for example, France's birth rate to that of other nations. These materials suggested that because of abortion, France would be weak compared to other global powers. There was a racial element to this material as well, since the fear stoked was not only that France as a nation would be surpassed but also that whiteness would be overtaken by other races. See Fonds Fonctionnement de l'assistance aux mères et nourrissons (1926–1936), DZ/AN/17E/3275, National Archives of Algeria, Algiers.

60. "The Women Thieves," *al-Najah*, September 18, 1925.

61. Brian McDonald, *Alice Diamond and the Forty Elephants: The Female Gang That Terrorised London* (London: Milo, 2015).

62. *al-Najah*, August 15, 1924, 8.

63. Omar Carlier, "Le café maure. Sociabilité masculine et effervescence citoyenne (Algérie XVIIe–XXe siècles)," *Annales Histoire, Sciences Sociales* 45, no. 4 (1990): 975–1003.

64. "Two Sayings about Women," *al-Shihab*, September 22, 1927.

65. al-Gharbi, "La femme musulmane"; Abdelhafidh ben El-Hachemi, "Religion Doesn't Demand That of Us."

66. "al-Banat al-Jahilat" [Ignorant girls], *al-Bassair*, April 29, 1938.

67. Séti B. M., "La voix d'une sœur," *La Défense*, May 4, 1934.

68. Publication of Alliance Nationale contre la Dépopulation, box ASP/60/2112, Direction de l'Intérieur et des Beaux-Arts, Gouvernement d'Algérie, AN Algeria.

69. *al-Najah*, May 16, 1928.

70. Judith Walkowitz, *City of Dreadful Delight: Narratives of Sexual Danger in Late-Victorian London* (Chicago: University of Chicago Press, 1992), 125.

71. Fatma Zohra Benaik, interviewed virtually by Sara Rahnama, March 4, 2019.

72. Dahbia Lounas, interviewed virtually by Sara Rahnama, October 31, 2021.

73. While the Qur'an mandated that Muslims leave a portion of their inheritance to daughters (albeit half of that allotted to male heirs, as given in Surah 4:11), Kabyle tribal agreement in place since 1748 disinherited women entirely. Ali Hacène, a judicial interpreter within the French colonial courts, wrote that the inferiority of women broadly in Kabylia could be traced back to the single issue of their disinheritance. He wrote that most of the Kabyle population was against women's disinheritance but were bound to the custom, although some went around it by giving money to their daughters before their death. Others reported that even non-Kabyle Algerians had begun this practice of disinheriting their daughters. Ali Hacène, "La femme kabyle: son rôle social en Kabylie, ce qu'il est et ce qu'il doit être," *L'Écho Indigène*, September 12, 1934.

74. Etty Terem, *Old Texts, New Practices: Islamic Reform in Modern Morocco* (Stanford, CA: Stanford University Press, 2014), 136.

75. "The Desirable Goal," *al-Najah*, December 15, 1926.

76. "Ouargla," *al-Najah*, February 24, 1928.

77. Vince, *Our Fighting Sisters*, chapter 1.

78. Caroline de la Brac Perrière, *Derrière les héros: les employées de maison musulmanes en service chez les Européens à Alger pendant la guerre d'Algérie, 1954–1962* (Paris: Harmattan, 1987), 54.

79. Alys Eve Weinbaum, Lynn M. Thomas, Priti Ramamurthy, Uta G. Poiger, and Madeleine Yue Dong, eds., *The Modern Girl around the World: Consumption, Modernity, and Globalization* (Durham, NC: Duke University Press, 2008).

80. The anxiety around modernity producing sexually unrestrained women is not restricted to colonial Algeria. As Durba Mitra has analyzed, such anxieties were formative in colonial India as well. Durba Mitra, *Indian Sex Life: Sexuality and the Colonial Origins of Modern Social Thought* (Princeton, NJ: Princeton University Press, 2020).

3. The Educated Muslim Woman and Algeria's Path to Progress

1. "Ta'lim al-Banat Fard" [Education for girls is an obligation.], *La Lutte Sociale*, July 13, 1937.

2. Jomier, "Muslim Notables," 8.

3. "Taʻlim al-Banat wa-l-Sufur" [The education of girls and unveiling], *al-Balagh al-Jazairi*, November 28, 1930, 1.

4. Shenila Khoja-Moolji, *Forging the Ideal Educated Girl: The Production of Desirable Subjects in Muslim South Asia* (Oakland: University of California Press, 2018), 4.

5. Mathéa Gaudry, "L'Instruction de la femme indigène," *L'Afrique française: bulletin mensuel du Comité de l'Afrique française et du Comité du Maroc*, December 1935.

6. Charles-Robert Ageron, *Modern Algeria: A History from 1830* (Trenton, NJ: Africa World Press, 1992), 71.

7. McDougall, *History of Algeria*, 146.

8. Fleischmann, "Other 'Awakening,'" 106.

9. Kateb, *Européens, "Indigènes" et Juifs en Algérie*, 255, 256.

10. Gaudry, "L'Instruction de la femme indigène."

11. This technical training, however, enabled massive waves of migration of Muslim men to France between the 1920s and the early 1950s. Eric Deroo, *Colonial Culture in France since the Revolution* (Bloomington: Indiana University Press, 2014), 372–79.

12. Maurice Viollette, *L'Algérie vivra-t-elle?: Notes d'un ancien gouverneur général* (Paris: Félix Alcan, 1931), 211.

13. Quoted in Gaudry, "L'Instruction de la femme indigène."

14. Alongside training schools for girls existed similar workshops for older women. The city of Bousaada, for example, had two of these workshop schools for women. One was attached to and administrated by the school for Muslim boys, while the other was a professional education center for working with wool specifically run directly by local administrators. 26–27 Alg ALGER 2I 50, Administration des indigènes du territoire civil, communes mixtes, Administration des indigènes, Préfecture d'Alger, ANOM.

15. Letter from the Commissary of Police of the City of Oran (M. le Blanc) to the Prefect of Indigenous Affairs, August 26, 1935, Archives of the Wilaya of Oran, Algeria.

16. A. Léon, *Colonisation, enseignement et éducation: étude historique et comparative* (Paris: Éditions L'Harmattan, 1991).

17. Julia Clancy-Smith, *Rebel and Saint: Muslim Notables, Populist Protest, Colonial Encounters* (Algeria and Tunisia, 1800–1904) (Berkeley: University of California Press, 1997), 34.

18. "Nasa'ih Islahiyya Hariyya bi-l-Iʻtibar hawla Mashruʻat Sumuw al-Wali al-ʻAm li-Tahsin Halat al-Ahali al-Muslimin" [Reforming advice worth considering about the projects of Violette to ameliorate the situation of Muslim inhabitants], *al-Najah*, December 22, 1925.

19. "al-Taʻlim al-Sinaʻi - Taraqqihi fi al-Umam al-Ukhra - Taʻlim al-Banat" [Vocational training - It's development in other nations - The education of girls], *al-Najah*, November 23, 1923.

20. "Hawla Ihdath Kulliya Kubra li-Taʻlim al-Sana'iʻ al-Nisa'iyya" [About the establishment of a great college for feminine vocational training], *al-Shihab*, January 21, 1926.

21. "Artisanat, travail de la laine, main d'œuvre féminine . . ." 1927–1939, ANOM ALG ALGER 2I/50, Administration des indigènes du territoire civil, communes mixtes, Administration des indigènes, Préfecture d'Alger, ANOM.

22. Nadia Mamelouk, "Anxiety in the Border Zone: Transgressing Boundaries in *Leïla: revue illustrée de la femme* (Tunis, 1936–1940) and in *Leïla: Hebdomadaire Tunisien Indépendant* (Tunis, 1940–1941)" (PhD diss., University of Virginia, 2008), 119.

23. Jaouida Chaouch Sellami, "Fondation: Contexte socio-politique, national et international," in *Dar el Bacha: Reflet d'un siècle, 1900–2000* (Tunis: Éditions Caractères, 2000), 17–41.

24. "Des écoles pour nos filles," *La Voix des Humbles*, November 1925, 20–25.

25. Mohand Lechani, "La famille indigène en Algérie," *La Voix des Humbles*, May 1931, 10–15.

26. *al-Najah*, October 4, 1929.

27. *La Voix des Humbles*, December 1934.

28. Houria Ameur, "La femme musulmane dans l'Afrique du Nord," *La Voix Indigène*, July 18, 1929.

29. "Admission de jeunes Musulmanes," Letter from the Sous-Prefect of Philippeville to the Prefect of Indigenous Affaires in Constantine, August 22, 1939, SDR 58, Fonds Service des Reforms, Archive of the Wilaya of Constantine, Algeria.

30. Charlotte Courreye, "L'Association des Oulémas Musulmans Algériens et la construction de l'État algérien indépendant: fondation, héritages, appropriations et antagonismes (1931-1991)" (PhD diss., Université Sorbonne, 2016), 363.

31. Courreye, "L'Association des Oulémas Musulmans Algériens et la construction de l'État algérien indépendant," 362.

32. Merad, *Le réformisme musulman en Algérie de 1925 à 1940* (Paris: Mouton, 1967), 327.

33. "Des écoles pour nos filles."

34. Ali Merad, *Ibn Bâdîs: Commentateur du Coran* (Paris: Paul Guethner, 1971), 238.

35. Ben Badis, *al-Shihab*, April 1939, 112, quoted in Merad, *Le réformisme musulman en Algérie*, 330.

36. Omnia Shakry, "Schooled Mothers and Structured Play: Child Rearing in Turn-of-the-Century Egypt," in *Remaking Women*, ed. Lila Abu-Lughod (Princeton, NJ: Princeton University Press, 1998), 150.

37. Nova Robinson, *Truly Sisters: Arab Women and International Women's Rights* (forthcoming), 132, 136, 109.

38. "La femme musulmane: lettre ouverte aux dames françaises du Congrès de Constantine," *La Voix Indigène*, March 10, 1932.

39. Seghir Hacène, "Le Congrès de Constantine," *La Voix Indigène*, April 7, 1932.

40. Hamed Largueche, "La femme musulmane," *La Voix Indigène*, May 5 1932, 2.

41. Hacène's response is reprinted in Surkis, *Sex, Law, and Sovereignty in French Algeria*, 291.

42. Nadia Mamelouk, "*Leïla*: 1936–1941 bien plus qu'une revue féminine," in *Leïla: Revue illustrée de la femme, 1936–1941*, ed. Hafedh Boujmil (Tunis: Éditions Nirvana, 2007), 12, 15.

43. Colonel Chérif Cadi, "Pour la femme musulmane," *La Voix Indigène*, May 19, 1932.

44. Colonel Cadi, *La Voix Indigène*, July 8, 1929.

45. Faissal Abualhassan, "Generating Frenchness: Tensions of Race and Civilization in Chérif Cadi's *Terre d'Islam* (1925)," Johns Hopkins African History Seminar, 2019, 9.

46. Abou-Ezzohra, "En instruisant nos filles nous deviendrons meilleurs, extrait d'un discours prononcé à l'occasion d'un mariage," *La Voix Indigène*, July 12, 1934.

47. Mohamed Saleh Ramdane, "Ta'lim al-Mar'a" [The education of women], *al-Bassair*, November 19, 1937.

48. The era in which the Muslims of Algeria "led" "the caravan of life" alluded to earlier periods of Islamic history, perhaps referring to the Islamic Golden Age during the Abbasid caliphate.

49. Muhammad bin Ahmad al Mansur, "Al-Mar'a al-Djaza'iriyya al-Haditha wa-l-Kitaba fi al-Suhuf" [The modern Algerian woman and writing in newspapers], *al-Bassair*, November 11, 1938.

50. "La renaissance de la femme irakienne," originally printed in *La Voix des Humbles* and later reprinted in the reformist *La Défense*, April 13, 1934; "The Modern Eastern Uprising in the Country of Afghanistan," *al-Shihab*, November 24, 1927.

51. Séti BM, "La voix d'une sœur," *La Défense*, May 4, 1934.

52. Séti BM, "La voix d'une sœur."

53. Kamel Kateb, *École, population et société en Algérie* (Paris: L'Harmattan, 2005), 45.

54. Courreye, "L'Association des Oulémas Musulmans Algériens et la construction de l'État algérien indépendant," 94, 95, 96, 362.

55. "al-Tabarru'at li-Tashyid Jami' Mila al-Hurr wa-Madrasatiha al-Hurra," *al-Bassair*, August 20, 1937.

56. "Siham fi Qulub al-Hasidin" [Arrows in the hearts of the envious], *al-Bassair*, May 3, 1938.

57. "La fête de la Kheira," ANOM ALG ALGER 4I/183, Service des liaisons nord-africaines, Administration des indigènes, Préfecture d'Alger, ANOM.

58. al-Mansur, "al-Mar'a al-Jaza'iriyya."

59. Al Kinti, ["The modern eastern uprising in the country of Afghanistan,"] *al-Shihab*, November 24, 1927.

60. Mohamed Hamed Filaji, "La femme musulmane," *La Défense*, November 2, 1934; "The Situation of Muslims in Russia: A Conversation with the Delegate in the Conference of Mecca," *al-Shihab*, July 15, 1926.

61. "Ruqi al-'Alam al-Islami bi-Ta'lim al-Mar'a" [The Rise of the Muslim world by Women's Education], *al-Najah*, October 5, 1927.

62. Bouchène et al., *Histoire de l'Algérie à la période coloniale*.

63. "Talaq Mustafa Kemal Atatürk" [The divorce of Mustafa Kemal Atatürk], *al-Shihab*, November 26, 1925.

64. *L'Ikdam*, November 10, 1922, quoted in Asseraf, *Electric News in Colonial Algeria*, 138.

65. Abdelhafidh ben El-Hachemi, "Fi Bahr al-Siyasa: al-Hadith 'an Turkia wa-Mustaqbaliha al-Muzdahir" [In the Sea of Politics: A Talk about Turkey and Her Flourishing Future], *al-Najah*, October 19, 1923.

66. "al-Imtiyazat al-Ajnabiyya bi-Faris" [Special treatment of foreigners in Persia], *al-Najah*, May 20, 1928.

67. *El Ouma*, December 10, 1938, quoted in Asseraf, *Electric News in Colonial Algeria*, 139.

68. Malek Bennabi, *Islam in History and Society*, trans. Asma Rashid (Islamabad: Islamic Research Institute, 1988), 4.

69. Asseraf, *Electric News in Colonial Algeria*, 127–29.

70. Such articles included but were not limited to El-Hachemi, "Fi Bahr al-Siyasa: al-Hadith 'an Turkia" [In the Sea of Politics: A Talk about Turkey], *al-Najah*, August 15, 1924; "Feminine Politics in Turkey," *al-Najah*, March 6, 1925; "About the Feminist Movement in Turkey," *al-Najah*, May 8, 1927; Benriba, "Féminisme et instruction (Turquie et Algérie)," *La Voix des Humbles*, October 1930; Jean Melia, "Le Réveil de'l'Islam Algérien," *La Voix Indigène*, May 24, 1934.

71. Such articles included but were not limited to "Rawdat al-Adab: al-Mar'a al-'Iraqiyya" [The Garden of Education: the Iraqi woman], *al-Shihab*, May 20, 1926; "The Industrial Education of Women: Its Advancements in Other Nations, and the Education of Girls," *al-Najah*, November 23, 1923; *al-Najah*, October 2, 1927; "The Modern Eastern Uprising in the Country of Afghanistan," *al-Shihab*, November 24, 1927; *al-Najah*, September 16, 1931; Filaji, "La femme musulmane"; Sarah Graham-Brown, "Women's Activism in the Middle East: A Historical Perspective," in Joseph and Slyomovics, *Women and Power in the Middle East*, 23–33.

72. Salah Labdi, "La femme musulmane," *La Défense*, November 9, 1934.

73. El-Hachemi, "Fi Bahr al-Siyasa: al-Hadith 'an Turkia."

74. Benriba, "Féminisme et instruction."

75. "La Renaissance de la femme irakienne," *La Défense*, April 13, 1934.

76. "Opinion of the Muslim World on the Education of Women."

77. Lechani, "La Famille indigène en Algérie," 14; Abou-Ezzohra, "En instruisant nos filles nous deviendrons meilleurs," 2.

78. Abou-Ezzohra, "En instruisant nos filles nous deviendrons meilleurs," 2.

79. al Mansur, "al-Mar'a al-Djaza'iriyya."

80. "Al-taalim al-sanaaii trquya."

81. Faris Haddad, "Ta'thir al-Mar'a fi al-Hayat al-Ijtima'iyya" [The influence of women on the social body], *al-Shihab*, December 6, 1926; Abderrahman Yalaoui, "Du mariage à la polygamie," *La Voix Indigène*, January 21, 1932; Séti B., "La voix d'une sœur," *La Défense*, May 4 and 25, 1934; Abou-Ezzohra, "En instruisant nos filles nous deviendrons meilleurs," 2; "Les Jeunes Algériens pour l'émancipation de la femme musulmane," *La Défense*, July 19, 1939.

82. "al-Mujaddidun," *al-Balagh al-Djaziri*, April 10, 1931.

83. François Psalty, "L'Émancipation de la femme turque," *L'Écho de la presse musulmane* (originally *Annales de Turquie*), January 24, 1936.

84. Abou-Ezzohra, "En instruisant nos filles nous deviendrons meilleurs," 2.

85. Benriba, "Féminisme et instruction."
86. "Échos d'Orient," *L'Égyptienne*, May 1938, 38.
87. Hannun, "States of Change," 198.
88. Mohammad Lamine Lamoudi, "Al-Mar'a al-Jaza'iriyya al-Algerianah" [The Muslim Algerian woman], *al Islah*, November 28, 1929.
89. Ahmed Smaili, "Chez les peuples: Égypte: Islam et le féminisme," *La Lutte Sociale*, November 21, 1936.
90. McDougall, *History of Algeria*, 152.
91. Kateb, *Ecole, population et société en Algérie*, 43.
92. Muhammad al-Bashir al-Ibrahimi, "Al-taqrir al-adabi" [Literary report], *al-Bassair*, October 15, 1951.
93. Courreye, "L'Association des Oulémas Musulmans Algériens et la construction de l'État algérien indépendant," 366-71, photograph on 370.
94. Zuhur Wunisi, 'Abra al-zuhūr wa-l-aswāk, 131-32, quoted in Courreye, "L'Association des Oulémas Musulmans Algériens et la construction de l'État algérien indépendant," 161.
95. Sophia Mo, "Reading Motherhood at the Margins of Algerian Feminist Retellings of Resistance" (paper presented at the annual meeting of the Middle East Studies Association, Denver, Colorado, December 3, 2022).
96. Zuhur Wunisi, "al-Mar'a al-Muslima wa-l-Haraka al-Kashfiyya" [The Muslim woman and the Scout Movement], *al-Hayat* 4 (October/November 1955): 7-8.
97. Merad, *Ibn Bâdîs*, 216.

4. The Haik, the Hat, and the Gendered Politics of the New Public

1. "Turid al-Hadara?" [You want civilization?], *al-Najah*, March 13, 1927.
2. I use "hat" in this chapter as a translation of the Arabic native category *qubba'a*, which means simply "hat," as opposed to the other forms of men's headwear that could also be referred to as hats.
3. The corpus of materials that Algerian thinkers envisioned as part of sharia included the Quran, hadith, and Sunna (prophetic sayings) texts.
4. Thomas Wide, "Astrakhan, Borqa', Chadari, Dreshi: The Economy of Dress in Early-Twentieth-Century Afghanistan," in *Anti-Veiling Campaigns in the Muslim World: Gender, Modernism and the Politics of Dress*, ed. Stephanie Cronin (New York: Routledge, 2014), 165-203; Marie Grace Brown, *Khartoum at Night: Fashion and Body Politics in Imperial Sudan* (Stanford, CA: Stanford University Press, 2017); Reina Lewis, *Muslim Fashion: Contemporary Style Cultures* (Durham, NC: Duke University Press, 2015); Saba Mahmood, *The Politics of Piety: The Islamic Revival and the Feminist Subject* (Princeton, NJ: Princeton University Press, 2005).
5. While these actors never explicitly defined modernity, they tended to describe it in terms of modernization, technology, urbanization, and an expansion of resources.
6. Vince, *Our Fighting Sisters*, 140-79; Douglas Northrop, *Veiled Empire: Gender and Power in Stalinist Central Asia* (Ithaca, NY: Cornell University Press,

2016); Mayanthi Fernando, *The Republic Unsettled: Muslim French and the Contradictions of Secularism* (Durham, NC: Duke University Press, 2014); Neil MacMaster, *Burning the Veil: The Algerian War and the Emancipation of Muslim Women* (New York: Manchester University Press, 2009); Joan Wallach Scott, *The Politics of the Veil* (Princeton, NJ: Princeton University Press, 2007); John Bowen, *Why the French Don't Like Headscarves: Islam, the State, and Public Space* (Princeton, NJ: Princeton University Press, 2007); Ryme Seferdjeli, "'Fight with Us, Women, and We Will Emancipate You': France, the FLN and the Struggle over Women during the Algerian War of National Liberation" (PhD diss., London School of Economics, 2005); Beth Baron, *Egypt as a Woman: Nationalism, Gender, and Politics* (Los Angeles: University of California Press, 2005); Mahmood, *Politics of Piety*; Winifred Woodhull, "Unveiling Algeria," *Genders* 10 (Spring 1991): 112-31; Assia Djebar, *Femmes d'Alger dans leur appartement* (Paris: Des Femmes, 1980).

7. On the broader historiography on men's dress and comportment, see Hoda Elsadda, "The New Man," in *Gender, Nation, and the Arabic Novel in Egypt, 1892-2008* (Syracuse, NY: Syracuse University Press, 2012): 38-58; Hanan Kholoussy, "The Grooming of Men," in *For Better, for Worse: The Marriage Crisis That Made Modern Egypt* (Stanford, CA: Stanford University Press, 2010), 23-48; Omar Carlier, "Messali et son look. Du 'jeune Turc' citadin au za'im rural, un corps physique et politique construit à rebours?" in *Le corps du leader: Construction et représentation dans les pays du Sud*, ed. Omar Carlier and Raphaëlle Nollez-Goldbach (Paris: Harmattan, 2008), 263-99; Deniz Kandiyoti, "Gendering the Modern: On Missing Dimensions in the Study of Turkish Modernity" and Resat Kasaba, "Kemalist Certainties and Modern Ambiguities," in *Rethinking Modernity and National Identity in Turkey*, edited by Bozdogan, Sibel and Resat Kasaba (Seattle: University of Washington Press, 1997).

8. The late Saba Mahmood's *Politics of Piety* challenged this insistence on hijab as stagnant symbol of religion. She demonstrated how for the Egyptian women's mosque movement, the hijab represented an evolving relationship between self and piety. See also Nilüfer Göle, who further deconstructed the idea of the hijab's particularism by arguing that secular and religious individuals alike engage in self-fashioning in ways that reflect a particular relationship to modernity and politics. Nilüfer Göle, "Manifestations of the Religious-Secular Divide: Self-State and the Public Sphere," in *Comparative Secularisms in a Global Age*, ed. Linell E. Cady and Elizabeth Shakman Hurd (New York: Palgrave Macmillan, 2010), 48.

9. Hannun, "States of Change," 2.

10. *al-Najah*, February 5, 1928.

11. Wilson Chacko Jacob, *Working Out Egypt: Effendi Masculinity and Subject Formation in Colonial Modernity, 1870-1940* (Durham, NC: Duke University Press, 2011), 199.

12. Haj, *Reconfiguring Islamic Tradition*, 148.

13. Jacob, *Working Out Egypt*, 207, 222.

14. Terem, *Old Texts, New Practices*, 14, 18.

15. Yasmine Nachabe, "Marie al-Khazen's Photographs of the 1920s and 1930s" (PhD diss., McGill University, 2011), 122.

16. Jacob, *Working Out Egypt*, 189.
17. Katherine Ann Wiley, "The Materiality and Social Agency of the Malahfa (Mauritanian Veil)," *African Studies Review* 62, no. 2 (2019): 149–74.
18. Dahbia Lounas, interviewed virtually by Sara Rahnama, October 31, 2021.
19. Assia Djebar's 1985 novel, *L'Amour, la fantasia*, offers a fictional exploration of this relationship between political conquest and the violent exploitation of female bodies. Assia Djebar, *L'Amour, la fantasia* (Paris: J. C. Lattès, 1985).
20. Aurelie Perrier, "Intimate Matters: Negotiating Sex, Gender and the Home in Colonial Algeria, 1830–1914" (PhD diss., Georgetown University, 2014).
21. Lazreg, *Eloquence of Silence*, 53.
22. Edward McAllister, "Yesterday's Tomorrow Is Not Today: Memory and Place in an Algiers Neighbourhood" (PhD diss., University of Oxford, 2015).
23. Christopher Breward, *Fashioning London: Clothing and the Modern Metropolis* (London: Berg, 2004).
24. Weinbaum et al., *Modern Girl around the World*.
25. Pessah Shinar, *Modern Islam in the Maghrib* (Jerusalem: Hebrew University of Jerusalem, 2004), 270.
26. Various payment receipts, IBA ASP 2 103, Fonds Beaux Arts, National Archives of Algeria, Algiers (hereafter AN).
27. Kamel Chachoua, *L'Islam kabyle: religion, état et société en Algérie* (Paris: Maisonneuve & Larose, 2001), 194.
28. Chachoua, 195.
29. Sheikh Abu Ya'la al-Zawawi, "al-Mar'a al-Turkiyya wa-l-Hijab" [The Turkish woman and the hijab], *al-Najah*, December 29, 1925.
30. *al-Bassair*, January 29, February 5, March 5, March 12, March 19, April 2, April 9, 1937.
31. Mustafa Ibn Hallush, "Hawla 'Adat al-Hijab," *al-Bassair*, April 2, 1937.
32. Mustafa Ibn Hallush, "Hijab al-Mar'a 'Ada la Din" *al-Bassair*, January 29, 1937.
33. Hamza Bukusha, "Hijab al-Mar'a Dīn wa-l-Mubalagha fihi 'Ada Sharifa fi al-Islam wa-qablahu," *al-Bassair*, March 5, 1937.
34. "Huquq al-Zawjayn" [The rights of the married couple], *al-Balagh al-Jazairi*, March 11, 1932, 1.
35. Mustafa Ibn Hallush, "Hawla 'Adat al-Hijab," *al-Bassair*, March 26, 1937.
36. Djamila Debèche, "L'Islam ne prescrit pas le port du voile à la femme musulmane," *La Justice*, February 20, 1937.
37. Beth Baron, *The Women's Awakening in Egypt: Culture, Society, and the Press* (New Haven, CT: Yale University Press, 1994).
38. Taciturne, "Le voile," *La Voix des Humbles*, November 1926, 16.
39. Omnia El Shakry, "Schooled Mothers and Structured Play: Child Rearing in Turn-of-the-Century Egypt," in Abu-Lughod, *Remaking Women*, 150.
40. Mohammed Benhoura, untitled editor's note, *La Justice*, February 20, 1937.

41. al-Zawawii, "Hawla Hijab al-Mar'a," *al-Bassair*, March 19, 1937.
42. Sheikh Abu Ya'la al-Zawawi, "al-Mar'a al-Turkiyya wa-l-Hijab," *al-Najah*, January 19, 1926.
43. "Al-Sufur wa-l-Tahdhir," *al-Shihab*, date unknown.
44. Shaykh Yahya Bin Muhammad al-Darraji, "al-Mar'a al-Jaza'iriyya wa-l-Hijab fi al-Shari'a al-Islamiyya" [The Muslim woman and hijab in Islamic Sharia], *al-Najah*, January 25, 1926.
45. al-Zawawii, "al-Mar'a al-Turkiyya wa-l-Hijab."
46. Debèche, "L'Islam ne prescrit pas le port du voile."
47. Debèche.
48. Baron, *Women's Awakening in Egypt*, 49.
49. Carlier, "Messali et son look," 278, 282–83.
50. Clancy-Smith, "A Woman without Her Distaff," 29.
51. Carlier, "Messali et son look," 282, 283.
52. Colonna, *Instituteurs algériens, 1883–1939* (Algiers: 1975), 16.
53. Tina Mai Chen, "Dressing for the Party: Clothing, Citizenship, and Gender-formation in Mao's China," *Fashion Theory* 5, no. 2 (2001): 143–71.
54. Jeremy Rich, "Civilized Attire: Refashioning Tastes and Social Status in the Gabon Estuary, 1870–1914," *Cultural and Social History* 2 (2005): 189–213.
55. Kathy Piess, *Cheap Amusements: Leisure in Turn-of-the-Century New York* (Philadelphia: Temple University Press, 1986), 63.
56. Jeremy Rich, "Gabonese Men for French Decency: The Rise and Fall of the Gabonese Chapter of the Ligue des Droits de l'Homme, 1916–1939," *French Colonial History* 13 (2012): 23–53.
57. Mary Louise Roberts, *Civilization without Sexes: Reconstructing Gender in Postwar France, 1917–1927* (Chicago: University of Chicago Press, 1994).
58. "Mustafa Kamal wa-l-Qubba'a," *al-Najah*, December 25, 1925.
59. Brown, *Khartoum at Night*, 31, 164–65.
60. *al-Najah*, July 29, 1927.
61. "Shabab al-Yawm wa-l-Din" [The youth of today and religion], *al-Balagh al-Jazairi*, February 19, 1932.
62. "Qubba'a," *al-Shihab*, July 22, 1926.
63. Shakib Arslan, "Jam'iyyat Talabat Shimal Ifriqiya" [The Association of North African students], *al-Shihab*, April 1937.
64. Jacob, *Working Out Egypt*, 210.
65. "Qubba'a."
66. "Labs al-Qubba'a," "Turid al-Hadara," *al-Najah*, March 13, 1927.
67. "Sahifat al-Najah," *al-Balagh al-Jazairi*, October 17, 1930.
68. "Labs al-Qubba'a."
69. "al-'Ulama' wa-l-Qubba'a" [The ulama and the hat], *al-Najah*, February 10, 1928.
70. "Labs al-Qubba'a" [Wearing the hat], *al-Shihab*, July 19, 1926.
71. "al-Taqlid al-a'ma fi Ism al-Hadarah" [Blind copying in the name of civilization], *al-Bassair*, October 23, 1935.
72. "Libs al-Qubba'a" [Wearing the hat], *al-Shihab*, July 15, 1926.
73. James McDougall, *History and the Culture of Nationalism in Algeria*.

74. Rashid, "al-Tarbush wa-l-'Amama" [The tarbush and the '*amama*], *al-Najah*, September 25, 1925.
75. Jacob, *Working Out Egypt*, 224.
76. Rashid, "al-Tarbush wa-l-'Amama."
77. "Libs al-qubba'a," *al-Shihab*, July 19, 1926.
78. Arslan, "Jam'iyyat Talabat Shimal Ifriqiya."
79. "Ra'iy hawla al-Tarbush," *al-Shihab*, April 29, 1926.
80. Salah al-Abdi, "Taqlid al-Taqlid," *al-Bassair*, October 30, 1936.

81. Emna Ben Miled has analyzed how veiling similarly emerged in the Mediterranean region as a cultural practice, unattached to any religion. Emna Ben Miled, *Les Tunisiennes ont-elles une histoire?* (Tunis: Les Presses de l'Imprimerie Simpact, 1998).

82. Laura Bier, "Feminism, Solidarity, and Identity in the Age of Bandung: Third World Women in the Egyptian Women's Press," in *Making a World after Empire: The Bandung Moment and Its Political Afterlives*, ed. Christopher Lee (Athens: Ohio University Press, 2010), 143-72; Mounira Charrad, "From Nationalism to Feminism: Family Law in Tunisia," in *Family in the Middle East: Ideational Change in Egypt, Iran, and Tunisia*, ed. Kathryn Yount and Hoda Rashad (New York: Routledge, 2008), 111-36; Anupama Roy, *Gendered Citizenship: Historical and Conceptual Explorations* (Hyderabad: Orient Longman, 2005); Jane Freedman and Carrie Tarr, *Women, Immigration and Identities in France* (London: Bloomsbury Academic, 2000); Partha Chatterjee, *The Nation and Its Fragments: Colonial and Postcolonial Histories* (Princeton, NJ: Princeton University Press, 1993); Chandra Mohanty, "Under Western Eyes: Feminist Scholarship and Colonial Discourses," *Feminist Review* 30 (1988): 61-88.

83. Djamila Debèche, "La femme musulmane dans la société," *Terres d'Afrique*, 1946.

5. French Feminists and the New Imperial Feminism

1. al-Gharbi, "La femme musulmane," *La Défense*, December 7, 1934.
2. Marie Bugéja, "La femme musulmane," *La Défense*, December 14, 1934.
3. Margaret Cook Andersen, *Regeneration through Empire: French Pronatalists and Colonial Settlement in the Third Republic* (Lincoln: University of Nebraska Press, 2015); Jennifer Boittin, "Feminist Mediations of the Exotic: French Algeria, Morocco, and Tunisia, 1921-1939," *Gender and History* 22, no. 1 (April 2010): 131-50; Sara L. Kimble, "Emancipation through Secularization: French Feminist Views of Muslim Women's Condition in Interwar Algeria," *French Colonial History* 7 (2006): 109-28.

4. Mrinalini Sinha has noted, "The further point of bringing British and Indian feminisms into the same field of analysis, however, is to demonstrate their co-implication in the history of the combined but uneven evolution of a system whose economic, political, and ideological reach was worldwide." Mrinalini Sinha, "Mapping the Imperial Social Formation: A Modest Proposal for Feminist History," *Signs* 25, no. 4 (Summer 2000): 1077-82.

5. C. Senieh, "Le Prophète a-t-il voulu l'asservissement de la femme musulmane?" *La Française*, March 19, 1932; "Le salut de femmes turques," *La Française*,

April 15, 1933; "Chez les féministes de l'Europe Orientale," *La Française*, September 30, 1933; Cécile Brunschvicg, "Les progrès du féminisme en Turquie," *La Française*, November 8, 1933; "À propos des étudiantes turques," *La Française*, November 24, 1934; "Femmes turques d'aujourd'hui" and Andrée Barras, "La femme turque émancipée," *La Française*, April 13, 1935; "La Turquie d'Atatürk," *La Française*, March 22, 1936.

6. Elsa Mornay, "La femme, l'Islam, et les derniers harems," *Minerva*, April 28, 1934.

7. Germaine Malaterre-Sellier, "La libération des femmes musulmanes," *La Française*, April 15, 1933 (later reprinted in *La Voix des Humbles*, July 1933).

8. Robinson, *Truly Sisters*, 2.

9. Robinson, *Truly Sisters*, chapter 3; Charlotte Weber, "Unveiling Scheherazade: Feminist Orientalism in the International Alliance of Women, 1911–1950," *Feminist Studies* 27, no. 1 (2001): 150; Fleischmann, *The Nation and Its "New" Women*; Badran, *Feminists, Islam, and Nation: Gender and the Making of Modern Egypt* (Princeton, NJ: Princeton University Press, 1996), 232–36.

10. "Une Française fait depuis quatre ans partie de la délégation française à la Société des Nations," *La Française*, April 12, 1937.

11. G. Buzenet, "Les journées féministes du Maroc," *La Française*, April 14, 1934.

12. Abou-Ezzohra, "Instruisons nos filles ... et nous deviendrons meilleurs: extrait d'un discours prononcé en Algérie à l'occasion d'un mariage musulman" [Educate our daughters ... and we become better: Excerpt from a speech given in Algeria on the occasion of a Muslim wedding], *La Française*, November 24, 1934.

13. "Le Congrès d'Istamboul: L'Orient et l'Occident coopèrent," *La Française*, June 8, 1935.

14. Boittin, "Feminist Mediations of the Exotic."

15. Germaine Malaterre-Sellier, "En Tunisie," *La Française*, May 21, 1932.

16. "Le Congrès d'Istamboul."

17. Jane Bagnault, "Les femmes françaises et le problème musulman," *La Française*, February 15, 1936.

18. "L'Enseignement des Indigènes: Entretien avec M. le Recteur Hardy," *L'Écho Indigène*, July 4, 1934.

19. Clancy-Smith, "A Woman without Her Distaff," 34.

20. "*Femmes de Demain* vous présente quelques-unes de ses collaboratrices habituelles" [*Femmes de Demain* presents to you some of its regular contributors], *Femmes de Demain*, November 14, 1935.

21. Vonnick, "Fête de bienfaisance à Constantine" [Celebration of Charity in Constantine], *Femmes de Demain*, May 15, 1936.

22. Vonnick, "Chez les petites Musulmanes" [At the Home with the Little Muslim Girls], *Femmes de Demain*, March 15, 1936.

23. A. Lafuente, "L'Aiguille musulmane: lettre ouverte à Mme Malaterre-Sellier," *La Française*, April 15, 1933; Ghabrial, "Le 'fiqh francisé'?"; Rachid, "Une grande Française Madame Aurelie Tidjani," *L'Écho Indigène*, January 10, 1934. For more on Aurélie Picard, see Ursula Kingsmill Hart, *Two Ladies of Algerie: The Lives of Aurelie Picard and Isabelle Eberhardt* (Athens: Ohio University Center for International Studies, 1987).

24. Letter from Jeanne Bottini-Honot to Joseph Brenier, April 23, 1939, 20140057/20/365, La Ligue de l'Enseignement, Archives Nationales de France, Pierrefitte-sur-Seine, France.

25. "Une Conférence de Mme Bottini," *La Défense*, January 25, 1935.

26. Letter from Jeanne Bottini-Honot to Joseph Brenier, April 23, 1939.

27. Sakina Messaadi, *Nos Sœurs Musulmanes, ou, Le mythe féministe, civilisateur, évangélisateur du messianisme colonialiste dans l'Algérie colonisée* (Houma, 2001), 40.

28. "Une conférence de Mme Bottini."

29. "Une lettre de femme indigène," *La Française*, February 28, 1931.

30. Peter Knauss, *The Persistence of Patriarchy: Class, Gender, and Ideology in Twentieth-Century Algeria* (New York: Praeger, 1987), 56.

31. Rosalia Bentami, *L'Enfer de la Casbah*, 15.

32. Bentami, 15.

33. Lucienne Jean-Darrouy, "Le statut personnel et la femme musulmane," *Femmes de Demain*, March 15, 1937.

34. Marie Bugéja, "La femme musulmane: Mon but dans l'évolution de la femme musulmane algérienne," *L'Écho Indigène*, February 7, 1934.

35. Marie Bugéja, "Pour l'évolution des femmes musulmanes," *La Française*, April 28, 1934.

36. Letter from the Mayor of Montgolfier to the Prefect of the Department of Oran, July 19, 1934, Direction de l'Interieur et des Beaux-Arts, Gouvernement d'Algérie, AN Algeria, pp. 2–4.

37. On medical services for Algeria's rural Muslim population, see Claire Fredj, "L'administration française et les soins aux 'indigènes': la mise en place de la 'triade médicale' dans l'Algérie des années 1920," in *Les savoirs de l'administration: Histoire et société au Maghreb du XVIe au XXe siècle*, ed. Elboudrari Hassan and Norman Daniel (Casablanca: Fondation du roi Abul Aziz, 2015), 119–36.

38. Madame Toubab, "La F dans la vie coloniale," *L'Action Nouvelle*, July 1, 1933.

39. Paule L. Becquet de Nodreat, "La Clinique indigène d'Alger," *La Française*, March 19, 1932.

40. "La Femme française aux colonies" [The French woman in the colonies], *Femmes de Demain*, June 1, 1936.

41. Malaterre-Sellier, "La Libération des femmes musulmanes."

42. This perspective may have been informed by her engagement with delegates from British colonies at international conferences. "Le congrès d'Istamboul: L'Orient et l'Occident coopèrent," *La Française*, June 8, 1935.

43. Jane Bagnault, "Le suffrage féminin et le problème algérien," *Femmes de Demain*, April 20, 1936.

44. Hubertine Auclert, *Les Femmes arabes en Algérie* (Paris: Société d'Éditions Littéraires, 1900), 63, quoted in Lazreg, *Eloquence of Silence*, 50.

45. Lucienne Jean-Darrouy, "À nos lectrices et à nos lecteurs" [To our female readers and our male readers], *Femmes de Demain*, November 14, 1935.

46. Cécile Brunschvicg, "La Situation des femmes en Algérie," *La Française*, February 28, 1931.

47. George R. Trumbull, *An Empire of Facts: Colonial Power, Cultural Knowledge, and Islam in Algeria, 1870–1914* (New York: Cambridge University Press, 2009), 36, 182.

48. Yaël Simpson Fletcher, "'Irresistible Seductions': Gendered Representations of Colonial Algeria around 1930," in *Domesticating the Empire: Race, Gender, and Family Life in French and Dutch Colonialism*, ed. Julia Clancy-Smith and Frances Gouda (Charlottesville: University of Virginia Press, 1998), 204.

49. Amélie-Marie Goichon, *La Vie féminine au Mzab* (Paris, 1927), vii–viii, quoted in Çelik, *Urban Forms*, 91.

50. Mary Roberts, *Intimate Outsiders: The Harem in Ottoman and Orientalist Art and Travel Literature* (Durham, NC: Duke University Press, 2007).

51. Other scholars have written extensively about Bugéja—notably Jeanne Bowlan and Sakina Messaadi. See Messaadi, *Nos Sœurs Musulmanes*; Jeanne M. Bowlan, "Civilizing Gender Relations in Algeria: The Paradoxical Case of Marie Bugéja, 1919–39," in Clancy-Smith and Gouda, *Domesticating the Empire*, 175–92; Sakina Messaadi, *Les Romancières coloniales et la femme colonisée: contribution à une étude de la littérature coloniale en Algérie dans la première moitié du XXe siècle* (Algiers: Entreprise nationale du livre, 1990); Lazreg, *Eloquence of Silence*, 94–95.

52. Marie-Louise Armand, "Bibliographie," *Bulletin de la Société de Géographie d'Alger et de l'Afrique du Nord* (1938): 265.

53. Some of the books she authored included *Nos sœurs musulmanes* (1921), *Visions d'Algérie* (1929), and *Énigme musulmane* (1938).

54. Bugéja, "La Femme musulmane: Mon but dans l'évolution de la femme musulmane algérienne"; Marie Bugéja, "La Femme musulmane," *La Défense*, December 14, 1934; Marie Bugéja, "La Femme musulmane," *La Défense*, January 18, 1935; Rabah Zenati, "Les Femmes musulmanes: à Madame Marie Bugéja," *La Voix Indigène*, December 1932.

55. Marie Bugéja, "La Femme musulmane: Mon but dans l'évolution de la femme musulmane algérienne."

56. Jeanne Bottini-Honot, *Parmi des inconnus* (Constantine: Éditions de l'Académie Numidia, 1929), 10.

57. Bottini-Honot, 35.

58. Trumbull (*Empire of Facts*, 183) described the amateur and professional ethnographies that depicted various regions of Algeria as "ethnographic tourism," which often involved the objectification of male and female bodies and did not always operate according to the logics of heterosexual desires.

59. Brunschvicg, "La Situation des femmes en Algérie."

60. Brunschvicg.

61. Jeanne Bottini-Houot (*sic*), "Le Féminisme en Algérie," *La Française*, July 15, 1933.

62. Bagnault, "Les Femmes françaises et le problème musulman."

63. "Pour la femme kabyle," *La Française*, November 23, 1929.

64. Bottini-Houot (*sic*), "Le Féminisme en Algérie."

65. Malaterre-Sellier, "En Tunisie."

66. Brunschvicg, "La Situation des femmes en Algérie."

67. Lafuente, "L'Aiguille musulmane."

68. Bottini-Houot (sic), "Le Féminisme en Algérie."
69. "Pour la femme kabyle," *La Française*, November 23, 1929.
70. Seghir Hacène, "Le Congrès de Constantine," *La Voix Indigène*, April 7, 1932.
71. Bottini-Houot (sic), "Le Féminisme en Algérie."
72. Paule Husset, "Elles et nous" [Them and us], *Femmes de Demain*, October 1, 1936.
73. "Pour la femme kabyle"; Mohammed Taouti, "Une opinion des milieux indigènes d'Algérie sur la femme musulmane" [An opinion from the indigenous milieu of Algeria on the Muslim woman], *La Française*, March 14, 1931; Abou-Ezzohra, "Instruisons nos filles."
74. Malaterre-Sellier, "La Libération des femmes musulmanes."
75. Mohammed Taouti, "Une opinion."
76. Senieh, "Le Prophète a-t-il voulu l'asservissement de la femme musulmane?"
77. "Le Droit de vote et la femme musulmane" [The right to vote and the Muslim woman], *Femmes de Demain*, February 15, 1937.
78. "Les Femmes musulmanes et le projet Violette" [Muslim women and the Violette Project], *Femmes de Demain*, March 1, 1937.
79. Lucienne Jean-Darrouy, "Musulmans, vos femmes aussi sont des êtres humains . . ." [Muslim men, your wives are also human beings . . .], *Femmes de Demain*, April 1, 1937.
80. C. Fel, "La Situation sociale de la Musulmane d'Algérie," *La Française*, April 5, 1931.
81. Bagnault, "Les Femmes françaises et le problème musulman."
82. Bagnault.
83. Jeanne Bottini-Honot, "Instruction des filles indigènes: Congrès des femmes méditerranéennes," *La Voix Indigène*, January 1933.
84. Bottini-Honot, *Parmi des inconnus*, 30, 31.
85. Lucienne Jean-Darrouy, *Femmes de demain*, November 14, 1935.
86. Husset, "Elles et nous."
87. "L'Union franco-musulmane," *Femmes de Demain*, March 15, 1937.
88. Paule Husset, "À l'Union féminine franco-musulmane [On the feminine Franco-Muslim]," *Femmes de Demain*, July 8, 1937.
89. Bagnault, "Les Femmes françaises et le problème musulman."
90. Jeanne Bottini-Houot (sic), "Une o œuvre féminine à Sétif," *La Française*, June 17, 1933.
91. Bugéja, "La Femme musulmane," *La Défense*, December 14, 1934.
92. Yvonne de Bruillard, "La Question féminine arabe jugée par un Arabe de treize ans," *La Française*, March 19, 1932.
93. Henriette Sauret, "Orientales et Occidentales," *La Française*, April 5, 1931.
94. Bowlan, "Civilizing Gender Relations in Algeria," 186.
95. C. Fel, "La Situation sociale de la musulmane d'Algérie," *La Française*, April 5, 1931.
96. Brunschvicg, "La Situation des femmes en Algérie."

97. Lucienne Jean-Darrouy, "View of a Woman: To Be or Not to Be a Citizen," *Femmes de Demain*, February 1, 1937.
98. Bagnault, "Les Femmes françaises et le problème musulman."
99. Husset, "Elles et nous."

6. Muslim Women Address the Nation

1. Mademoiselle K. A., [Letter to the editor], *as-Salam*, May 1, 1947.
2. Houria, "Le Mariage musulmane," *as-Salam*, July 1, 1947. The critiques of colonialism within discussions about women occurred outside of the press as well. In May 1948 Mademoiselle Guerab held a conference about the emancipation of the Muslim woman at the Cercle Cligny. Among the causes of the Muslim woman's inferiority, Guerab cited "the consequences of colonialism," including prejudice and a lack of educational opportunities. Anissa, "Autour d'une conférence," *as-Salam*, July 1948.
3. Fatima Zohra Guechi, *La Presse algérienne de langue arabe 1946–1954: enjeux politiques et jeux de plumes* (Constantine: Bahaeddine, 2009), 286.
4. This mirrors the process Partha Chatterjee has described in colonial Bengal. He identified two phases: the first in the late nineteenth century when "the women question" was hotly debated, and the second in the twentieth century when nationalism had become increasingly the dominant ideological issue. He wrote that within these periods, women's possibilities changed as they became educated in larger numbers. The particular forms of patriarchy they faced also changed, as did the types of demands being made on women. See Partha Chatterjee, "The Nationalist Resolution of the Women's Question," in *Recasting Women: Essays in Indian Colonial History*, ed. Kumkum Sangari and Sudesh Vaid (New Delhi: Zubaan, 1990), 233–53.
5. MacMaster, *Burning the Veil*.
6. Laura Bier, "Modernity and the Other Woman: Gender and National Identity in the Egyptian Women's Press, 1952-1967," *Gender and History* 16, no. 1 (2004): 99–112; Marilyn Booth, "Women in Islam: Men and the 'Women's Press' in Turn-of-the-20th-Century Egypt," *International Journal of Middle East Studies* 33, no. 2 (May 2001): 171–201; Baron, *Women's Awakening in Egypt*.
7. Gokchen was the world's first female fighter pilot and one of the adopted daughters of Mustafa Kemal Atatürk.
8. Anissa, "Chronique d'Anissa," *as-Salam*, September 1, 1946.
9. Anissa, *as-Salam*, November 1936.
10. [Letter to the editor], *as-Salam*, June 1947.
11. Jaime Wadowiec, "Muslim Algerian Women and the Rights of Man: Islam and Gendered Citizenship in French Algeria at the End of Empire," *French Historical Studies* 36, no. 4 (Fall 2013): 649–76.
12. Terrence Peterson, "Counterinsurgent Bodies: Social Welfare and Psychological Warfare in French Algeria, 1956–1962" (PhD diss., University of Wisconsin–Madison, 2015).
13. Newell, *Power to Name*.

14. Khider was involved with Messali Hadj's Mouvement pour le triomphe des libertés démocratiques, while Ferhat Abbas was leader of a rival nationalist group, the Union démocratique du manifeste algérien—both political parties established in 1946. "Notre avenir dépend de notre jeunesse estudiantine: il faut l'aider!" *as-Salam*, February 15, 1947.

15. In July 1947 the Association of Muslim Algerian Women was founded to advocate for "the education of the Muslim woman to accelerate her evolution." In May 1948 a group of Muslim teachers and students in Algiers banded together to create the Association of the Arab Algerian Young Woman, which similarly vowed to develop "Arab and Islamic education to benefit Muslim Algerian young women." Associations, ANOM ALG ALGER 4I/184, Service des liaisons nord-africaines, Administration des Indigènes, Préfecture d'Alger, ANOM.

16. *Le problème de l'enseignement en Algérie* (Algiers: Baconnier, 1960), 13, 32.

17. Gosnell, *Politics of Frenchness in Colonial Algeria*, 47.

18. *al-Bassair*, January 19, 1948.

19. Ouanassa Siari Tengour, "Les Écoles coraniques (1930-1950): portée et signification," *Insaniyat* 6 (1998): 85-95.

20. Fatma Zohra Benaik, interviewed digitally by Sara Rahnama, March 4, 2019.

21. Dahbia Lounas, interviewed virtually by Sara Rahnama, October 31, 2021.

22. Halima Benabed, [Letter to the editor], *L'Action*, September 1947.

23. Madame H. S., "The Actual State of the Evolution of the Muslim Woman," *as-Salam*, May 1950.

24. [Letter to the editor], *as-Salam*, March 1, 1947.

25. B. M. A, [Letter to the editor], *as-Salam*, May 1, 1947.

26. Guechi, *La Presse algérienne de langue arabe*, 284.

27. "A Little Savoir-Vivre," *as-Salam*, May 15, 1948.

28. Anissa, "Chronique d'Anissa," *as-Salam*, September 1, 1946.

29. Anissa, "Les Fleurs de l'amitié," *as-Salam*, December 1946.

30. Anissa, *as-Salam*, October 15, 1946.

31. Anissa, "Les fleurs de l'amitié," *as-Salam*, December 1, 1946, March 1, 1947.

32. S. H. Bintou Chaab, [Letter to the editor], *as-Salam*, March 15, 1947.

33. Anissa, *as-Salam*, April 15, 1948.

34. [Letter to the editor], *as-Salam*, May 1, 1947.

35. Mademoiselle Chérifa B., [Letter to the editor], *as-Salam*, June 1, 1947.

36. [Letter to the editor], *as-Salam*, March 15, 1947.

37. Smain H., "Crisis of Marriage in Algeria: A Reply to Mademoiselle Sylviane," *as-Salam*, May 1950.

38. Mademoiselle Leila, [Letter to the editor], *as-Salam*, April 1947.

39. Lounas interview.

40. Anissa, "Chronique d'Anissa," *as-Salam*, September 1, 1946.

41. Afaneh Najmabadi, *Women with Mustaches and Men without Beards: Gender and Sexual Anxieties of Iranian Modernity* (Berkeley: University of California Press, 2005), 202.

42. "Call in Favor of the Students," *as-Salam*, July 1946.

43. Brian Harrison, *Peaceable Kingdom: Stability and Change in Modern Britain* (New York: Oxford University Press, 1982), 161.
44. Khadidja, [Letter to the editor], *as-Salam*, May 15, 1947.
45. Madame H. S., "The Actual State of the Evolution of the Muslim Woman," *as-Salam*, May 1950.
46. B. M. A.
47. Mademoiselle Chérifa B.
48. Mademoiselle H. Said, [Letter to the editor], *as-Salam*, July 1, 1947.
49. Vince, *Our Fighting Sisters*.
50. [Letter to the editor], *as-Salam*, February 15, 1947.
51. [Letter to the editor], *as-Salam*, January 15, 1947.
52. Houria Illal, [Letter to the editor], *as-Salam*, January 15, 1947; Asnia H. M., *as-Salam*, May 1950.
53. Asnia H. M.
54. Taleb Selim, [Letter to the editor], *as-Salam*, March 1, 1947.
55. Abdelkader Haddadi, [Letter to the editor], *as-Salam*, March 1, 1947.
56. B. M. A.
57. Partha Chatterjee, *The Nation and Its Fragments: Colonial and Postcolonial Histories* (Princeton, NJ: Princeton University Press, 1993).
58. Nedjma Gamar, [Letter to the editor], *as-Salam*, April 1947.
59. "A Man and His Wife," *as-Salam*, February 1, 1947.
60. "The Muslim Woman and Her Evolution," *as-Salam*, February 1, 1947.
61. S. H. Bintou Chaab.
62. [Letter to the editor], *as-Salam*, May 15, 1947.
63. Mademoiselle Mina, [Letter to the editor], *as-Salam*, March 1, 1947.
64. Mohammed-Lamine Boutaleb, [Letter to the editor], *as-Salam*, December 1, 1947.
65. Mademoiselle H. Said.
66. Khouira B., [Letter to the editor], *as-Salam*, April 1950.
67. Mademoiselle Chérifa B.
68. Mademoiselle H. Said.
69. Khouira B.
70. Asnia H. M.
71. Madame H. S.
72. Djamila Débêche (*sic*), "Islam Does Not Prescribe Wearing the Veil to the Muslim Woman," *La Justice*, February 20, 1937.
73. McDougall, *History of Algeria*, 179.
74. Djamila Debèche, *Les grandes étapes de l'évolution féminine en pays d'Islam* (Nevers: Imprimerie Chassaing, 1959).
75. Zineb, "Khadidja Bent Khoualid: Épouse du Prophète," *L'Action*, September 1947; "Au Palais de Haroun-Er-Rachid," *L'Action*, October 1947.
76. Djamila Debèche, "Le Mouloud: Le 20 avril 571 de l'ère chrétienne naissait à la Mecque Mohammed," *L'Action*, February 1948.
77. Djamila Debèche, *Aziza*, trans. Zahia Smail Salhi in *Women Writing Africa: The Northern Region*, ed. Fatima Sadiqi, Amira Nowaira, Azza El Kholy, and Moha Ennaji (New York: Feminist Press / City University of New York, 2009), 193–97.

78. "La Correspondance de nos lecteurs," *L'Action*, January 1948, March 1948.
79. French colonial surveillance reports never mentioned that Anissa was of European origin.
80. Anissa, "Nour El Mahal: Enquête épistolaire sur le mariage mixte," *Salam Ifrikya*, May 1950.

Conclusion

1. M. Chakib, "Gala de l'Association des femmes musulmanes algériennes," *L'Algérie Libre*, February 26, 1954.
2. MacMaster, *Burning the Veil*, 46.
3. Letter from Governor-General Roger Léonard to the Minister of the Interior in Paris, March 12, 1952, IBA/ASP/EL/10/1052, Citoyenne de statut civil local—électorat, AN.
4. Zahia Smail Salhi, "The Algerian Feminist Movement between Nationalism, Patriarchy and Islamism," *Women's Studies International Forum* 33, no. 2 (2010): 113-24; Chérifa Benabdessadok, "Tradition et modernisme: Un faux débat?" in *Présences de femmes* (Algiers: Office des publications universitaires, 1984), 7-11; Chafika Dib-Marouf, *Fonctions de la dot dans la cité algérienne: Le cas d'une ville moyenne: Tlemcen et son "Hawz"* (Algiers: Office des publications universitaires, 1984); Souad Khodja, *Les Algériennes du quotidien* (Algiers: Enterprise Nationale du Livre, 1985).
5. Danièle Djamila Amrane-Minne, *Des Femmes dans la guerre d'Algérie* (Paris: Karthala, 1994); Diane Sambron, *Femmes musulmanes: guerre d'Algérie, 1954-1962* (Paris: Éd. Autrement, 2007); Vince, *Our Fighting Sisters*.
6. Goswami, "AHR Forum."
7. Kateb Yacine, *Le Poète comme un boxer: entretiens 1958-1989* (Paris: Editions du Seuil, 1994).
8. Sarah Ghabrial, "Le 'fiqh francisé'?"
9. Jomier, "Muslim Notables."
10. Lucie Ryzova, *The Age of Efendiyya: Passages to Modernity in National-Colonial Egypt* (New York: Oxford University Press, 2014), 9.

Bibliography

Secondary Sources

Abualhassan, Faissal. "Generating Frenchness: Tensions of Race and Civilization in Chérif Cadi's *Terre d'Islam* (1925)." Johns Hopkins African History Seminar, 2019.

Abu-Lughod, Lila. *Remaking Women: Feminism and Modernity in the Middle East.* Princeton, NJ: Princeton University Press, 1998.

Ageron, Charles-Robert. *Les Algériens musulmans et la France (1871–1919).* Vol. 2. Paris: Presses universitaires de France, 1968.

———. *Modern Algeria: A History from 1830.* Trenton, NJ: Africa World Press, 1992.

Ahmad, Attiya. *Everyday Conversions: Islam, Domestic Work, and South Asian Migrant Women in Kuwait.* Durham, NC: Duke University Press, 2017.

Amrane-Minne, Danièle Djamila. *Des Femmes dans la guerre d'Algérie.* Paris: Karthala, 1994.

Andersen, Margaret Cook. *Regeneration through Empire: French Pronatalists and Colonial Settlement in the Third Republic.* Lincoln: University of Nebraska Press, 2015.

Asseraf, Arthur. *Electric News in Colonial Algeria.* New York: Oxford University Press, 2019.

Ayalon, Ami. *The Press in the Arab Middle East: A History.* New York: Oxford University Press, 1995.

———. *Reading Palestine: Printing and Literacy, 1900–1948.* Austin: University of Texas Press, 2004.

Badran, Margot. "Between Secular and Islamic Feminism/s: Reflections on the Middle East and Beyond." *Journal of Middle East Women's Studies* 1, no. 1 (2005): 6–28.

———. *Feminism in Islam: Secular and Religious Convergences.* London: Oneworld, 2009.

———. *Feminists, Islam, and Nation: Gender and the Making of Modern Egypt.* Princeton, NJ: Princeton University Press, 1996.

Baron, Beth. *Egypt as a Woman: Nationalism, Gender, and Politics.* Los Angeles: University of California Press, 2005.

———. *The Women's Awakening in Egypt: Culture, Society, and the Press.* New Haven, CT: Yale University Press, 1994.

Benabdessadok, Chérifa. "Tradition et modernisme: Un faux débat?" In *Présences de femmes.* Algiers: Office des publications universitaires, 1984, 7–11.

Ben Miled, Emna. *Les Tunisiennes ont-elles une histoire?* Tunis: les Presses de l'Imprimerie Simpact, 1998.
Bennoune, Mahfoud. *The Making of Contemporary Algeria, 1830–1987.* Cambridge: Cambridge University Press, 2002.
Betts, Raymond. *Assimilation and Association in French Colonial Theory, 1890–1914.* Lincoln: University of Nebraska Press, 2004.
Bier, Laura. "Feminism, Solidarity, and Identity in the Age of Bandung: Third World Women in the Egyptian Women's Press." In *Making a World after Empire: The Bandung Moment and Its Political Afterlives*, edited by Christopher Lee. Athens: Ohio University Press, 2010, 141–72.
———. "Modernity and the Other Woman: Gender and National Identity in the Egyptian Women's Press, 1952–1967." *Gender and History* 16, no. 1 (2004): 99–112.
Blévis, Laure. "La Citoyenneté française au miroir de la colonisation: étude des demandes de naturalisation des 'sujets français' en Algérie coloniale." *Genèses* 53 (2003): 25–47.
Boittin, Jennifer. "Feminist Mediations of the Exotic: French Algeria, Morocco, and Tunisia, 1921–1939." *Gender and History* 22, no. 1 (April 2010): 131–50.
Booth, Marilyn. "Women in Islam: Men and the 'Women's Press' in Turn-of-the-20th-Century Egypt." *International Journal of Middle East Studies* 33, no. 2 (May 2001): 171–201.
Bouchène, Abderrahmane, Jean-Pierre Peyroulou, Ouanassa Siari Tengour, and Sylvie Thénault. *Histoire de l'Algérie à la période coloniale, 1830–1962.* Paris: Éditions La Découverte, 2012.
Bowen, John. *Why the French Don't Like Headscarves: Islam, the State, and Public Space.* Princeton, NJ: Princeton University Press, 2007.
Bowlan, Jeanne M. "Civilizing Gender Relations in Algeria: The Paradoxical Case of Marie Bugéja, 1919–39." In Clancy-Smith and Gouda, *Domesticating the Empire*, 175–92.
Bozdogan, Sibel, and Resat Kasaba, eds. *Rethinking Modernity and National Identity in Turkey.* Seattle: University of Washington Press, 1997.
Breward, Christopher. *Fashioning London: Clothing and the Modern Metropolis.* London: Berg, 2004.
Brown, Marie Grace. *Khartoum at Night: Fashion and Body Politics in Imperial Sudan.* Stanford, CA: Stanford University Press, 2017.
Butler, Judith. "Contingent Foundations: Feminism and the Question of 'Postmodernism.'" In *Feminists Theorize the Political*, edited by Judith Butler and Joan Wallach Scott. New York: Routledge, 1992.
Carby, Hazel. "Policing the Black Woman's Body in an Urban Context." *Critical Inquiry* 18, no. 4 (Summer 1992): 738–55.
Carlier, Omar. "Le Café maure. Sociabilité masculine et effervescence citoyenne (Algérie XVIIe–XXe siècles)." *Annales. Histoire, Sciences Sociales* 45, no. 4 (1990): 975–1003.
———. "Medina and Modernity: The Emergence of Muslim Civil Society in Algiers between the Two World Wars." In Çelik et al., *Walls of Algiers*, 62–86.

———. "Messali et son look. Du "jeune Turc" citadin au za'im rural, un corps physique et politique construit à rebours?" In *Le Corps du leader: construction et représentation dans les pays du Sud*, edited by Omar Carlier and Raphaëlle Nollez-Goldbach. Paris: Harmattan, 2008, 263-299.

Çelik, Zeynep. "A Lingering Obsession: The Houses of Algiers in French Colonial Discourse." In Çelik et al., *Walls of Algiers*, 134-60.

———. *Urban Forms and Colonial Confrontations: Algiers under French Rule*. Berkeley: University of California Press, 1997.

Çelik, Zeynep, Julia Clancy-Smith, and Frances Terpak, eds. *The Walls of Algiers*. Seattle: University of Washington Press, 2009.

Chachoua, Kamel. *L'Islam kabyle: religion, état et société en Algérie*. Paris: Maisonneuve & Larose, 2001.

Charrad, Mounira. "From Nationalism to Feminism: Family Law in Tunisia." In *Family in the Middle East: Ideational Change in Egypt, Iran, and Tunisia*, edited by Kathryn Yount and Hoda Rashad. New York: Routledge, 2008, 111-36.

Chatelain, Marcia. *South Side Girls: Growing Up in the Great Migration*. Durham, NC: Duke University Press, 2015.

Chatterjee, Partha. *The Nation and Its Fragments: Colonial and Postcolonial Histories*. Princeton, NJ: Princeton University Press, 1993.

———. "The Nationalist Resolution of the Women's Question." In *Recasting Women: Essays in Indian Colonial History*, edited by Kumkum Sangari and Sudesh Vaid, 233-53. New Delhi: Zubaan, 1990.

Chen, Tina Mai. "Dressing for the Party: Clothing, Citizenship, and Genderformation in Mao's China." *Fashion Theory* 5, no. 2 (2001): 143-71.

Christelow, Allan. *Muslim Law Courts and the French Colonial State in Algeria*. Princeton, NJ: Princeton University Press, 1985.

Clancy-Smith, Julia. "The House of Zainab: Female Authority and Saintly Succession in Colonial Algeria." In *Women in Middle Eastern History Shifting Boundaries in Sex and Gender*, edited by Nikki R. Keddie and Beth Baron. New Haven, CT: Yale University Press, 1991, 254-74.

———. *Rebel and Saint: Muslim Notables, Populist Protest, Colonial Encounters (Algeria and Tunisia, 1800–1904)*. Berkeley: University of California Press, 1997.

———. "A Woman without Her Distaff: Gender, Work, and Handicraft Production in Colonial North Africa." In Meriwether and Tucker, *Social History of Women and Gender*, 25-62.

Clancy-Smith, Julia, and Frances Gouda. *Domesticating the Empire: Race, Gender, and Family Life in French and Dutch Colonialism*. Charlottesville: University of Virginia Press, 1998.

Cole, Joshua. "À chacun son public: politique et culture dans l'Algérie des années 1930." *Sociétés and Représentations* 38 (February 2014): 21-51.

———. *Lethal Provocation: The Constantine Murders and the Politics of French Algeria*. Ithaca, NY: Cornell University Press, 2019.

Colonna, Fanny. *Instituteurs algériens, 1883–1939*. Paris: Presses de la Fondation nationale des sciences politiques, 1975.

———. "Training the National Elites in Colonial Algeria, 1920-1954." *Historical Social Research* 33 (2008): 285-95.

Conklin, Alice. *A Mission to Civilize: The Republican Idea of Empire in France and West Africa, 1895–1930.* Stanford, CA: Stanford University Press, 1997.

Courreye, Charlotte. *L'Algérie des Oulémas: Une histoire de l'Algérie contemporaine (1931–1991).* Paris: Éditions de la Sorbonne, 2020.

———. "L'Association des Oulémas Musulmans Algériens et la construction de l'État algérien indépendant: fondation, héritages, appropriations et antagonismes (1931-1991)." PhD diss., Université Sorbonne, 2016.

Davis, Muriam Haleh. *Markets of Civilization: Islam and Racial Capitalism in Algeria.* Durham, NC: Duke University Press, 2022.

Debèche, Djamila. *Les grandes étapes de l'évolution féminine en pays d'Islam.* Nevers: Imprimerie Chassaing, 1959.

———. *Aziza.* Translated by Zahia Smail Salhi in *Women Writing Africa: The Northern Region,* edited by Fatima Sadiqi, Amira Nowaira, Azza El Kholy, and Moha Ennaji. New York: Feminist Press / City University of New York, 2009, 193-97.

Deroo, Eric. *Colonial Culture in France since the Revolution.* Bloomington: Indiana University Press, 2014.

Dib-Marouf, Chafika. *Fonctions de la dot dans la cité algérienne: le cas d'une ville moyenne: Tlemcen et son "Hawz."* Algiers: Office des publications universitaires, 1984.

Djebar, Assia. *Femmes d'Alger dans leur appartement.* Paris: Des Femmes, 1980.

———. *L'Amour, la fantasia.* Paris: J. C. Lattès, 1985.

Drew, Allison. *We Are No Longer in France: Communists in Colonial Algeria.* Manchester: Manchester University Press, 2017.

Dunwoodie, Peter. *Francophone Writing in Transition: Algeria, 1900–1945.* New York: Peter Lang, 2005.

Elsadda, Hoda. *Gender, Nation, and the Arabic Novel in Egypt, 1892–2008.* Syracuse, NY: Syracuse University Press, 2012.

El Shakry, Omnia. "Schooled Mothers and Structured Play: Child Rearing in Turn-of-the-Century Egypt." In Abu-Lughod, *Remaking Women,* 126-70.

Evans, Martin. *Algeria: France's Undeclared War.* New York: Oxford University Press, 2012.

Fernando, Mayanthi. *The Republic Unsettled: Muslim French and the Contradictions of Secularism.* Durham, NC: Duke University Press, 2014.

Fleischmann, Ellen. *The Nation and Its "New" Women: The Palestinian Women's Movement, 1920–1948.* Los Angeles: University of California Press, 2003.

———. "The Other 'Awakening': The Emergence of Women's Movements in the Modern Middle East, 1900-1940." In Meriwether and Tucker, *Social History of Women and Gender,* 89-139.

Fletcher, Yaël Simpson. "'Irresistible Seductions': Gendered Representations of Colonial Algeria around 1930." In Clancy-Smith and Gouda, *Domesticating the Empire,* 193-210.

Fredj, Claire. "L'Administration française et les soins aux 'indigènes': la mise en place de la 'triade médicale' dans l'Algérie des années 1920." In *Les savoirs de l'administration. Histoire et société au Maghreb du XVIe au XXe siècle,* edited

by Elboudrari Hassan and Norman Daniel. Casablanca: Fondation du roi Abul Aziz, 2015, 119–36.
Freedman, Jane, and Carrie Tarr. *Women, Immigration and Identities in France*. London: Bloomsbury Academic, 2000.
Fromage, Julien. "Innovation politique et mobilisation de masse en 'situation coloniale': un 'printemps algérien' des années 1930." PhD diss., École des hautes études en sciences sociales, 2012.
Ghabrial, Sarah. "Le 'fiqh francisé'?: Muslim Personal Status Law Reform and Women's Litigation in Colonial Algeria (1870–1930)." PhD diss., McGill University, 2014.
———. "Gender, Power, and Agency in the Historical Study of the Middle East and North Africa." *International Journal of Middle East Studies* 48, no. 3 (August 2016): 561–64.
———. "'Muslims Have No Borders, Only Horizons': A Genealogy of Border Criminality in Algeria and France, 1848–Present." In *Decolonising the Criminal Question: Colonial Legacies, Contemporary Problems*, edited by A. Aliverti, H. Carvalho, A. Chamberlen, and M. Sozzo. Oxford: Oxford University Press, 2023, 145–61.
Göle, Nilüfer. "Manifestations of the Religious-Secular Divide: Self-State and the Public Sphere." In *Comparative Secularisms in a Global Age*, edited by Linell E. Cady and Elizabeth Shakman Hurd. New York: Palgrave Macmillan, 2010, 41–53.
Gosnell, Jonathan. *The Politics of Frenchness in Colonial Algeria, 1930–1954*. Rochester, NY: University of Rochester Press, 2002.
Goswami, Manu. "AHR Forum: Imaginary Futures and Colonial Internationalisms." *American Historical Review* 117, no. 5 (December 2012): 1461–85.
Graham-Brown, Sarah, "Women's Activism in the Middle East: A Historical Perspective." In Joseph and Slyomovics, *Women and Power in the Middle East*, 23–33.
Guechi, Fatima Zohra. *La Presse algérienne de langue arabe 1946–1954: enjeux politiques et jeux de plumes*. Constantine: Bahaeddine Edition, 2009.
Haj, Samira. *Reconfiguring Islamic Tradition: Reform, Rationality, and Modernity*. Stanford, CA: Stanford University Press, 2009.
Hale, Bradley Rainbow. "The Soul of Empire: The Society of Missionaries of Africa in Colonial Algeria, 1919–1939." PhD diss., University of Connecticut, 2005.
Hammad, Hanan. *Industrial Sexuality: Gender, Urbanization, and Social Transformation in Egypt*. Austin: University of Texas Press, 2016.
Hannun, Marya. "States of Change: Women, Islamic Reform, and Transregional Mobility in the Making of 'Modern' Afghanistan." PhD diss., Georgetown University, 2021.
Harrison, Brian. *Peaceable Kingdom: Stability and Change in Modern Britain*. New York: Oxford University Press, 1982.
Hart, Ursula Kingsmill. *Two Ladies of Algerie: The Lives of Aurelie Picard and Isabelle Eberhardt*. Athens: Ohio University Center for International Studies, 1987.

Hassett, Donal. *Mobilizing Memory: The Great War and the Language of Politics in Colonial Algeria, 1918–39*. Oxford: Oxford University Press, 2019.

Hijab, Nadia. "Women and Work in the Arab World." In Suad and Slyomovics, *Women and Power in the Middle East*, 41–51.

Hirsch, Hadas. "Veiling." In *Encyclopedia of Jews in the Islamic World*, edited by Norman A. Stillman. Leiden: Brill, 2010.

Hunter, Tera. *To 'Joy My Freedom: Southern Black Women's Lives and Labors after the Civil War*. Cambridge, MA: Harvard University Press, 1998.

Ihaddaden, Zahir. *Histoire de la presse indigène en Algérie des origines jusqu'en 1930*. Algiers: ENAL, 2003.

Jacob, Wilson Chacko. *Working Out Egypt: Effendi Masculinity and Subject Formation in Colonial Modernity, 1870–1940*. Durham, NC: Duke University Press, 2011.

Jayawardena, Kumari. *Feminism and Nationalism in the Third World*. London: Zed, 1986.

Jomier, Augustin. "Muslim Notables, French Colonial Officials, and the Washers of the Dead: Women and Gender Politics in Colonial Algeria." *French Politics, Culture and Society* 39, no. 1 (2021): 9–33.

Joseph, Suad, and Slyomovics, Susan, eds. *Women and Power in the Middle East*. Philadelphia: University of Pennsylvania Press, 2001.

Jureidini, Ray. "Sexuality and the Servant: An Exploration of Arab Images of the Sexuality of Domestic Maids Living in the Household." In *Sexuality in the Arab World*, edited by S. Khalaf and J. Gagnon. London: Saqi Books, 2006, 130–51.

Kahlenberg, Caroline. "New Arab Maids: Female Domestic Work, 'New Arab Women,' and National Memory in British Mandate Palestine." *International Journal of Middle East Studies* 52 (2020): 449–67.

Kallander, Amy Aisen. *Tunisia's Modern Woman: Nation-Building and State Feminism in the Global 1960s*. New York: Cambridge University Press, 2021.

Kassamali, Sumayya. "Migrant Worker Lifeworlds of Beirut." PhD diss., Columbia University, 2017.

Kateb, Kamel. *École, population et société en Algérie*. Paris: L'Harmattan, 2005.

———. *Européens, "Indigènes" et Juifs en Algérie (1830–1962)*. Paris: Éditions de l'Institut national d'études démographiques, 2001.

Katz, Ethan. *The Burdens of Brotherhood: Jews and Muslims from North Africa to France*. Cambridge, MA: Harvard University Press, 2015.

Khodja, Souad. *Les Algériennes du quotidien*. Algiers: Entreprise nationale du livre, 1985.

Khoja-Moolji, Shenila. *Forging the Ideal Educated Girl: The Production of Desirable Subjects in Muslim South Asia*. Oakland: University of California Press, 2018.

Kholoussy, Hanan. "The Grooming of Men." In *For Better, For Worse: The Marriage Crisis That Made Modern Egypt*. Stanford, CA: Stanford University Press, 2010, 23–48.

Kimble, Sara L. "Emancipation through Secularization: French Feminist Views of Muslim Women's Condition in Interwar Algeria." *French Colonial History* 7 (2006): 109–28.

Knauss, Peter. *The Persistence of Patriarchy: Class, Gender, and Ideology in Twentieth-Century Algeria*. New York: Praeger, 1987.
Krik, Hagit. "The Female Imperial Agent and the Intricacies of Power: British Nurses in Mandate Palestine." *Journal of Middle East Women's Studies* 18, no. 1 (March 2022): 12-35.
Lazreg, Marnia. *The Eloquence of Silence: Algerian Women in Question*. New York: Routledge, 1994.
Léon, A. *Colonisation, enseignement et éducation: étude historique et comparative*. Paris: Editions L'Harmattan, 1991.
LeTourneau, Roger. "Social Change in the Muslim Cities of North Africa." *American Journal of Sociology* 60, no. 6 (May 1955): 527-35.
Lewis, Reina. *Muslim Fashion: Contemporary Style Cultures*. Durham, NC: Duke University Press, 2015.
MacMaster, Neil. *Burning the Veil: The Algerian War and the "Emancipation" of Muslim Women, 1954-62*. New York: Manchester University Press, 2009.
Mahmood, Saba. *The Politics of Piety: The Islamic Revival and the Feminist Subject*. Princeton, NJ: Princeton University Press, 2005.
Makdisi, Jean Said, Noha Bayoumi, and Rafif Rida Sidawi, eds. *Arab Feminisms: Gender and Equality in the Middle East*. New York: IB Tauris, 2014.
Mamelouk, Nadia. "Anxiety in the Border Zone: Transgressing Boundaries in *Leïla: revue illustrée de la femme* (Tunis, 1936-1940) and in *Leïla: Hebdomadaire Tunisien Indépendant* (Tunis, 1940-1941)." PhD diss., University of Virginia, 2008.
———. "*Leïla*: 1936-1941 bien plus qu'une revue féminine." In *Leïla: Revue illustrée de la femme, 1936-1941*, edited by Hafedh Boujmil. Tunis: Editions Nirvana, 2007.
Marynower, Claire. *L'Algérie à gauche (1900-1962): socialistes à l'époque coloniale*. Paris: Presses Universitaires de France, 2018.
———. "'À nos sœurs indigènes . . . le meilleur de notre affection': militantes socialistes dans l'Oranie des années 1930." *Genre and Colonization* 1 (Spring 2013): 192-231.
———. "Réformer l'Algérie? Des militants socialistes en 'situation coloniale' dans l'entre-deux-guerres." *Histoire/Politique* 1, no. 13 (2011): 112-24.
McAllister, Edward. "Yesterday's Tomorrow Is Not Today: Memory and Place in an Algiers Neighbourhood." PhD diss., University of Oxford, 2015.
McDonald, Brian. *Alice Diamond and the Forty Elephants: The Female Gang That Terrorised London*. London: Milo, 2015.
McDougall, James. *History and the Culture of Nationalism in Algeria*. New York: Cambridge University Press, 2006.
———. *A History of Algeria*. Cambridge: Cambridge University Press, 2017.
Merad, Ali. *Ibn Bâdîs: Commentateur du Coran*. Paris: Paul Guethner, 1971.
———. *Le réformisme musulman en Algérie de 1925 à 1940*. Paris: Mouton, 1967.
Meriwether, Margaret L., and Judith E. Tucker, eds. *Social History of Women and Gender in the Modern Middle East*. Boulder, CO: Westview, 1999.
Mernissi, Fatima. *Beyond the Veil: Male-Female Dynamics in a Modern Muslim Society*. Bloomington: Indiana University Press, 1987.

Messaadi, Sakina. *Nos Sœurs musulmaness, ou, Le mythe féministe, civilisateur, évangélisateur du messianisme colonialiste dans l'Algérie colonisée*. Algiers: Éditions Distribution Houma, 2001.

———. *Les romancières coloniales et la femme colonisée: contribution à une étude de la littérature coloniale en Algérie dans la première moitié du XXe siècle*. Algiers: Entreprise nationale du livre, 1990.

Meynier, Gilbert. *L'Algérie révélée: La guerre de 1914–1918*. Paris: Editions Bouchene, 2015.

Milani, Farzaneh. *Words, not Swords: Iranian Women Writers and the Freedom of Movement*. Syracuse, NY: Syracuse University Press, 2011.

Miliani, Hadj, and Samuel Sami Everett. "Marie Soussan: A Singular Trajectory." In *Jewish-Muslim Interactions: Performing Cultures between North Africa and France*, edited by Samuel Sami Everett and Rebekah Vince. Liverpool: Liverpool University Press, 2020, 81–100.

Mitra, Durba. *Indian Sex Life: Sexuality and the Colonial Origins of Modern Social Thought*. Princeton, NJ: Princeton University Press, 2020.

Mo, Sophia. "Reading Motherhood at the Margins of Algerian Feminist Retellings of Resistance." Paper presented at the annual meeting of the Middle East Studies Association, Denver, Colorado, December 3, 2022.

Moghadam, Valentine. "Feminism, Legal Reform, and Women's Empowerment in the Middle East and North Africa." *International Social Science Journal* 59, no. 191 (2008): 9–16.

Mohanty, Chandra. "Under Western Eyes: Feminist Scholarship and Colonial Discourses." *Feminist Review* 30 (1988): 61–88.

Moradian, Manijeh. *This Flame Within: Iranian Revolutionaries in the United States*. Durham, NC: Duke University Press, 2022.

Nachabe, Yasmine. "Marie al-Khazen's Photographs of the 1920s and 1930s." PhD diss., McGill University, 2011.

Najmabadi, Afsaneh. *Women with Mustaches and Men without Beards: Gender and Sexual Anxieties of Iranian Modernity*. Berkeley: University of California Press, 2005.

Nead, Lynda. *Victorian Babylon: People, Streets and Images in Nineteenth-Century London*. New Haven, CT: Yale University Press, 2000.

Newell, Stephanie. *The Power to Name: A History of Anonymity in Colonial West Africa*. Athens: Ohio University Press, 2013.

Nightingale, Carl. *Segregation: A Global History of Divided Cities*. Chicago: University of Chicago Press, 2012.

Nord, Deborah Epstein. *Walking the Victorian Streets: Women, Representation, and the City*. Ithaca, NY: Cornell University Press, 1995.

Northrop, Douglas. *Veiled Empire: Gender and Power in Stalinist Central Asia*. Ithaca, NY: Cornell University Press, 2016.

Panchasi, Roxanne. *Future Tense: The Culture of Anticipation in France between the Wars*. Ithaca, NY: Cornell University Press, 2009.

Perrier, Aurelie. "Intimate Matters: Negotiating Sex, Gender and the Home in Colonial Algeria, 1830–1914." PhD diss., Georgetown University, 2014.

Perrière, Caroline de la Brac. *Derrière les héros: les employées de maison musulmanes en service chez les Européens à Alger pendant la guerre d'Algérie, 1954–1962*. Paris: Harmattan, 1987.

Peterson, Derek, Steph Newell, and Emma Hunter, eds. *African Print Cultures: Newspapers and Their Publics in the Twentieth Century.* Ann Arbor: University of Michigan Press, 2016.
Peterson, Terrence. "Counterinsurgent Bodies: Social Welfare and Psychological Warfare in French Algeria, 1956–1962." PhD diss., University of Wisconsin-Madison, 2015.
Piess, Kathy. *Cheap Amusements: Leisure in Turn-of-the-Century New York.* Philadelphia: Temple University Press, 1986.
Prochaska, David. *Making Algeria French: Colonialism in Bône, 1870–1920.* New York: Cambridge University Press, 1990.
Pursley, Sara. *Familiar Futures: Time, Selfhood, and Sovereignty in Iraq.* Stanford, CA: Stanford University Press, 2019.
Rich, Jeremy. "Civilized Attire: Refashioning Tastes and Social Status in the Gabon Estuary, 1870–1914." *Cultural and Social History* 2 (2005): 189–213.
——. "Gabonese Men for French Decency: The Rise and Fall of the Gabonese Chapter of the Ligue des Droits de l'Homme, 1916–1939." *French Colonial History* 13 (2012): 23–53.
Roberts, Mary. *Intimate Outsiders: The Harem in Ottoman and Orientalist Art and Travel Literature.* Durham, NC: Duke University Press, 2007.
Roberts, Mary Louise. *Civilization without Sexes: Reconstructing Gender in Postwar France, 1917–1927.* Chicago: University of Chicago Press, 1994.
Roberts, Sophie B. *Citizenship and Antisemitism in French Colonial Algeria, 1870–1962.* New York: Cambridge University Press, 2017.
Robinson, Nova. *Truly Sisters: Arab Women and International Women's Rights* (forthcoming).
Rogers, Rebecca. *A Frenchwoman's Imperial Story: Madame Luce in Nineteenth-Century Algeria.* Stanford, CA: Stanford University Press, 2013.
Roy, Anupama. *Gendered Citizenship: Historical and Conceptual Explorations.* Hyderabad: Orient Longman, 2005.
Ruedy, John. *Modern Algeria.* Bloomington: Indiana University Press, 1992.
Ryzova, Lucie. *The Age of Efendiyya: Passages to Modernity in National-Colonial Egypt.* New York: Oxford University Press, 2014.
Sadiqi, Fatima, Amira Nowaira, Azza El Kholy, and Moha Ennaji, eds. *Women Writing Africa: The Northern Region.* New York: Feminist Press / City University of New York, 2009.
Sambron, Diane. *Femmes musulmanes: guerre d'Algérie, 1954–1962.* Paris: Éd. Autrement, 2007.
Scott, Joan Wallach. *The Politics of the Veil.* Princeton, NJ: Princeton University Press, 2010.
Seferdjeli, Ryme. "'Fight with Us, Women, and We Will Emancipate You': France, the FLN and the Struggle over Women during the Algerian War of National Liberation." PhD diss., London School of Economics, 2005.
Sellami, Jaouida Chaouch. "Fondation: Contexte socio-politique, national et international." In *Dar el Bacha: Reflet d'un siècle, 1900–2000.* Tunis: Editions Caractères, 2000.
Shinar, Pessah. *Modern Islam in the Maghrib.* Jerusalem: Hebrew University of Jerusalem, 2004.

Silver, Chris. *Recording History: Jews, Muslims, and Music across Twentieth-Century North Africa*. Stanford, CA: Stanford University Press, 2022).
Sinha, Mrinalini. "Mapping the Imperial Social Formation: A Modest Proposal for Feminist History." *Signs* 25, no. 4 (Summer 2000): 1077–82.
Smail Salhi, Zahia. "The Algerian Feminist Movement between Nationalism, Patriarchy and Islamism." *Women's Studies International Forum* 33, no. 2 (2010): 113–24.
Spevack, Aaron. *The Archetypal Sunni Scholar: Law, Theology, and Mysticism in the Synthesis of al-Bajuri*. Albany: State University of New York Press, 2014.
Surkis, Judith. *Sex, Law, and Sovereignty in French Algeria, 1830–1930*. Ithaca, NY: Cornell University Press, 2019.
Tengour, Ouanassa Siari. "Les Écoles coraniques (1930–1950): portée et signification." *Insaniyat* 6 (1998): 85–95.
Terem, Etty. *Old Texts, New Practices: Islamic Reform in Modern Morocco*. Stanford, CA: Stanford University Press, 2014.
Trumbull, George R. *An Empire of Facts: Colonial Power, Cultural Knowledge, and Islam in Algeria, 1870–1914*. New York: Cambridge University Press, 2009.
Tucker, Judith E. "The Arab Family in History: 'Otherness' and the Study of the Family." In *Arab Women: Old Boundaries, New Frontiers*, edited by Judith E. Tucker. Bloomington: Indiana University Press, 1993, 195–207.
Vince, Natalya. *Our Fighting Sisters: Nation, Memory, and Gender in Algeria, 1954–2012*. Manchester: Manchester University Press, 2015.
Wadowiec, Jaime. "Muslim Algerian Women and the Rights of Man: Islam and Gendered Citizenship in French Algeria at the End of Empire." *French Historical Studies* 36, no. 4 (Fall 2013): 649–76.
Walkowitz, Judith. *City of Dreadful Delight: Narratives of Sexual Danger in Late-Victorian London*. Chicago: University of Chicago Press, 1992.
Weber, Charlotte. "Unveiling Scheherazade: Feminist Orientalism in the International Alliance of Women, 1911–1950." *Feminist Studies* 27, no. 1 (2001): 125–57.
Weil, Patrick. *Qu'est-ce qu'un Français? Histoire de la nationalité française depuis la Révolution*. Paris: Éditions Grasset & Fasquelle, 2002.
Weinbaum, Alys Eve, Lynn M. Thomas, Priti Ramamurthy, Uta G. Poiger, and Madeleine Yue Dong. *The Modern Girl around the World: Consumption, Modernity, and Globalization*. Durham, NC: Duke University Press, 2008.
Wide, Thomas. "Astrakhan, Borqa', Chadari, Dreshi: The Economy of Dress in Early-Twentieth-Century Afghanistan." In *Anti-Veiling Campaigns in the Muslim World: Gender, Modernism and the Politics of Dress*, edited by Stephanie Cronin. New York: Routledge, 2014, 165–203.
Wiley, Katherine Ann. "The Materiality and Social Agency of the Malaḥfa (Mauritanian Veil)." *African Studies Review* 62, no. 2 (2019): 149–74.
Woodhull, Winifred. "Unveiling Algeria." *Genders* 10 (Spring 1991): 112–31.
Yacine, Kateb. *Le Poète comme un boxer: entretiens 1958–1989*. Paris: Editions du Seuil, 1994.

Primary Source Publications

L'Action
L'Action Nouvelle
L'Algérie Libre
al-Balagh al-Jazairi
al-Bassair
Bulletin de la Société de géographie d'Alger et de l'Afrique du Nord
La Défense
L'Écho de la Presse Musulmane
L'Écho Indigène
L'Entente franco-musulmane
Femmes de Demain
La Française
L'Ikdam
al-Islah
La Justice
La Lutte Sociale
Minerva
al-Najah
Oran Républicain
El Ouma
al-Salam
al-Shihab
La Voix des Humbles
La Voix Indigène

Primary Source Monographs and Novels

Baroy, Marie. "Rôle du travail de la femme dans l'évolution sociale de la Casbah." Master's thesis, Université de Alger, 1943.
Bel, Marguerite A. *Les arts indigènes féminins en Algérie*. Algiers: Ouvrage publié sous les auspices du Gouvernement Général de l'Algérie, 1939.
Bennabi, Malek. *Islam in History and Society*. Translated by Asma Rashid. Islamabad: Islamic Research Institute, 1988.
———. *Mémoires d'un témoin du siècle: l'enfant, l'étudiant, l'écrivain*. Algiers: Samar éditions, 1965.
Bentami, Rosalia. *L'Enfer de la Casbah*. Algiers: Impr. du Lycée, 1936.
Borrmans, Maurice. "La femme de ménage musulmane en service dans les familles européennes." Master's thesis, University of Algiers, 1955.
Bottini-Honot, Jeanne. *Parmi des inconnus*. Constantine: Éditions de l'Académie Numidia, 1929.
Bugéja, Marie. *Énigme musulmane*. Algiers: Editions de France, 1938.
———. *Nos sœurs musulmanes*. Algiers: Editions de France, 1921.
———. *Visions d'Algérie*. Algiers: Editions de France, 1929.

Cadi, Cherif. *Terres d'Islam*. Paris: Charles-Lavauzelle, 1916.
Faci, Saïd. *L'Algérie sous l'égide de la France contre la féodalité algérienne*. Toulouse, 1936.
———. *Mémoire d'un instituteur algérien d'origine indigène*. Constantine: Attali, 1931.
Goichon, Amélie-Marie. *La Vie féminine au Mzab*. Paris, 1927.
Laloë, G. *Enquête sur le travail des femmes indigènes à Alger*. Algiers: Typographie Adolphe Jourdan, 1910.
Lechani, Mohand *Le Malaise algérien*. Algiers: Pfeifer et Assant, 1939.
Lefèvre, Laure. "Recherches sur la condition de la femme kabyle." PhD diss., Université d'Alger, 1939.
Viollette, Maurice. *L'Algérie vivra-t-elle?: notes d'un ancien gouverneur général*. Paris: Félix Alcan, 1931.
al-Zawawi, Shaykh Abu Yaʿla. *al-Islam al-sahih*. Cairo: al-Manar Press, 1926.
Zenati, Rabah. *Bou-el-Nour*. Algiers: La Maison des Livres, 1945.

Archives Consulted

Archives of the Wilaya of Algiers
Archives of the Wilaya of Constantine
Archives of the Wilaya of Oran
Archives of the Archdiocese of Algiers
Archives nationales d'Algérie (Algiers)
Archives nationales de France (Pierrefitte)
Archives nationales d'Outre-Mer (Aix-en-Provence)
Archives nationales de Tunisie (Tunis)
Bibliothèque nationale de France

Oral Interviews

Benaik, Fatma Zohra. Interviewed virtually by Sara Rahnama. March 4, 2019.
Lounas, Dahbia. Interviewed virtually by Sara Rahnama. October 31, 2021.

Index

Page numbers in *italics* refer to figures and tables.

Abbas, Ferhat, 27, 30–31, 129, 162, 173, 212n14
Abbasid caliphate, 119, 176, 200n48
Abduh, Muhammad, 9, 85, 107
Abdul-Hamid, 96
Abou-Ezzohra, 1–2, 7, 90, 97–98, 135, 147
activism, 10, 23, 46–49, 58–59, 71, 116, 138, 143, 152, 173, 181–82. *See also* anti-colonial nationalism; feminism; French feminists
AEMAN, 121, 124, 181
Afghanistan, 3–4, 6, 32, 40, 93–94, 96, 99, 106–7
agency, 15, 184
agricultural labor, 20, 50–51, 53–54, 56, 68, 80
Ahmad, Fadila, 155
Ahmad, Sayyid ʿAbd al-Qadir bin Si, 69
Aicha, Lalla (Moroccan princess), 157
Akbou (commune in Kabylie), 43
al-Ajyal, 107
Alawiyya order, 31–32, 38, 76
al-Balagh al-Jazairi, 31, 66, 76, 85, 102, 113, 121–22
al-Bassair, 19, 22, 30, 69, 76, 90–91, 93, 97, 102, 111–12, 114–15, 125, 155, 162
al-Darraji, Yahya bin Muhammad, 63, 115
al-Din, Nazira Zein, 107
al-Fajr, 125
al-Fatat, 35
al-Fath, 121
Algerian War of Independence, 10, 12–14, 29, 73, 104–5, 110, 129, 175, 179, 181–82. *See also* anti-colonial nationalism
al-Gharbi, 60, 69, 130–31, 146
Algiers: casbah (neighborhood), 52, 57, 111, 139; domestic workers in, 55, 59; schools in, 80
al-Hajwi, Muhammad, 108

al-Hayat, 102
Alif-Ba theater troupe, 58–59
Al Islah, 99
Aliwa, Sheikh Ahmad Ben, 31
al-Mahdi al-Wazzani, 70
al Manar, 155, 164–65
al-Maqqari, Ahmad Ibn Muhammad, 119
al-Masreyyah, 36
al-Moudjahid, 102
al-Najah, 23, 32–33, 35, 38, 44, 63, 65, 67–68, 70–71, 76, 81–82, 84, 94–97, 103, 106–7, 111–12, 115, 119–23
al-Namri, Ali bin Ahmad bin Muhammad, 63, 66–67
al-Oqbi, Tayyib, 114, 163
al-Shihab, 22, 30, 34–35, 68–69, 76, 82, 86, 93, 115, 124–25
al Shula, 155
al-Zawawi, Abu Yaʾla, 32, 111–12, 115
Amazigh, 6, 41, 109
Ameur, Houria, 84, 88, 93
Ameur, Tahar, 147
anti-colonial nationalism, 5, 9, 11–14; censorship and, 35; domestic workers and, 71–73; forms of dress and, 104–5, 108, 122–26, 129; Muslim press and, 23; Muslim reformists and, 30–31, 122–25, 155; postwar period, 158–59; unveiling and, 104–5, 153, 179; women fighters, 102, 165, 179; women's advancement and, 13–14, 153, 155, 167, 179, 181–83, 185. *See also* Algerian War of Independence
Arab culture, 6; modernization and, 63; past glory of, 91, 94, 123, 127
Arabic-language press, 14–15, 30, 32, 94, 110, 190n19
Arslan, Shakib, 121, 124
artisanal work, 54–56, 80–82, 92–93, 100, 137

227

INDEX

as-Salam, 154–61, *157–58*, *160*, 164–73, 175–79
assimilation: education and, 84, 128, 140, 165, 173; ethnographies and, 143–44; forms of dress and, 104–5, 120–22, 125–29, 153, 172; French army and, 153; Muslim men, 84, 126, 144, 156, 172, 176, 179; nationalism and, 28, 129, 169, 172–73, 179, 184; opposition to, 64–65, 76, 82, 93, 125, 127, 156, 159, 164–67, 169, 176; support for, 14, 23–24, 27–31, 38, 49, 59–62, 73, 78, 89–90, 184; women's advancement and, 14, 48–49, 181. *See also* citizenship and naturalization
association (with French culture), 27
Association des oulémas musulmans algériens (AOMA), 30–31, 44, 101–2, 162
Association of Muslim Algerian Women (AFMA), 180–82, 212n15
Association of Schoolteachers of Indigenous Origin (AIOIA), 23, 38–39, 76, 183–84
associations, 25, 43, 46, 73, 92–93, 145, 162, 212n15
Atatürk, Mustafa Kemal, 3–4, 32, 40, 94–96, 99, 107, 118–22, 126, 128, 133, 148, 159, 175. *See also* Turkey
atheism, 121–22
Auclert, Hubertine, 141
Aziza (Debèche), 174, 176

Bachtarzi, Mahieddine, 44–46
Bagnault, Jane, 136, 141, 149–50, 152
Bahri, Younès, 35
Bakr, Asma bint Abi, 102
Baroy, Marie, 55
Battle of Algiers, 114
Battle of Algiers, The (1966 film), 110, 179
beauty culture, global, 158–59, 166
Begarra, Joseph, 25
Bel, Marguerite, 20
Benabdessadok, Chérifa, 183
Benabed, Halima, 163–64
Benaik, Fatma Zohra, 70, 163
Ben Badis, Abdelhamid, 18, 30–32, 34–35, 39, 43–44, 85–86, 101–2, 112
Bendiab, Abderrahim, 26–27
Bendjelloul, Mohammed Salah, 29, 31
Ben Drahou, Rahma, 47–49, *49*, 57–61, 71, 73, 181, 193n2

Benhoura, Mohammed, 114
Benlabed family, 32
Bennabi, Malek, 34–35, 95
Benriba, 96, 99
Bentami, Rosalia, 133, 139–40
Ben Yamina (café), 34–35
"Berber." *See* Amazigh
Bertrand, Cyprienne, 90
Bey, Salah, 1
Blum-Violette Law (1936), 5, 147–48, 155
bodies, 11, 48–49, 59–74, 126, 137, 204n19, 209n58. *See also* dress
Bottini-Honot, Jeanne, 137–39, 143–46, 149–50
Bouhedja, Hadj Youcef, 84
Boumendjel, Messali Hadj Ahmed, 25
Boutaleb, Mohammed-Lamine, 172
Bouzareah, 23, 25, 28, 38
Brenier, Joseph, 138
Bruillard, Yvonne de, 151
Brunschvicg, Cécile, 132, 135, 142, 144, 151
Bugéja, Marie, 130–33, 139–40, 146, 151
Bukusha, Hamza, 112–13, 115, 126–27

Cadi, Chérif bin Larbi, 89–90
cafés: French, 111; masculine culture of, 34–35, 55, 68, 73
Carioca, Tahia, 157
casbah (in Algiers), 52, 57, 111, 139
censorship, 28–29, 35–36, 161, 184
Cercle du Progrès, 46, 149
Chamia, Ratiba, 45
charity, 43, 145, 150
Chassériau, Charles Frédéric, 180
chastity, 93, 172
Chateaubriand, 58
Chentouf, Mamia, 180–82
cinema culture, 165
citizenship and naturalization, 5, 27–28, 31–32, 90, 132, 147–48, 155
civilization: French, 132–35, 140–41, 153; Islamic/Arab, 85–88, 91, 94, 120, 123, 127, 181, 200n48; modernity and, 27, 98–100, 119–20, 122. *See also* modernity
civilizing mission, colonial, 16, 141–42, 146
class: colonial economy and, 50–51; French women and, 146; in interwar period, 19–21; social mobility, 24–25; urbanization and, 64; women's

INDEX   229

advancement and, 38, 56, 62–69.
  See also elite Muslims; middle-class
  Muslims; working-class Muslims
clothing industry, 52–53. See also dress
Code de l'indigénat (Native code), 5, 28–29
codes of conduct, 165–66, 169, 179, 185.
  See also propriety and impropriety
communist groups, 25, 31, 33, 71
communist press, 33, 48, 76
conferences, 43, 46, 87, 134–35, 145–47,
  149–50, 176, 208n42, 211n2
Constantine, 23, 28, 34–35, 39, 78
consumption, 20–21, 73, 110
corruption, 82, 97, 100, 102

Debèche, Djamila, 113–16, 124, 127–28,
  173–78, *174, 178,* 183
Demour, Maryse, 140
Dib-Marouf, Chafika, 183
divorce, 3, 86, 99–100
Djebar, Assia, 204n19
doctors, female, 45, 67, 94, 132, 136, 140,
  150, 162
domestic workers, 47–74; anti-colonial
  nationalism and, 71–73; assimilation
  and, 59–62; gender of, 51, *53,* 54;
  mobility and visibility of, 47–50,
  56–74, 130; modern subject formation
  and, 185; physical safety of, 69–71;
  public life and, 10; radio broadcasts
  and, 35; settler views of, 151
Douifi, Melika, 57–59
dowry, 86, 92
dress, 103–29; Algeria's future and,
  103–6, 122–28, 172; custom and,
  105–6, 110, 112–16, 118, 125–28;
  domestic workers and, 185; education
  and, 100; European-style, 6, 26, *26,*
  37, 104–5, 107, 120–22, 125–26, 151,
  153, 172, 176; gender relations and,
  104; global beauty culture, 158–59,
  166; identity and, 107–8, 118, 121,
  123, 126, 172, 185; men's clothing and
  hats, 103–8, 116–22, 125–29, 202n2;
  Middle Eastern, 106–9, 166; modernity
  and, 103, 105, 119–24, 126–27, 129;
  Muslim culture and tradition, 103,
  116–23, 125–29; nationalism and,
  104–5, 108, 122–26, 129; settler
  colonialism and, 116, 118, 120–21,
  185; stereotypes about, 37, 129,
  142; women in public life and, 127;
  women's styles of hijab, 48, 98, 103–6,
  109–16, 125–28. See also veiling
Dupré, Jeanne, 90
Dyab, Layla, 155

economy, colonial, 4, 6; class and, 50–51;
  gender dynamics and, 65; limitations
  of, 71, 139; rural-to-urban migration
  and, 50–56; women's labor and, 81. See
  also labor
education, 75–102; about French culture,
  28–29, 81, 136; European settlers
  and, 100, 149; language and, 172;
  modern subject formation and, 185.
  See also Islamic education; schools;
  schoolteachers; women's education
effendis, 185
Egypt: colonialism in, 3; forms of
  dress, 106–8, 121, 166, 185, 203n8;
  Muslim reform movement, 7; women's
  advancement, 4, 6, 32, 45, 56, 94,
  96, 113, 116, 132, 134–35, 153, 176;
  women's education, 2, 4, 89, 91, 98;
  women's journals, 35
Egyptian Feminist Union (EFU), 4,
  35–36
El-Hachemi, Abdelhafidh ben, 32–33, 39,
  63–65, 67, 69, 95–96
elite Muslims, 1–2, 19–21, 23–24, 35–36,
  50, 64, 73, 90, 143–48, 171, 177
El Kheira Association, 46, 92–93
El Madani, Tawfiq, 111
El Ouman, 95
equality. See gender equality
ethnographies, amateur, 130–31, 139–40,
  142–44, 159, *160,* 209n58
Étoile nord-africaine, 33, 46, 182
European colonialism, 3, 87, 95, 128, 135.
  See also settler colonialism
European norms, 49, 59–64, 93, 119–26,
  159, 173, 176. See also assimilation
European women's rights, 67–68,
  99–100, 114–16, 140–41, 153

family, 8–9, 16, 27, 55, 65, 73, 81, 169,
  176, 184. See also gender relations;
  marriage; motherhood; patriarchy
Fanon, Franz, 110, 178
fashion, 37, 61, 107, 117, 125, 166. See
  also dress
fatwas, 41, 85, 104, 107–8
Favre, Lucienne, 151

Fédération des élus indigènes algériens (Federation of Indigenous Elected Officials), 29–30, 37–38, 155, 190n26
feminism: definitions of, 8–9; as future possibility, 7–17, 183–86; global, 206n4; imperial, 132, 152–53; Islamic, 9, 12, 176, 181; in late twentieth century, 183; Muslim press and, 23, 89–90 (*see also* Muslim press); organized movements, 4, 6, 9, 96, 132, 212n15; secular, 9. *See also* French feminists; gender equality; maternal feminism; state feminism; women's advancement
feminist press, 33–34. *See also* "Women's Page"
Femmes de Demain, 33, 136, 139, 141, 146–50, 152
Femmes nouvelles, 161
Filastin, 36–37
Foudhaili, Essaida, 89
France: Algerian Muslim migration to, 5, 51; birth rate, 67, 196n59; claims to civilizational superiority, 132–35, 140–41, 153; culture and society, 11, 28–29, 81, 136. *See also* French feminists; settler colonialism
Franco-Muslim Feminine Union, 149–50
French Army, Psychological Warfare Bureau, 153, 161
French feminists, 130–53; amateur ethnographers, 142–44; efforts against settler prejudice, 148–52; as intermediaries, 130–32, 135, 140; as intermediaries to elite Muslims, 144–48, 152; Middle Eastern women's rights and, 132–35, 141; publications, 33–34 (see also *specific newspapers*); settler-colonial context and, 152; social services and, 135–42. *See also* European women's rights
French-language press, 14–15, 24, 30, 32, 37, 83, 88, 110, 190n19
French League for Education, 138
French Union for Women's Suffrage (UFSF), 132–33, 135, 137–38, 142, 144–45
frivolity, 50, 64, 159, 165–67
Front de libération nationale (FLN, National Liberation Front), 25, 102, 105, 110, 114, 182–83
futures, 10–17, 61, 103, 183–86

Gamar, Nedjma, 171
Gaudry, Mathéa, 78
gender equality, 1–14. *See also* feminism; women's advancement
gender relations: in Europe, 67–68, 99–100, 114–16, 151–52; forms of dress and, 104; harmony in, 165; in marriage, 86, 156, 171–72; power dynamics in, 10, 20, 43, 50, 55–56, 62–69, 71–74, 104–5, 142, 156, 168, 172, 184. *See also* masculinity; patriarchy
geographic location of Algeria, 6
Goichon, Amélie-Marie, 142
Gokchen, Sabiha, 159, 211n7
Greece, 96, 125, 127
Green Mosque (Constantine), 85
Guiga, Bahri, 89

Hacène, Ahmed, 25
Hacène, Ali, 25, 88, 197n73
Hacène, Amar, 25
Hacène, Seghir, 88–89, 93, 146
Haddadi, Abdelkader, 171
hadith literature, 15, 18, 37, 41. *See also* Islamic knowledge
Hadj, Messali, 46, 116, 173, 176, 181–82, 212n14
haiks, 45, 56, 71, 109–16, 126, 129, 153, 168, 195n45; images of, 44, 72, 158. *See also* veiling
hair: covering of, 56, 110, 126–27, 158 (*see also* hijabs); styles of, 37, 61
Hamoud, Nefissa, 180–81
Hardy, Georges, 81
harem, 37, 47–48, 143. *See also* sequestration
headwear: ideologies and, 105–6; men's, 103, 105, 107, 117–19, 123–27, 129. *See also* haiks; hijab; veiling
hijabs, 48, 98, 103–6, 109–16, 126
Hocine, Baya, 71
honor, 64–66, 75, 98, 112–13, 116, 127, 156, 169–70
Husset, Paule, 146, 149–50, 152

Ibn Arabi, 113
Ibn Hallush, Mustafa, 112, 115, 127
Ibrahimi, Bashir al, 31, 162
identity: Algerian, 2–3, 14, 31, 38, 85–86, 105, 122–23, 183; Arab, 121, 183; dress and, 107–8, 118, 121, 123, 126, 172, 185; feminism as, 184; Muslim, 29–31,

38, 41–42, 82, 85–86, 93, 98, 106, 120, 126–27, 172, 181, 183. *See also* Muslim culture
Ighilahriz, Louisette, 10
imperial feminism, 132, 152–53
India, 96, 135, 197n80
Indonesia, 165
inheritance, 70, 77, 86, 98–99, 197n73
internationalism, 11, 104, 129, 132, 152–53, 183, 186
international news, 73, 156
Iran, 3–4, 6, 32, 95–96, 109, 135, 168
Iraq, 2–3, 11, 19, 32, 96, 98
Islam: feminism in, 9, 12, 176, 181; flexibility of, 127; past glory of, 85–88, 91, 181, 200n48; personal legal status, 27–28; renaissance of, 2, 33, 35, 86–87, 90–91, 158, 164, 168. *See also* Muslim culture; Muslim press; social uplift
Islamic education, 78, 85–86, 90, 162–63, 212n15
Islamic knowledge: defined, 7; on forms of dress, 104–8, 112–16, 119–22, 127, 174; laypeople's engagement with, 85–86; modernity and, 123–24; woman question and, 15, 37–38, 40–41, 63; women's education and, 76–78, 85–89

Jean-Darrouy, Lucienne, 139, 141, 147–49, 151
Jews, 39, 45, 195n45
Jonnart Law (1919), 5
Jordan (as Transjordan), 3

Kabyle population, 43, 52, 70, 85, 111, 145, 197n73
Kahena, 41
Kessous, Mohamed el Aziz, 33
Khadija (wife of Prophet Muhammad), 176
Khadija, Lalla, 41, 43
Khan, Amanullah, 3–4, 93, 96, 99, 122
Khan, Sayyid Ahmad, 107
Khider, Mohamed, 162, 212n14
Khodja, Souad, 183
Ksentini, Rachid, 45

labor, 5, 19–20, 50–55, 65. *See also* agricultural labor; domestic workers; women's labor
L'Action, 113, 163–64, 173–78, 183
La Défense, 18–19, 22, 27, 30–31, 69, 91, 96, 99, 130–31, 137, 143

La Dépêche Algérienne, 147
La Française, 33, 134, 136, 138–40, 145–47, 149, 151–52
L'Afrique du Nord illustrée, 44, 45
L'Afrique française, 46
La Justice, 113–14, 174
L'Algérie Libre, 181
La Lutte Sociale, 76, 100
La Mazière, Alice, 145
Lamoudi, Lamine, 18, 27, 31, 99
La Presse Marocaine, 19
Largueche, Hamed, 87, 89
La Voix des Humbles, 19, 22–30, 26, 32, 37, 39–40, 76, 82–83, 89, 92, 96–97, 99, 114, 127, 133, 174, 184, 191n37
La Voix Indigène, 1, 22, 25, 27, 30, 32–33, 37, 61, 76, 83–84, 87–90, 93, 97, 143, 147
La Voix Libre, 30
Lebanon, 3–4, 6, 35, 96, 107–8
Lechani, Mohand, 25, 83
L'Echo d'Alger, 139
L'Echo de la presse musulmane, 174
L'Echo Indigène, 29, 88, 137, 143
L'Égyptienne, 4, 35–36, 40, 99
Leïla (Debèche), 174, 176
Leïla (periodical), 36, 89
L'Entente franco-musulmane, 29, 37, 67
Léonard, Roger, 182
Le Petit Niçois, 178
Les Archives des luttes des femmes en Algérie (The archive of women's struggle in Algeria), 183
LeTourneau, Roger, 13
Liberté, 46
Libya, 3
licentiousness, 57, 85, 93, 170
L'Ikdam, 95
literacy, 13, 25, 34, 66, 92, 148, 162–63, 190n19
Livre de l'Algérie, 111
L'Oréal advertisement, *158*
Lounas, Dahbia, 21, 40, 70, 109, 163

makeup, 64, 110, 166
malahfa, 109
Malaterre-Sellier, Germaine, 133–35, 141, 145, 147
Mami ben Allaoua, Smaïl, 32–33, 35, 44, 65, 67, 95
Mansur, Muhammad bin Ahmad al-, 91, 97
Marçais, William, 142

marriage: mixed (Muslim-European), 172–73, 177–78; personal advertisements for, 177. *See also* family; gender relations
masculinity, 67–68, 105, 108, 123, 165
maternal feminism, 138–40, 152
Mauritania, 109
medical care, 136, 140, 152
men, Muslim: café culture and, 34–35, 55, 68, 73; clothing and hats, 103–8, 116–22, 125–29, 202n2; education, 80–81; employment, 65; migration to France, 5, 51. *See also* gender relations; masculinity
Mernissi, Fatima, 63
Mesli, Fadéla, 29
Messika, Habiba, 45
middle-class Muslims, 6, 20, 24–25, 50–51, 118
Middle East: links to Algeria, 126; news from, 32, 40, 77, 89, 94, 183; use of term, 3; women's advancement in, 2–9, 35–38, 40, 93–98, 116, 132–35. *See also* Afghanistan; Egypt; Iran; Iraq; Tunisia; Turkey
migration: to France, 5, 51; rural-to-urban, 50–56, 75–76
Millet, René, 82
Minerva, 133
misogyny: French colonial ideas about (*see* stereotypes); Islam and, 63, 90, 147, 181; patriarchy and, 151
mobility, women's, 47–50, 56–74, 130, 196n49
"modern girls," 10, 73–74
modernity, 2–7, 12, 94, 175–76; definitions of, 202n5; forms of dress and, 103, 105, 116, 119–24, 126–27, 129; men's anxieties about, 63–67, 185. *See also* civilization
modesty, 98, 113, 166, 168–69, 172
Mogannam, Matiel, 37
morality, 62–69, 98. *See also* licentiousness; promiscuity; propriety and impropriety
Mornay, Elsa, 133
Morocco, 3, 108, 125, 127, 134–35
Mostaganem, 31, 167, 171
motherhood, 165, 167–68; education and, 43, 91, 101
Mouvement pour le triomphe des libertés démocratiques (Movement for the Triumph of Democratic Liberties, MTLD), 165. *See also* PPA-MTLD
Muhammad (Prophet), 18, 37, 41, 87, 89, 114, 176
musical culture, 45
Muslim, use of term, 2–3. *See also* Islam
Muslim culture, 49, 82, 120–21, 136, 139, 142. *See also* identity; Islamic education; Islamic knowledge
Muslim press: female contributors, 25–26, *26*, 37–38, 84, 154–79; female readers, 35; growth of, 19, 21–23; ideological groups and communities, 14–16, 22–34, 46; readership, 34–35; reliability of sources, 161; unattributed articles, 33–34, 161; wire news and, 32, 40. *See also* censorship; *specific publications*
Muslim reformist movement, 6–7, 14; associations, 46; fatwas and, 104; Islamic knowledge and, 40–41, 114; nationalism and, 30–31, 122–25, 155; origins of, 30; publications, 22, 40; in rural areas, 39–40; schools, 75, 92, *101*, 162–64; science and, 113; Sufi critiques of, 31; woman question and, 18–19, 38–43; women's education and, 38, 78, 84–93
Mussot, Yvonne, 33, 48–49, 60–61, 195n45
Mzabi women, 15, 43, 61, 75, 142, 184

Nahda ("awakening"), 35
nationalism. *See* Algerian War of Independence; anti-colonial nationalism
naturalization. *See* citizenship and naturalization
Nawfal, Hind, 35
"new women," 10, 73–74, 171
North Africa, 6, 13, 32, 45–46, 56, 87, 92, 95, 105, 107, 121, 133–34, 161, 163
Noureddine, Aldjia, 162

Office of Familial Action, 69
Opéra of Algiers, 180–81
Oran républicain, 33, 47–48, *49*, 58, *61*, 194n5
Orientalism, 5–6, 11, 36–38, 47–48, 114, 144. *See also* stereotypes
Ottoman Empire, 3, 6, 117, 123
Oussedik, M. Meziam, 145

INDEX   233

Pahlavi, Reza Shah, 3-4, 96
Pakistan, 165
Palestine, 3-4, 6, 35-37, 56, 107, 134
pan-Arabism, 35
Panchasi, Roxanne, 11
Parti communiste algérien (Algerian Communist Party, PCA), 25, 33
Parti du peuple algérien (Algerian People's Party, PPA), 155, 181-82
patriarchy, 105, 182, 211n4; challenges to, 108 (*see also* feminism); essentialist, 31, 42, 50, 66-67, 74, 76-77; French women and, 151-52; social equilibrium and, 165
personal legal status, 27-28
political participation, 8-9, 46, 190n26
political parties, 20, 25, 30, 46, 71, 212n14
polygamy, 3, 27, 141, 151
Popular Front, 20, 71, 72
possibility, methodology of, 13
poverty, 51, 130, 139, 151
power relations, 104, 184; colonialism and, 57, 98, 118-21. *See also* gender relations
PPA-MTLD, 181-82
press. *See* censorship; feminist press; international news; Muslim press; settler press
progress, 7, 28, 60, 98-100, 128, 181
promiscuity, 63, 66, 141
property rights, 77, 99-100
propriety and impropriety, 62-69, 76, 166, 170. *See also* modesty; morality; respectability; sexuality
prostitution, 57, 109-10, 120, 196n49
public life, women's participation in, 8, 10, 13-14, 20-21, 43-46, 56, 61-69, 73-74, 180-81, 185-86; education and, 182; forms of dress and, 127; as government leaders, 8-9; heterosocial spaces, 6, 65, 68, 166-67; veiling and, 112-16. *See also* cafés; political participation

Qadiriyya order, 31
Qur'an, 15, 37, 41, 78. *See also* Islamic knowledge

Rachid, Zineb, 156
Radio Ptt d'Alger, 174
Rahmaniyya order, 31, 43

Ramdane, Mohamed Saleh, 67, 90
reformist movement. *See* Muslim reformist movement
religion. *See* Islam; Islamic knowledge; Muslim culture; Muslim reformist movement; Sufism
resistance, 35, 96, 110, 184. *See also* anticolonial nationalism
respectability, 71, 118, 156, 161, 168-69, 173
Rida, Rashid, 85, 113, 120, 122
rural areas, 20, 48, 50-51, 56, 81, 130. *See also* agricultural labor

Sarkar, Benoy Kumar, 11
Saudi Arabia, 95
Sauret, Henriette, 151
schools: artisanal, 80-82, 92-93, 100, 137; created by French feminists, 137, 145, 148-49, 151; French colonial, 23, 25, 28, 38, 78-80, 79-80, 83, 92, 100-101, 120, 136-42, 159, 162, 191n37, 198n14; Islamic, 163 (*see also* Islamic education); numbers of, 78-80, 79-80. *See also* education; women's education
schoolteachers: assimilation and, 29; associations, 38-39, 155; female, 7, 101, 137, 145, 148-49, 151; nationalism and, 29; publications by, 22-30, 32; woman question and, 38, 42, 76-78, 83-84, 183-84
Section Française de l'Internationale Ouvrière (SFIO), 25, 39, 71
secularism, 9, 40, 95-96, 118, 126, 128, 138, 203n8
segregation, informal, 4, 52, 57
sequestration, 5, 37, 48-49, 60-62, 142-44, 147, 152, 172. *See also* harem
settler colonialism, 3-5, 21, 28-29, 51, 71, 179; bureaucracy, 25, 29, 80, 120; *Code de l'indigénat* (Native code), 5, 28; criticism of, 69, 88-89, 98-100, 135-42, 146, 154-55, 183-84, 211n2; education, 100, 149; feminist possibility and, 10-14; forms of dress and, 116, 118, 120-21, 185; laws, 5, 28, 51, 77-78; population, 187n5; segregation and, 52, 57, 131; state archives, 14-16; upward mobility, 51; use of term, 187n5; women's advancement and, 4-6, 38, 71, 175-76

INDEX

settler press, 21–22, 33
sexual harassment, 69–71
sexuality, 5, 27, 56, 93, 144, 172. See also licentiousness; promiscuity; propriety and impropriety
Shabiba school, 46, 163
Sharawi, Huda, 4, 36, 106–7
sharia, 121–22, 126, 202n3
shrines, 39, 42, 48
Sidi Ramadan mosque, 32, 111
"sisterhood," 159. See also "Women's Page"
Smaili, Ahmed, 100
social change in interwar Algeria, 19–21, 73–74, 185. See also dress; education; labor; modernity; urbanization; women's advancement
social divisions, 8, 15, 50, 184–86
socialists, 18, 25, 33, 39, 42, 71, 89
social uplift: colonial economy and, 71; Muslim reform and, 87 (see also Muslim reformist movement); through women's education, 32–33, 60, 162; women's advancement and, 6–7, 11–12, 32–33, 38, 85, 91, 97, 100, 159, 164
Souk-Ahras, 143–44, 149
Soussan, Marie, 45, 58
state feminism, 4, 6, 9. See also Egypt; Turkey
stereotypes: about forms of dress, 37, 129, 142; about Muslim women, 5, 13, 37–38, 47–48, 60; "backwardness" or "primitivism," 7, 37, 87, 94, 105, 114, 143–44; Muslims as misogynistic, 9, 13, 37–38, 47–48, 77, 82, 84, 86–88, 99–100, 116, 153, 182, 184. See also Orientalism
street harassment, 156, 167, 169–71
Sudan, 120
suffrage, 3–4, 98–100, 133, 140–41. See also French Union for Women's Suffrage
Sufism, 30–31, 37, 39–40, 42–43, 48, 84, 86, 90, 121. See also zawiyas
Sunna texts. See Islamic knowledge
superstition, 100, 113, 151
surveillance, French colonial, 15–16, 28, 32, 161, 184
Syria, 2–4, 6, 32, 35, 96, 98

Tahrat, Larbi, 25
Taleb, Selim, 170–71
Taliana, Dalila, 45
Tarahoui, Djemila, 161
Tarzi, Suraya, 106
Tatouti, Mohammed, 147
teachers. See schoolteachers
theater performances, 43–45, *44*, 58–59
Tidjani, Aurélie Picard, 137
Tijaniyya order, 31, 43
Tounsia, Louisa, 45
tradition, 7; education and, 25; forms of dress and, 103, 116–23, 125–29; nationalism and, 124–25; women's role as bearers of, 127–28
Transvaal fatwa, 107
travel literature, 143–44
Tunisia, 3, 32, 36, 45, 82–83, 89, 96, 135
Turkey: independence, 95; men's headwear, 103, 106–7, 109, 118–19, 126; modernization, 103, 111, 118–22, 128; state feminism and women's advancement, 2–4, 6, 32, 68, 98–99, 111, 116, 132–35, 148, 153, 175–76; women's education, 2, 91, 94–96. See also Atatürk, Mustafa Kemal

Umayyad caliphate, 119
umma (global community of Muslims), 87, 91, 93, 95, 108, 112, 122, 155
Union démocratique du manifeste algérien (UDMA), 30–31
Union populaire algérienne (UPA), 30
United Nations, 134
unveiling, 101, 126–29; anxieties about, 63–64, 105, 115, 125, 166; campaigns for, 3, 168–69; in the Middle East, 106–7, 112; street harassment and, 170–71; women's advancement and, 49–50, 60–62, *61*, 89, 128, 139, 153–54, 159. See also veiling
urbanization, 6, 20–21; domestic workers and, 71; gender norms and, 55–56; overpopulation and, 194n14; rural-to-urban migration, 50–56, 75–76; social changes and, 41, 64–67. See also Algiers; cafés

veiling: as cultural practice, 206n81; face veil, 36, 56, 106, 109–10, 113, 123, 126–27; ideologies and, 105–6; Islam and, 48, 174; nationalism and, 104–5, 153, 178–79; sexual violence and, 109–10; styles of, 41, 56, 109. See also haiks; hijabs; unveiling

vieux turbans ("old turbans"), 19, 24. *See also* elite Muslims
Violette Project, 151
Viollette, Maurice, 80
voting rights. *See* suffrage

wars. *See* Algerian War of Independence; World War I
Westernization, 119–25. *See also* assimilation; European norms
"woman question" debates, 1–7, 18–19; in Algerian Muslim press, 38–43; in the Middle East, 35–38; in Muslim public life, 43–46
women's advancement: anti-colonial nationalism and, 13–14, 153, 155, 167, 179, 181–83, 185; assimilation and, 14, 48–49, 181; civilization and modernity, 6–7, 11–12, 32–33, 38, 40–42, 65, 98–100; class and, 38, 56, 62–69; education and, 2, 69, 128, 131, 154–55, 159 (*see also* women's education); employment and mobility (*see* domestic workers); in Middle Eastern countries, 2–8, 32, 35–38, 40, 45, 56, 68, 93–99, 111, 113, 116, 132–35, 148, 153, 175–76; postwar period, 154–79; settler colonialism and, 4–6, 38, 71, 175–76; social uplift and, 6–7, 11–12, 32–33, 38, 85, 91, 97, 100, 159, 164; unveiling and, 49–50, 60–62, *61*, 89, 128, 153–54, 159 (*see also* dress). *See also* feminism
women's education: access to, 1–2, 5–9, 13, 41, 88; anxieties about, 18, 31, 63, 75–78, 102, 164, 167; assimilation and, 84, 128, 140, 165, 173; colonial, 78–83; dress and, 100; in Egypt, 36; French feminists on, 136–40; Islamic tradition and, 25; motherhood and, 43; postwar period, 161; precolonial, 78; professional training, 80; social uplift and, 32–33, 60, 162; women's advancement and, 2, 69, 128, 131, 154–55, 159. *See also* education; schools
women's labor, 6–9, 16–18, 47–74; gender relations and, 104; modern subject formation and, 185; statistics on, 52–55, *53–54*. *See also* agricultural labor; artisanal work; domestic workers
"Women's Page": in *as-Salam*, 154–61, 165–67, 171, 175, 177–79; in *Oran républicain*, 33, 48, 194n5
Women's Union (Syria and Lebanon), 4
working-class Muslims, 10, 20, 25, 39, 44, 48, 52, 56, 64, 74, 186. *See also* domestic workers; labor
World War I, 5, 51, 119
Wunisi, Zuhur, 8–9, 101–2

Yacine, Kateb, 183
Young Algerians, 29, 133, 139, 155, 184

Zainab, Lalla, 43
Zarrouk, Mahmoud, 36
zawiyas (Sufi institutions), 30, 39, 76, 78, 111
Zenati, Rabah, 1, 25–30, 33, 61–62, 88

www.ingramcontent.com/pod-product-compliance
Lightning Source LLC
Chambersburg PA
CBHW032037300426
44117CB00009B/1094